Paradise

The Trash Project

VOL III

Paradise

Ken Hollings

FIRST PUBLISHED BY
Strange Attractor Press in 2024,
in an unlimited paperback edition.

LAYOUT DESIGN BY
Tihana Šare and Baphorock.
TYPESET IN Tremolo & Typonine Sans.

ISBN: 978-1-913689-85-8

A CIP CATALOGUE RECORD for this book is available from the British Library.

DISTRIBUTED BY The MIT Press, Cambridge, Massachusetts. And London, England.

PRINTED AND BOUND IN Estonia by Tallinna Raamatutrükikoda.

STRANGE ATTRACTOR PRESS
BM SAP, London, WC1N 3XX UK,
www.strangeattractor.co.uk

The Trash
Project

VOL III

Paradise

Ken Hollings

You believe I run after the strange because I do not know the beautiful: no, it is because you do not know the beautiful that I seek the strange.

··· ✝ ···

Georg Christoph Lichtenberg,
The Waste Books

I wish to remain an eternal mystery to myself and to others.

··· ✝ ···

King Ludwig II of Bavaria,
letter to the actress Marie Dahn-Hausmann, *April* 27, 1876

Contents

Paradise

And he who employs aright these
memories is ever being initiated
into perfect mysteries and alone
becomes truly perfect.
But, as he forgets earthly
interests and is rapt in the divine,
the vulgar deem him mad,
and rebuke him; they do not see
that he is inspired.

Plato, Pheadrus

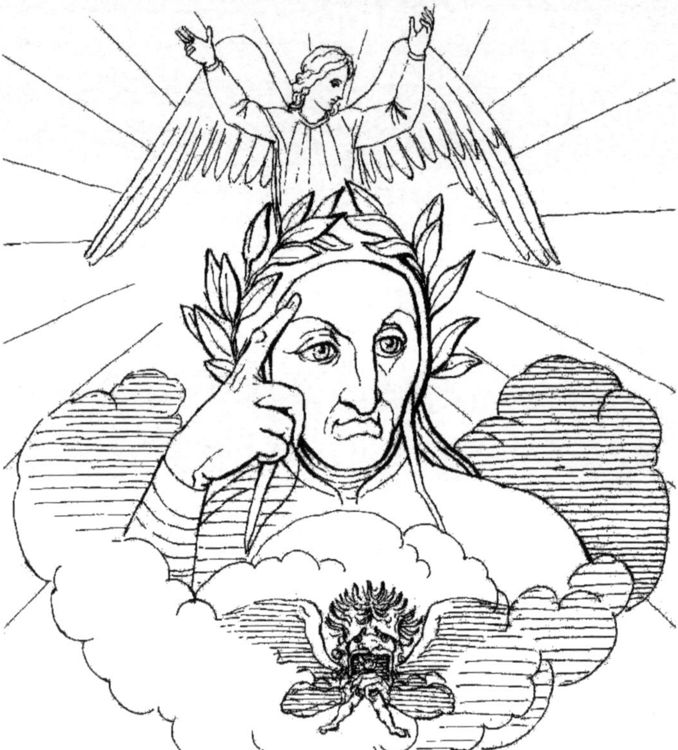

Introduction: To Remain an Eternal Mystery

When King Ludwig II of Bavaria famously revealed his desire 'to remain an eternal mystery to myself and to others', he was making a very specific literary reference. *The Bride of Messina,* a verse drama by the German poet Friedrich Schiller, has at its centre a young woman whose royal lineage is 'a secret to herself'. She is one of three children born to Princess Isabella of Messina. Fearing a prophecy that she will bring about the family's downfall, the mother hides the daughter away in a convent. The curse cannot be lifted, however. Her two brothers both die violently, having fallen in love with her, neither of them realising until it is too late that she is their sister. In a play that makes repeated reference to mysteries and secrets, this is the deepest and darkest of them all. What was it about this cruel narrative that spoke so clearly to Ludwig? How did he come to identify himself with the young woman's story? Perhaps the king saw his own destiny reflected in her doomed innocence. Perhaps he secretly envied her ability to bring down an entire royal house simply by being born. A king who lived for beauty alone, Ludwig would certainly have embraced the tragic poetry of such a fate. It was by following such lines of thought that I was able to formulate more fully something I had over the years come to identify as the Psychoanalysis of Trash. The fact that the young woman in Schiller's play is called Beatrice, the same name as Dante's spiritual guide in *Paradise*, made its connection with *The Trash Project* even clearer to me.

In *Purgatory*, the previous volume of this three-part series, I examined the processes and values involved in the transformation of matter from its base, corrupted nature into a noble, more refined one. In the third and final part, I do the exact opposite, considering instead how the deliberate exhausting of material riches can be seen as a form of Trash Aesthetics. My reworking of *Paradise* consequently tells the story of three kings who all share Beatrice's doomed innocence: unwittingly but wilfully squandering everything they have in a grand spectacle of waste. The Psychoanalysis of Trash begins and ends with the effects of this terrible curse.

The lives of Ludwig II of Bavaria, Elvis Presley and Michael Jackson are disasters that helped define their age. Ludwig reigned in the late nineteenth century when Europe's royal houses had already lost their former pre-eminence. By the middle of the following century, the democratic nations of the world needed a new kind of monarch, and Elvis was hailed as the King of Rock 'n' Roll. Then, as the twentieth century drew to its close, Michael Jackson proclaimed himself the King of Pop. All three had a great deal in common. Each gave themselves up to a profligacy so extreme that it would consume them entirely. Each of them would die before their time, physically and spiritually ravaged. Beset on all sides by scandals and debt, their lives ended dramatically but not well – or neatly. Theirs were essentially aesthetic deaths: on behalf of, and enabled by, art. No wonder their ostentatious extravagance was broadly condemned as a lapse in taste. In the face of such deaths, all taste is essentially bourgeois. *Paradise* can subsequently be seen as a gallery of the dead, with many of the faces in it appearing distorted and strange as a result. Or in the words of Ovid's Narcissus as he wasted away out of love for his own beauty: 'What I desire, I have. My very plenty makes me poor.'

It is this extreme squandering of the self that brings together two opposing concepts that are essential to the Psychoanalysis of Trash: sovereignty and disgrace. Everything that separates the one from the other starts to disappear when it comes to the individual impatient to satisfy their desires. Immediate gratification requires an equally immediate and unstinting outlay: something that remains relatively rare. The world is full of those who have amassed huge fortunes and perhaps enjoyed great fame but who carefully conserved what they had. Frank Sinatra, for example, may have been the Chairman of the Board and the Leader of the Rat Pack, but he was no sovereign. With his Mafia and White House connections, plus his widening business interests, Frankie never squandered more than he could afford, handing it out in the form of gifts to himself and his immediate circle after one of his violent rages. Sinatra's Las Vegas was a very different town from the one that Elvis Presley and Michael Jackson knew.

I had written about the correspondences between Elvis Presley and Michael Jackson long before I placed them both in *Paradise*. The first time was in the essay 'Electronically Yours, Eternally Elvis', published in the 1993 anthology *The Last Sex: Feminism and Outlaw Bodies*, edited by Arthur and Marilouise Kroker. That was back when Michael was still alive; and I was sketching out a draft of what would become my first book, *Destroy All Monsters*. The next occasion was at the request of Mark Fisher, who was preparing his volume *The Resistible Demise of Michael Jackson* in response to the King of Pop's death in 2009. 'And Tell Sad Stories of the Death of Kings' gave me the opportunity to re-examine the lives of Elvis and Michael from the standpoint of their respective endings. A constant theme running through these two essays, separated as they are by several years, was the idea that Michael and Elvis could only be understood in terms of a sovereignty that resided entirely within their bodies. Ludwig II's insistence upon exerting his own sense of majesty through aesthetic pleasures pursued to the point of bankruptcy only helped to broaden the connections between sovereignty and disgrace. Ludwig, Elvis and Michael were incapable of conserving their wealth or enjoying it peacefully. They could only spend freely and wastefully. In the end, the sovereign individual must dissipate themselves entirely. They can do nothing less. Privilege is the mean-spirited control of others, while sovereignty in its truest form is a massive disruptive outpouring of that privilege. It has no choice but to lose itself in what a society of onlookers might choose to call crime, which is also the punitive expression of disgrace.

This would be a good time to address what I mean by the term 'sovereignty', particularly with regard to its relationship with crime, disgrace and the Psychoanalysis of Trash. First of all, it should be clear that I do not think of sovereignty as being an exclusively pure expression of power, virtue or glorious stability. Quite the contrary: it refers to a dangerous, unstable state of being which challenges, exhilarates and, in the end, totally consumes the individual. This understanding has been informed by the writings of French philosopher Georges Bataille on the subject. In fact, I used some of his words to introduce the concept of sovereignty at a very precise moment in *The Trash Project*. Towards the middle of the 'Earthly *Paradise*' section that ends *Purgatory*, there are a few lines taken from a longer statement by Bataille on the deep divide separating the 'sovereign' individual from the 'subservient' crowds and how both parties detect the shameful odour of death clinging to the other. The quote is from Bataille's *The Accursed Share* and appears as an incomplete fragment in Essay XXX of *Purgatory*; you will find the concluding part in the correspondingly numbered essay in this current volume. Between these two specific interventions, the influence of *The Accursed Share* on the composition of *Paradise* can be keenly felt. For example, the intense incompatibility between the sovereign and the subservient helped me to identify an aristocratic element to Trash's sense of its own criminal license. This identification, as reflected in the examples of Ludwig II, Elvis Presley and Michael Jackson, had little or nothing to do with class. It was Bataille's definition of sovereignty as 'the negation of prohibition' that allowed me to see within the Psychoanalysis of Trash a very clear connection between sovereignty and disgrace as expressions of waste. Bataille's sovereign individual will always be used up and discarded. *The Accursed Share* is, if nothing else, a work of economic theory. 'The victim,' Bataille observes, 'is a surplus taken from the mass of useful wealth. And he can only be withdrawn from it in order to be consumed profitlessly and therefore utterly destroyed. Once chosen, he is the accursed share, destined for violent consumption. But the curse tears him away from the order of things; it gives him a recognizable figure, which now radiates intimacy, anguish, the profundity of living beings.'

How well Bataille's description of the sacrificial victim fits the lives of Ludwig, Elvis and Michael as much as their deaths. Like Beatrice, Schiller's tragic heroine, they had no choice but to be chosen. This curse is a necessary line of influence that has been passed on to them. However peaceful their everyday lives might have appeared on the surface, powerful material and cultural forces helped shape their fate. Ludwig, Elvis and Michael might have been celebrated or venerated in different ways, but there was only one way for each of them to fall: from sovereignty into disgrace and ridicule – and finally into Trash. Their shared fate is not related to any specific crimes, misdemeanours or transgressions but represents instead a collective pathology of sovereignty. All three of them have too much in common to allow for any other possibility.

In the end, this book is concerned with the Psychoanalysis of Trash rather than its cultural rehabilitation. Its aim has been to go deeper into Paradise, not higher. Continuing a theme taken up at the very end of *Purgatory*, the sovereignty of Ludwig II, Elvis Presley and Michael Jackson represents the transformation of Beatrice's doomed innocence into a monstrous one. Their extreme self-indulgence retains the memory of a prelapsarian existence: one in which sensory experience has not yet been co-opted or regulated by what Bataille designates 'the order of things'. *Paradise* for them is the complete return of the repressed that Trash Aesthetics has always hinted at. This means not only that these sovereigns are free in their monstrous innocence to desire that which is bad for them but also to act upon that desire by embodying it to the point of annihilating themselves. Consumption in their case is not a moment to be deferred, nor is it a functioning part of some self-regulating economic system. To consume, for them, means to be consumed in the same way that fire uses up everything it touches. This is why Michael Jackson makes his first grand entrance in *Paradise* crowned with flames, his hair set alight by an exploding magnesium flare during the filming of a Pepsi commercial. This self-consuming does not place Eros in contention with Thanatos, but rather with itself. The garish, dazzling coherence of the worlds that Ludwig, Elvis and Michael created around themselves was an attempt to recombine all those elements of their existence that had become fragmented and scattered by desire. More than the return of the repressed, they mark a regression back into it – in other words, its accommodation. However, this can only be for that one individual, who is then doomed by the sovereignty of their unique position. Seen in personal and mythological terms, this accommodation takes the form of what I have chosen to call 'The Trash Palace'.

There are many connections and similarities drawing Ludwig, Elvis and Michael into each other's presence; and I will reveal them over the course of this book. However, the one thing that most securely ties them together are the places they chose to call home. Neuschwanstein, Linderhof and Herrenchiemsee, Graceland, Hayvenhurst and Neverland have become as famous as their former occupants. Frequently regarded with disdain by the media and the public alike for their apparent lack of 'taste', these remain significant cultural sites that are impossible to view except from this scornful perspective. The Trash Palace seethes with the dark energies of pop culture. These can (and should) be seen as the return of the repressed experienced primarily as an environment. Resort hotels, casinos, night clubs and teenagers' bedrooms all offer milder versions of the same experience. Meanwhile, the gilded showrooms of dictators, oligarchs and thugs – from the crusted opulence of their Rococo interiors to the sumptuous red upholstery that looks like spilled blood – all share what HBO's John Oliver once called 'a design aesthetic that amounts to "Elvis tries to remember what Versailles looks like but can't."' It was Georges Bataille, however, who described Versailles as 'the most notable form – although in human terms it may not be the richest – that was given to the principle of a noble existence dedicated to the scorn of useful activity.' The Trash Palace gives shape to the inner life of the sovereign individual, however cruel or despotic that might have become. The Trash Palace is where kings always get their way: indulged and obeyed to the point of their own destruction. Alive with unexpressed desires and passions, Trash ruins any tidy sense of what culture can or ought to be. This has nothing to do with cheapness or vulgarity – splendour and opulence can also be the epitome of Trash. Consider, for example, the versions of the *'Tischlein-deck'-dich'* or 'Wishing Table' that Ludwig II had installed in his private dining rooms at Linderhof and Herrenchiemsee. Based on a Grimms' fairy tale that featured a table magically able to set itself with food and drink upon command, this mechanical version could be raised and lowered through the floor using winches, allowing Ludwig to dine completely alone. 'Nevertheless,' his cook would later recall, 'the dinners and suppers always have to be large enough to serve at least three or four people. This way, although the king always sits down to eat alone, he does not feel alone after all. He believes himself in the company of Louis XIV and Louis XV and their lady friends, Madame de Pompadour and Madame de Maintenon. He even greets them now and then and carries on conversations with them as though he really had them as his guests at table.' Eventually such extravagant indulgences would be turned against King Ludwig II and used to depose him. At the same time, they reveal how sovereignty provides not only a refuge from the subservient masses but also individual access to a world of renewed enchantment. Put simply: it is a way of escaping the order of things. Michael Jackson and Elvis Presley would have both understood that.

All three sovereign individuals managed to place themselves at the centre of their own particular universes: pulling people into orbit around them, some closer and tighter than others, but all accepting in the end that here was their new reality. This is a key to understanding the relationship between sovereignty and the Psychoanalysis of Trash. Anyone can be wilfully eccentric and go their own separate way; but it takes extraordinary personal power to convince everyone that what they are now expected to share should be considered 'normal'. Night becomes day from this point on; and it's only what lies outside the Trash Palace that seems weird and disturbing. The carefully ordered ascendancy of Dante's *Paradise* has a similarly unshakable certainty at its centre. Following the geocentric cosmology of the time, he organises the final part of *The Divine Comedy* around the Ptolemaic precept that the Earth was enclosed by a series of concentric crystal spheres, each large enough to contain all of the preceding ones. Each sphere is dedicated to a specific heavenly body and determines its motion through the firmament. Using the Earthly Paradise as some sort of mediaeval launch pad at the start of *Paradise*, a radiant Beatrice takes Dante upwards, rising from one crystal sphere to the next, until they reach the Empyrean, where he catches a glimpse of God as a tiny point of light moving the entire universe in perfectly balanced rotation.

The order in which these crystal spheres are stacked inside one another will be familiar to anyone who has read *Purgatory*, the second volume of my *Trash Project*, where I copied the order of the planets in the arrangement of the Terraces across the central part of the text. It remains the same for both books: the Moon, Mercury, Venus, the Sun, Mars, Jupiter, Saturn. The only difference is that in *Paradise* the seven spheres are enclosed by an eighth and ninth: namely, the Fixed Stars and the Primum Mobile. Beyond that, there is only God. In his version of *Paradise*, Dante tends to blur the transition from one sphere to the next – maybe in his version of Heaven things are encouraged to blend more harmoniously into each other. This is not an approach I have chosen to follow. My *Paradise* is organised instead around stories contained within stories, rather than spheres within spheres. The Psychoanalysis of Trash extends from Ludwig II to Elvis Presley, then their respective narratives are continued with Michael Jackson until the end. It also contains echoes, themes and recurrences from the previous two volumes in *The Trash Project* and is consequently best read more as a reflection of Hell than of Heaven.

'You have to be in Heaven to see Hell,' mutters the old writer from somewhere deep inside me; and I am not altogether certain Dante would have disagreed with this perception. When William Blake alluded to Hell as the perfect mould of Heaven, he might well have had *The Divine Comedy* in mind. The Nine Circles of Dante's *Inferno* find their exact counterpart in the Nine Crystal Spheres of his *Paradise*. Dante describes both as equally unbearable to the human senses. The physical sufferings of Hell find their counterpart in a Heaven where Beatrice's smile threatens to reduce Dante to ashes, and celestial voices have the power to render him senseless. Similarly, Dante's *Paradise*, like his *Inferno*, describes an eternity without hope: a theological virtue no longer necessary in Heaven and unconditionally withheld from those trapped in Hell. It could also be argued that Dante's *Paradise*, along with his *Inferno* and *Purgatory*, were written as reproaches to Bataille's 'order of things', which I understand to be the rigid hierarchy of values that material possessions impose upon our world rather than the ways in which objects can be classified and arranged – although neither is by any means excluded by the other.

Either way, we become trapped by our own errors of judgement. Meanwhile Dante remains obsessed with order. The one hundred cantos that make up *The Divine Comedy*, carefully distributed across all three of its parts, constitute a gird upon which themes, echoes, symmetries and inversions are constantly multiplied. The elegance of its overall design crosses centuries of taste and belief. Dante's strict structural example when applied to the planning of *The Trash Project* allowed me to take a more generative approach to my text. Uniformity and repetition can yield surprising results, especially when imposed upon a subject as unruly as Trash. Unexpected correspondences and variations would suddenly emerge. I frequently found myself playing spectator to a process that seemed to be running itself, establishing connections and framing new meanings without my assistance. At times it felt as if some decisions had already been made for me. However, it had never been my intention to rewrite or update *The Divine Comedy* but merely to use it as a compositional tool, so there was a great deal in Dante's original that I rejected out of hand. This has certainly been the case with *Paradise.* Lacking any of the tortures and torments that made *Inferno* and *Purgatory* so interesting, Dante's trip through the crystal spheres of Heaven is, by comparison, rather dull. The endless exclamations of harmony and joy, plus the continual overflowing of love, wisdom and light tend to pall after a while. Apparently, wickedness is not just essential to Trash but to Art itself. Who knew? Even from the perspective of Heaven, Dante cannot entirely free himself from vice, bitterly complaining from time to time about how badly things are going back on Earth. Parts of his *Paradise* are alive with recrimination, retaining a number of names and references from both *Inferno* and *Purgatory*. I have chosen to follow him in this. For example, the presence of Ludwig II relates back to *Purgatory* through his grandfather Ludwig I with his *Gallery of Beauties* and his disastrous affair with Lola Montez. Many figures already familiar to readers of the previous two volumes reappear in my version of *Paradise*; and a clear sense of continuity is intended to link all three parts of *The Trash Project*.

One of the things I have carried over from Dante's *Paradise* is his fascination with the number three, which held tremendous spiritual significance for him. I have responded to this not only by placing three kings at the heart of my narrative, but also in borrowing from the three volumes that make up Georges Bataille's *The Accursed Share*. Linguistically, Dante's *Paradise* contains a number of challenges. I have not followed his example of inventing my own words to describe the experience of life in Heaven, as I feel this a practice more suited to academics than to poets. I found Dante's use of repeated phrases far more interesting. The refrain 'And Elvis now knows' that starts each of the six paragraphs that make up Essay XX corresponds exactly to the repetition of a corresponding phrase in Canto XX of Dante's *Paradise*. Similarly, the nine rhetorical questions posed in Essays XXIV through XXVI have their counterparts in Dante's original. I have also made some attempt to replicate the acrostic that appears in Canto XIX of his poem; but where he uses it to spell out the word *'lue'*, meaning 'pestilence', mine spells out a name that had great importance for Ludwig II and those who came after him. Dante first uses this literary device in his *Purgatory*, and I reproduced the same effect there in three separate places, spread out evenly across the length of my version. A short *Trash Concordance*, detailing similar correspondences and parallels in the three volumes of my project, has been prepared to accompany the publication of *Paradise*.

This generative approach seemed appropriate to my subject. In this way I have attempted to build my own Trash Palace out of Paradise rather than merely discovering it there. By not conforming to established modes of critical inquiry I wanted to free Trash from the expectations and prejudices that have surrounded it. In the end, I'm still not sure if I can fully define Trash, but I have a better sense of its importance – certainly enough to see that Trash Aesthetics can express more than mere negation. Trash came into its own during the age of mechanical reproduction, which is also why I purposely chose to write about it from the perspective of a medieval Book of the Dead dedicated to the salvation of the human soul. Trash has always had a mythic dimension, which means it cannot be reduced to one clear narrative or meaning. At the same time, manifestations of Trash are elusive and abrasive, rubbing up all of our values the wrong way while evading classification. We have to be alone with Trash; no theory can offer an adequate substitute for direct experience. This, in the end, constitutes the 'resistance without the grounds to stand upon' that I mentioned at the end of my Introduction to *Purgatory*. I deliberately set out to offer a fragmented and partial account because I never wanted *The Trash Project* to be mistaken for something authoritative, comprehensive or objective – and, on reflection, I find it strange how often these terms end up seeming synonymous with each other. This has always been a personal reflection on a subject that has obsessed me for many years. If anything, its aim has been to *enhance* the direct experience of Trash rather than justify or explain it. I hope that my efforts provide the starting point for a broader, wider, more discursive debate in which other voices will wish to participate, either to correct me, amplify me, dismiss or criticise me. I don't care – this is only the beginning.

Every beginning has an end, however; and I have reached mine. Before leaving you in Paradise, I would like to take a few words to thank Rachel Hollings whose devotion to Ludwig II and his castles helped inspire the start of this book. I would also like to express my appreciation once again to Amanda and John Sutherell for kindly allowing me to use their cottage as a writer's retreat during the initial planning stages. Thanks are equally due to Jasmine Raznahan at *Noon* magazine and Reuben James and Albert Riera Galceran of *Emergent* for publishing early versions of material that have been reworked and included in the present volume. As always, I am grateful to the many who have shaped and influenced the final outcome, often without realising it. I am therefore happy to acknowledge the contributions of Roger K Burton and Alexia Marmara of the Horse Hospital, Lori E Allen and Deborah Wale of Tears|Ov, Philip Marshall, Beth Arzy and Ela Orleans – this would have been a very different, and perhaps lesser, book without them. I am particularly thankful to the tape composer Howlround for the unstinting joy he has always shown in Trash and for his companionship over the past four years. It is no secret that he and I have been performing and recording together as The Howling. The 'Trash List' that forms the basis for 'David Gest, Liza Minnelli, Michael Jackson and Elizabeth Taylor', The Howling's earliest composition, was originally compiled as part of *Inferno* but set aside when it no longer fitted into the book's overall structure. A studio version of the final piece can be found on our album *Incredible Night Creatures of the Midway*, available from The Tapeworm. When I first started work on *Inferno*, I had no idea where it would take me, and it's quite possible that I still don't really know. However, I was always very aware of the help and support shown to me by Mark Pilkington, Jamie Sutcliffe and Tihana Šare of Strange Attractor Press. They have never been in the least bit fazed by the demands of such an ambitious project and have done a truly magnificent job in turning it into a tangible reality. All three of them have earned their place in the Rose of Paradise.

Ken Hollings
Easter 2021 – Autumn 2024

Paradise

The Psychoanalysis of Trash

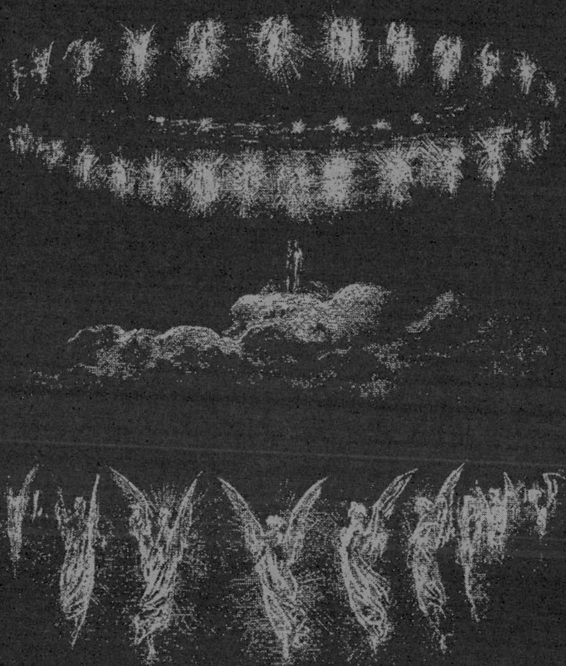

But a storm is blowing from Paradise, it has caught itself up in his wings and is so strong that the Angel can no longer close them. The storm drives him irresistibly into the future, to which his back is turned, while the rubble-heap before him grows sky-high. That which we call progress, is this storm.

··· + ···

Walter Benjamin, *The Concept of History*

If I say of individual love that it is outside history, this is insofar as what is individual is never manifest in history. Those men whose names fill our memories have nothing individual about them: their existence is given to us only to the extent that their identity corresponds with the general movement of history. They indeed rise up in isolation before our eyes, but it is the isolation of statues at the crossroads of history.

Georges Bataille, *The Accursed Share*

I

In the Shadow of the Earth

The Sublunar Paradise

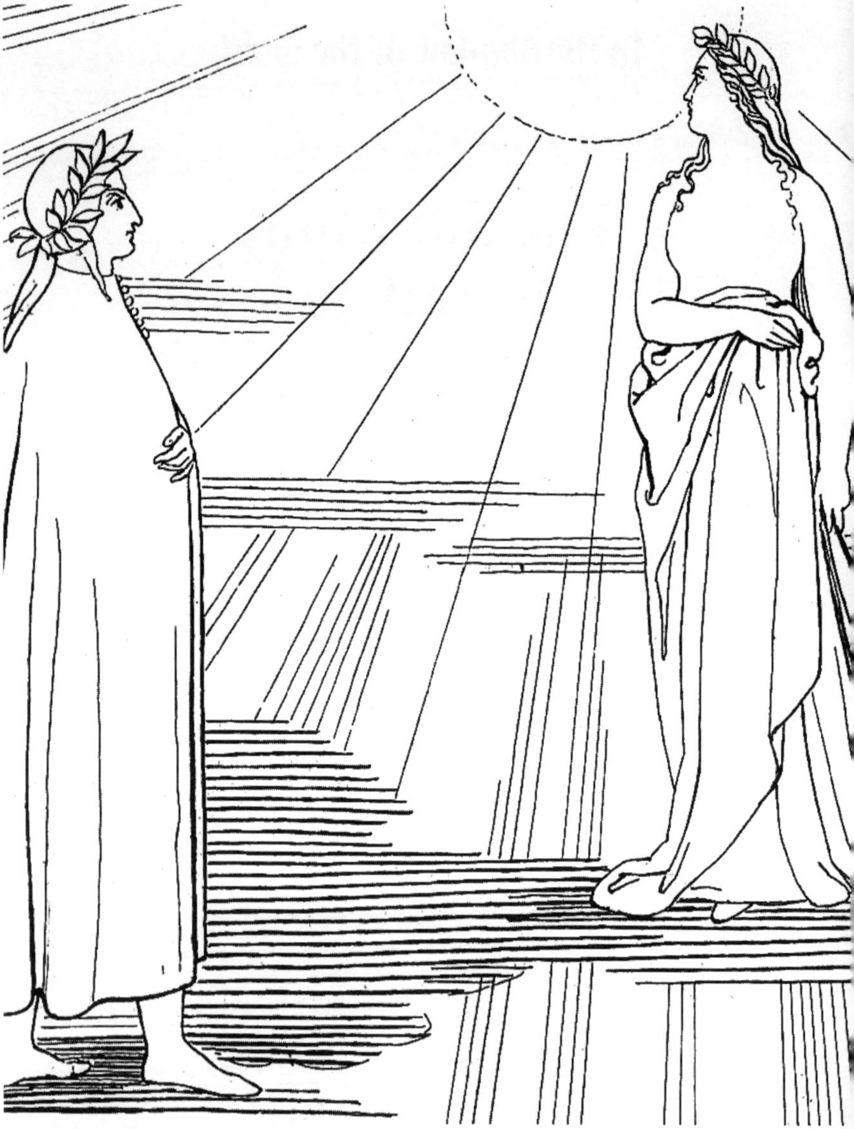

Leaving Earth and Water for Air and Fire

∴ ✝ ∴

And now I seem to be present at the dress rehearsal for some disastrous reoccurrence. Tannhäuser, poet and knight of the Holy Roman Empire, awakes to find himself where he has always been for as long as he can remember: bathed in the calm blue underground light of Venusberg. In this secret chamber, deep within a mountain located between Eisenach and Gotha in Thuringia, Tannhäuser first came to worship Venus, who invited the poet to stay, hidden away with her, far from the world. Together they share a life devoted to youth, beauty and love. Tannhäuser has no idea how long he has been lying here, dreaming in Venus' arms. He tells Venus his heart feels empty. He misses living aboveground – misses the sensation of *not* having everything his body and heart desires.

∴ ✝ ∴

Linderhof, the King's palace in southwest Bavaria, stands like a toy theatre in its own neatly landscaped gardens that blend into the forests and mountains beyond them as if this were a single place, isolated from the rest of the world: somewhere to be totally alone, gazing at the empty horizon. Started in 1870 and inspired by the Versailles of Louis XIV, Linderhof is a small Baroque confection set in white stone that is closer historically to the Playboy Mansion than the seventeenth-century palaces it copies. In a niche at the centre of its intricately gleaming façade, the allegorical figure Victory holds up two laurel crowns, one in each hand, barely glancing at the world below her. Walter Pater, whose writings on beauty influenced Wilde and Proust, once imagined the King as a 'northern Apollo' yearning for the light and warmth of the south. 'The god of light, coming to Germany from some more favoured world beyond it, over leagues of rainy hill and mountain, making soft day there: that had ever been the dream of the ghost-ridden yet deep-feeling and certainly meek German soul,' he wrote in 1887. A Greek temple sits above symmetrically terraced gardens laid out directly opposite the palace. The King had originally intended the circular temple to be dedicated to Apollo but decided that a marble statue of Venus should be placed there instead. Below the temple in the middle of a lower terrace is an arched alcove containing the sculpted bust of Queen Marie Antoinette of France.

Suddenly aware of the first leaves falling from trees that are still green, I can feel the summer ending. The moment is so precise and so immediately recognisable. Something in the air at Linderhof has changed. A storm is gathering over the King's palace, and there is the leaden, earthy smell of rain. Nobody knows what really goes on in Paradise – no mortal eye can fully comprehend it. Branches wave gently in the afternoon breeze.

Over the centuries Venusberg remained a Teutonic fantasy: a subterranean temple devoted to pagan urges and pleasures – the sins of youth, beauty and love. Its exact location is rumoured to be inside Hoerselloch: a cavern in deepest Thuringia. The entrance can still be visited to this day, the darkened cave entry sealed off from the world by metal bars. A published account dating from the time of Linderhof's construction reads as follows: 'In ancient days, according to the Thuringian Chronicles, bitter cries and long-drawn moans were heard issuing from this cavern; and at night wild shrieks, and the burst of diabolical laughter would ring out from it over the vale, and fill the inhabitants with terror. It was supposed that this hole gave admittance to Purgatory; and the popular but faulty derivation of Horsel was *Hore die Seele*, Hark, the Souls!'

⁂ ✝ ⁂

As above, so below. The King had his own Venusberg at Linderhof: an ornate underground grotto sunk into the slope behind his palace. Everything about it is fake. The dripstone cave it occupies was dug into the side of the green hill. An iron framework of struts and pillars is covered with canvas and cement, carefully sculpted then dusted with antimonite to look like stalactites. The whole edifice is supported by a single steel column, disguised as a central stalagmite, rising from the placid green surface of a subterranean lake. An artificial waterfall and mechanical waves add to the natural allure of the Venus Grotto. Here the King floats in a gilded boat shaped like a scallop shell, surrounded by live swans and garlands of ceramic flowers; in its prow a golden cherub aims his bow. Running the length of one wall, a painted backcloth shows Tannhäuser reclining at the feet of his goddess in Venusberg, dreamily watching a crowd of nymphs at play. A precise reflection of it floats upon the dimly lit water of the lake.

⁂ ✝ ⁂

Venus tells Tannhäuser he is free to leave any time he wishes; but the outside world no longer wants him. No priest will grant him absolution for his transgressions. Pope Urban IV, Chief of the Catholic Church, decrees that Tannhäuser will only be absolved of sin on the day that his papal staff sprouts leaves and bursts into flower. Sick to his soul, the poet returns to Venusberg, never to be seen again. After banishing Tannhäuser from his presence, the Pope's staff suddenly sprouts leaves and bursts into flower.

••• ✝ •••

The King ordered that his personal grotto be equipped with a machine programmed to produce a sequence of coloured lighting effects ending with a rainbow spreading itself over the Venusberg backdrop. A set of tinted glass discs rotate in front of twenty-four arc lamps: alternating shades of red, to represent Venusberg, and a blue reminiscent of the legendary water in the Grotta Azzurra on the island of Capri off the Italian coast. The Venus Grotto only makes sense when seen as the expression of a pure and precise intention: the King even sending one of his most trusted servants to Capri on two separate occasions to ensure the correct shade of blue was achieved.

••• ✝ •••

The lake, the cave, the painting and the lights offer him a private theatre for his own personal drama, which must be a poetic tragedy. In Venusberg all private desires and sensations yield to mythology and aesthetics.

••• ✝ •••

This subterranean grotto is the King's secret birth chamber. It allows him to experience once again life inside the womb: gently buoyed by the shining water, comforted by the restful air, warmed to a constant temperature by the fire of four hidden furnaces. The King can contemplate colours, sounds and the poetry of the senses. It's only as you pass down a long dark tunnel that takes you from the lake and out through an imitation limestone cleft in the hill, modelled directly on the entrance to Venusberg, that you realise how much it feels like being expelled from a uterus. The King has staged his own birth: forced out of the Venus Grotto into the cold afternoon air and the red glow of a distant sun.

••• ✝ •••

A heavy rainstorm sweeps into the area around Linderhof, cars throwing up great waves of spray along the motorway hard shoulder.

II

In the Shadow of the Earth

The First Sphere

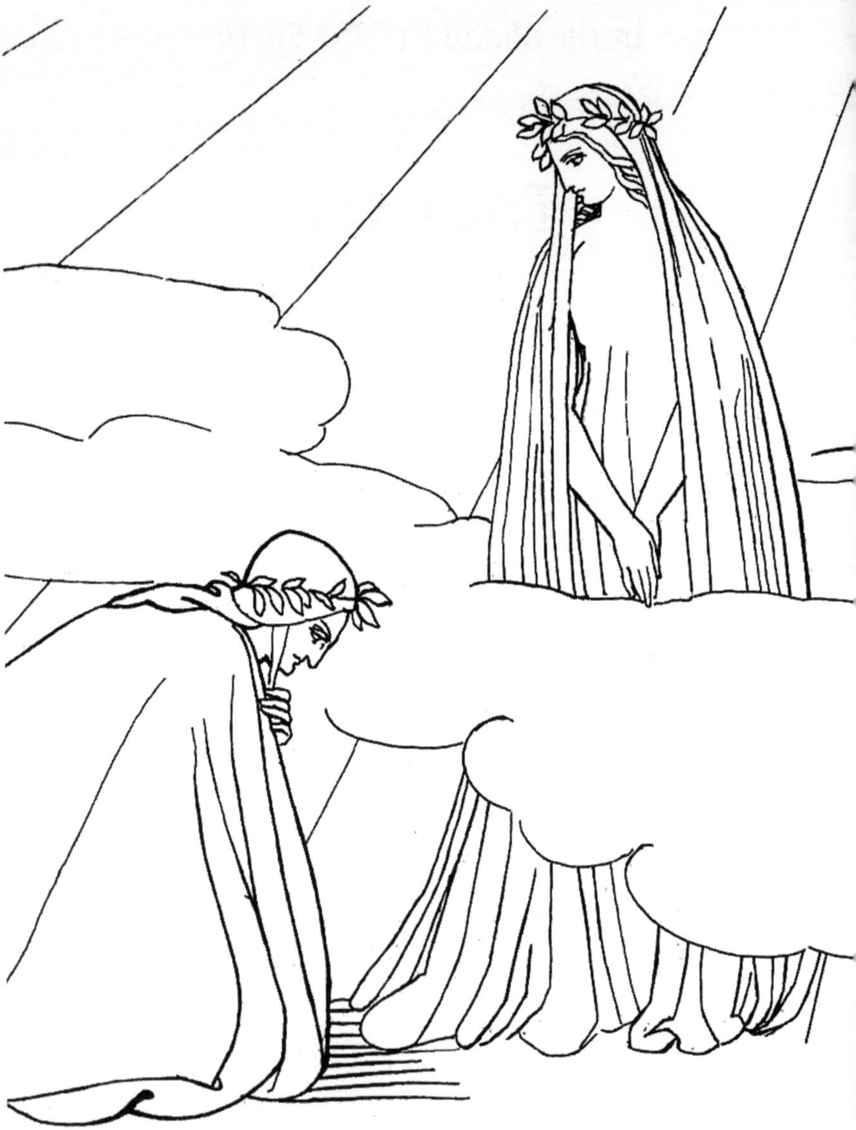

The Moon in Heaven

Ludwig II, the young king of Bavaria, was born in splendour on 25 August 1845 with the sun in Virgo and the moon in Scorpio, presiding over a personality that was passionate but withdrawn and aloof: a conjunction that produces great beauty and even greater tragedy. His horoscope directed him to a higher destiny; the French poet Paul Verlaine called him the nineteenth century's 'one true king'. He came into the world on the same date and at the same hour as his grandfather, King Ludwig I of Bavaria, descended from the House of Wittelsbach, and was named after him. Being born was his first public act as future king, male members of the court being on hand to witness the legitimacy of his succession. Ludwig's father was another Wittelsbach in a line that stretched back over the centuries. His mother was a Prussian princess. She gave birth to Ludwig at Schloss Nymphenburg on the outskirts of Munich, in a simple moss-green bedroom that still looks out over elaborate, strictly organised gardens.

··· ✝ ···

15.10.11 – Nymphenburg: walking in clear autumn sunlight through stables and gardens – huge black carp swimming in long straight waterways – swans on open lakes – trees a deep russet. Landscaped grounds experienced as a continuum in which the novelty of a constantly changing perspective is expected – giving way to pleasure, drama, surprise. The palace is dedicated to Flora, Roman goddess of flowers and spring, and her nymphs – a royal villa or maison de plaisance *in which one grand interior leads into another – intricate Baroque plasterwork, vivid painted ceilings crowded with mythological details spread themselves across every room, defying any camera to make sense of them. Hard not to see Ludwig's passion for visual excess originating here.*

··· ✝ ···

A name can shape a king's destiny more powerfully than any star. August 25 is not only Ludwig's birthday but also his name day, linking him directly to St Louis IX, France's only canonised king. 'Louis' being a common variant for 'Ludwig', the Northern Apollo is able to trace his royal ancestry all the way back to Ludwig of Kelheim, who is said to have been taken out of this world by one of Hassan-i Sabbah's secret assassins. Then there is St Ludwig, Landgrave of Thuringia; and Ludwig the Bavarian, the first Wittelsbach to rule the Holy Roman Empire; and Duke Ludwig the Rich, also of the House of Wittelsbach. And, with the inescapable logic of fate, Ludwig I of Bavaria had for his godfather Louis XVI of France, who died by the executioner's hand in Paris.

••• ✠ •••

Ludwig II believes in the significance of names and dates. They connect him to his past. Like so many monarchs before him, he will pass most of his life in palaces and castles, yearning for a different time. He understands the history and the beauty of being a king. The Holy Roman Empire still remains a very recent loss to him. But Ludwig also knows that he is the most lunar of monarchs, reflecting the borrowed light of his namesakes and antecedents. He is nothing but a copy of a copy, bearing the imprint of a splendour that disappeared from Europe long before his birth at Nymphenburg. Ludwig II feels the crushing weight of its absence.

••• ✠ •••

When Venus emerged fully formed from the waters of the Mediterranean, Jupiter turned the seafoam left in the wake of her birth into the first swan: a bird whose purity and sovereignty would transform it into Ludwig II's personal emblem. To understand the swan and the legend of its creation is to gain some sense of the young king's relationship with his past. He is an unstable form, an insubstantial echo, moulded by an authority that no longer exists. From the moment of his birth, Ludwig II finds himself trapped in a Hall of Mirrors where every appearance is distorted. Trash is the end of all repetition; it marks the draining away of an image's power – Trash is what comes after. Just as a line of endless reflections caught between two mirrors curves heavily away, swerving off into infinity, so a slow and steady downwards drag is continued through each copy.

Trash is the copy that ends all copying. The marble figure of Venus in her circular temple at Linderhof strikes a coy pose copied directly from a statue that appears in Antoine Watteau's *Pilgrimage to Cythera*, which in turn is an embellished copy of his earlier painting *The Embarkation for Cythera*. Both works are based upon the same theme: the pleasures of youth, beauty and love. The first version even features a golden boat very similar to the gilded scallop shell that floats in Ludwig's Venus Grotto. Watteau's paintings fell into disfavour during the French Revolution, Versailles and the French monarchy having become too closely associated with the Baroque style. Over a century later, Ludwig II, having been born into its wild uninhibited symmetries at Nymphenburg, has them faithfully copied at Linderhof. The allegorical figure of Victory holding her two laurel crowns echoes a painted ceiling at Nymphenburg depicting the goddess Flora in similar pose. A gilded statue of Flora reclines at the base of a fountain in the sunken gardens at Linderhof; two cherubs accompany her, covering their ears against the roaring of the water.

··· ✝ ···

The Baroque bathes everything in moonlight, encrusts each form in coral, like shadows rippling through water, waves and seaweed fronds doubling back on themselves. Capri's Grotta Azzurra, in whose colour the Venus Grotto at Linderhof is bathed, was once the personal swimming hole of the emperor Tiberius, as well as a marine temple dedicated to the Roman gods. Tiberius moved from the Roman capital to the island in 27 AD, setting up a secluded pleasure house in which to conduct secret orgies. According to the historian Suetonius, its bedrooms were furnished with the most salacious paintings and sculptures, as well as an extensive erotic library. The emperor arranged for boys and girls dressed as fauns or nymphs to offer themselves outside groves, bowers and grottoes on the island.

⁂

Ludwig II knows he started his life under a bad sign. Dark forces and voices come crowding in around him. As a baby, he is overcome by fever and cramps after his wet nurse dies of meningitis. He never fully recovers his health. A king must be an absence: perceptible only through the things he brings into being. The Baroque consequently reflects the instability of power barely held in check. In a larval frenzy, matter decomposes then rearranges itself: reaching out into the air, turning space and light into something cojoined, crystalline and rotten – each line a distraction to the eye, caught up in intricacies: confused, immersive and alive. According to Abbé Grégoire, Catholic priest and leading voice of the French Revolution: 'kings are to the moral order what monsters are to the physical order.'

⁂

'There were two souls in his breast,' wrote Ludwig von Bürkel, future Court Secretary to King Ludwig II. 'The soul of a tyrant and the soul of a child.'

III

In The Shadow of the Earth

The First Sphere Continued

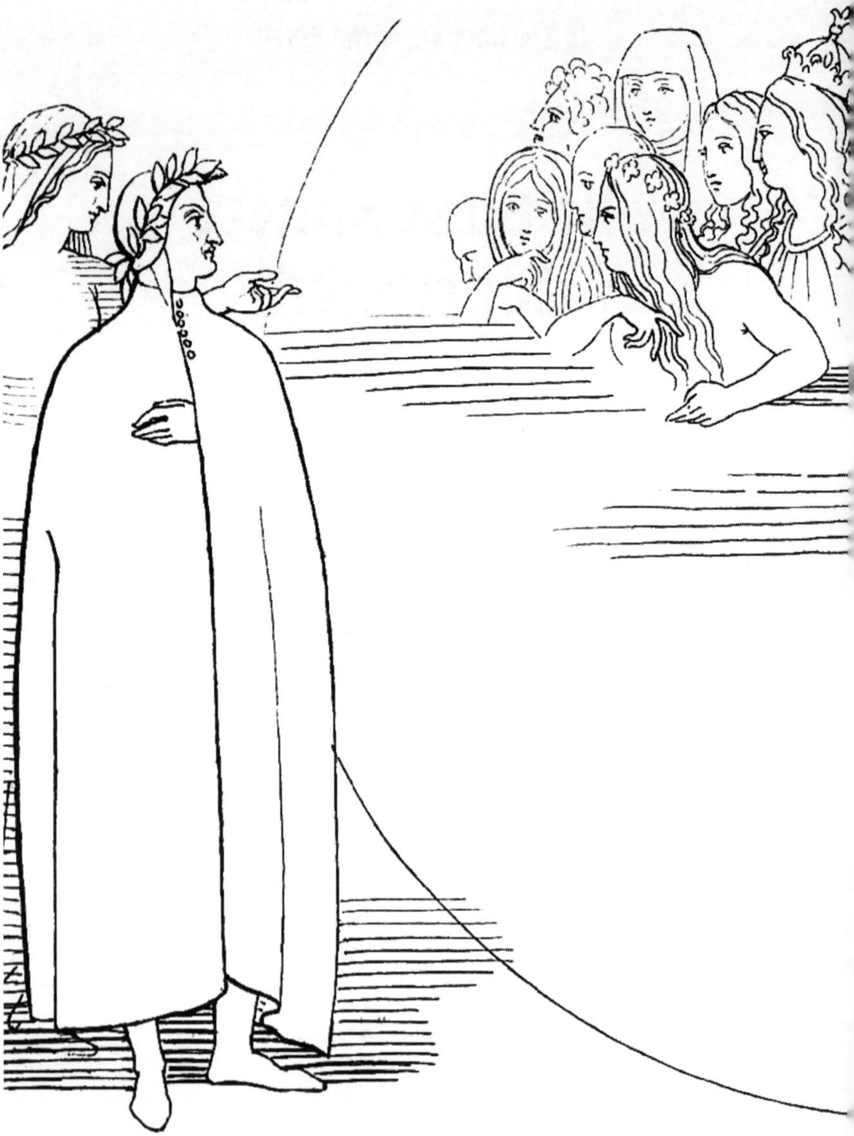

As a pearl set against the palest skin...

Imagine a pale child, plagued by headaches: capable of lying alone in a darkened room for hours at a time, entertained by his own thoughts. The child loves dressing up as a nun, loves playacting and stories – he meets Hans Christian Andersen, who cuts out paper dolls for his amusement. He loves reading, is kind and generous to others and has an imaginative inner life. 'Ludwig developed pleasure in art early on,' his mother recalls, 'he liked to build things, especially churches, monasteries and the like.' In a country where religious orders squandered their resources during the seventeenth century on a Baroque orgy of pilgrims' chapels and churches, Ludwig reconstructs the Holy Sepulchre out of wooden blocks and decorates it with lights. Pleasure for him is something solitary: detached from the world – affirming the right to exist on its own terms. His mother dresses him in a blue uniform – it is Ludwig's favourite colour. His father treats him condescendingly: rarely seeing him except when they encounter each other in palace corridors, granting him at most a cold word in passing. Ludwig's childhood is joyless and lonely. He knows he will be King of Bavaria one day and has to be prevented from tying up his young brother Otto and sentencing him to death for not showing proper deference. 'Read about Louis XIV,' he writes in his diary, 'the power of the ruler, a time of the flowering, the splendour of kingship, omnipotence in the feeling of being a king.'

••• ✝ •••

The term 'Baroque' is derived from an old Portuguese word for a misshapen or imperfect pearl. 'I am having them done up in the rich magnificent style that was fashionable when Louis XIV was on the throne; they make a sumptuous and splendid impression,' Ludwig II writes of his private apartments in the Residenz, the Wittelsbachs' Munich palace. 'One will feel completely transported back to the period of Louis XIV, to the time of the splendour of Versailles, which at that time was the most magnificent, splendid royal seat in Europe.' Louis XIV was a Virgo – just like him. The pearl is associated with the Moon, being irregular and inconstant: its reflected light shimmering like water.

••• ✝ •••

In 1864, following Maximilian II's sudden death, Ludwig ascends to the throne at age eighteen. He starts his reign on the same day Louis XIV started his: 10 March. Everyone is struck by the new king's youth and seriousness, his high moral purpose and passionate ideals. Ludwig's Minister of Justice will one day write of how 'he gloried passionately in everything beautiful, great and noble.' At his father's funeral, everyone remembers the young king's extraordinarily expressive and soulful eyes – they are the first things people notice about him. He is portrayed the year after his ascension gazing intently into the far distance: a dreamy adolescent in the blue uniform of a general, an ermine robe unfurling elegantly around his shoulders; in the shadows behind him sits the crown that Napoleon has forbidden any king of the former Holy Roman Empire to wear. What Ludwig cannot possibly imagine is how far his gaze will project into the future.

The coronation portrait is completed in 1865, but Ludwig never formally posed for it – the painter worked from a photograph instead. The one true king of this century is also the first true king of the Age of Mechanical Reproduction, which is also the age of kitsch; caught between ritual and politics, Ludwig's rule extends into picture postcards and photo albums, rotogravures and prints. From age thirteen until his death, Ludwig II's life is captured by court photographer Joseph Albert, who is present for many of its key moments. Ludwig learns to appreciate the power of this relatively new medium – quickly understands its power as a metaphor. 'My inner world is as sensitive as a photographic plate,' he confesses, 'even the slightest impression is indelibly inscribed there.' Shortly after Joseph Albert starts photographing him, Ludwig has his black hair elaborately curled and waved to give it more body and make his head appear bigger and therefore more in proportion with the rest of his physique. Soon the king insists upon having his hair styled every day – otherwise he claims he is unable to eat.

One of Ludwig's first acts as king is to summon Richard Wagner to Munich and offer the composer his support and protection. 'Alas he is so beautiful and gifted, soulful and magnificent, that I fear his life must fade away like a fleeting, divine dream in this cruel world,' Wagner writes after their first meeting. With Ludwig's help, *Tristan und Isolde*, a work hitherto considered impossible to perform, is finally staged, together with new productions of Wagner's earlier operas *Lohengrin* and *Tannhäuser*. 'I was transported into superterrestrial spheres, I breathed immeasurable bliss,' Ludwig enthuses to Wagner about his music. 'As you may imagine,' observes Wagner, 'his charming ignorance of real life – an ignorance that bears such promise – is bound to involve the young King in conflicts where circumstances make him behave with obvious weakness.' Under such circumstances, Wagner believes, his music – and his music alone – will save this pale and soulful child. Cosima Wagner records in her diary the composer's concern that, without the proper education, their own son Siegfried 'will become a dreamer, maybe an idiot, the sort of thing we see in the King of Bavaria.'

Forget about failed seriousness – Wagner's failed solemnity evokes Trash in the grandest manner. In an age of endless reproduction and applied industrial might, Wagner emerges as a manufacturer of divine sensation: something which sends his former friend and sometime admirer Friedrich Nietzsche into a frenzy of despair. Wagner becomes for him a degenerative nervous condition 'which has disguised itself here, both as an art and as an artist'. Sensuality, beauty and taste are forced to serve as sublime sedatives, leaving behind them the stupefied look of the almost sated. It is perhaps this aspect of Wagner's work that appeals most strongly to a teenage king whose music teacher positively rejoiced when royal duties obliged Ludwig to forego all further lessons. The pale child in his darkened room breathes 'immeasurable bliss' as if it were an anaesthetic.

··· + ···

According to Nietzsche's diagnosis, Wagner is the symptom of a far more prevalent disease. 'Owing to the very fact that nothing is more modern than this thorough morbidness, this dilatoriness and excessive irritability of the nervous machinery,' he writes, 'Wagner is the *modern artist par excellence*, the Cagliostro of modernity. All that the world most needs to-day, is combined in the most seductive manner in his art, – the three great stimulants of exhausted people: brutality, artificiality and innocence (idiocy).' However, it is precisely these qualities that excite the keenest interest when contemplating Trash's appeal today. Wagner tricks out his new Munich residence in lilac silks and purple velvet, decorating his 'Grail Room' with swathes of pink and yellow satin, a Turkish carpet and white flowered moire.

··· + ···

Sensation becomes a pathological condition whereby love, beauty and youth are transformed into brutality, artificiality and innocence (idiocy).

IV

In the Shadow of the Earth

The First Sphere Concluded

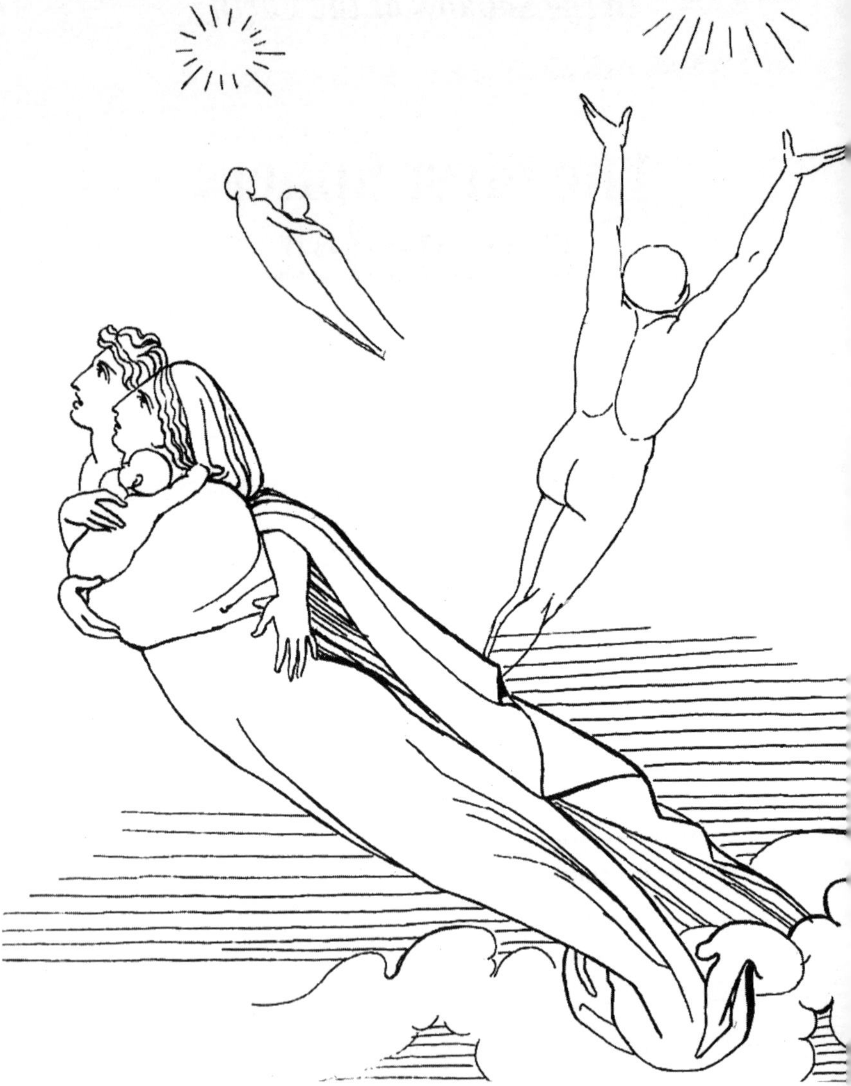

A royal cup of blood

I found myself returning Ludwig II's troubled stare one night. Propped up on my desk, a postcard reproduction shows him in front of Joseph Albert's camera again, one of two poses in the same straight-backed chair. His hair has been lacquered and styled into a complex fractal wave that sweeps up to the right and sharply down to the left; his arms are crossed in front of him, his hands balled into fists. As the camera turns him to stone, you can see Ludwig withdrawing from the world, glancing away: replacing himself with endless copies of the same image. Medusa's gaze confronts itself. 'Incidentally, his majesty has been photographed 82 times,' a visiting dignitary remarks after visiting Ludwig's Munich court. Trash cannot exist without mass production. Ludwig II is destined to become '*der kitsch könig* – his castles and palaces make him the international king of kitsch. There isn't a photograph of him in existence where he is not nervously willing himself to disappear: 'my nature is simply different from that of most of my fellow men,' he reveals, gazing into some unfathomable distance.

Another of Ludwig's early acts as king is to call for a list of all the horses in the royal stables, so he can personally try each one of them out for himself. Ludwig II thinks of horses as his friends. Riding offers an escape from the tedium of court life. Ancient myths and legends of the Grail Knights are more real and more beautiful to Ludwig than the daily transactions of his own cabinet. 'Our young man is becoming increasingly dreamy and unpredictable,' the king's circle of advisors confide uneasily to one another. Ludwig will make sure that the castles he builds are located as far from the Munich Residenz as royally possible.

'It is my intention to rebuild the old castle ruin of Hohenschwangau near the Pollat Gorge in the authentic style of the old German knights' castles,' Ludwig confides in a letter to Wagner. 'The location is one of the most beautiful one could find, holy and unapproachable.' As its name implies, the Schwangau region is renowned for its swans; they are everywhere the king looks – swimming on lakes, painted on walls, reproduced as cheap ceramic gimcracks. Ludwig sees himself as a modern Redeemer – of monarchy, of art and the spiritual culture of his kingdom. Isolated in the mountains with a ravine behind it, a steep ascent at the front and a view of distant fields and lakes, his reinvention of the medieval castle will be dedicated to the myth of the Holy Grail and to the divine right of kings. 'The Emperor Ludwig the Bavarian is said to have built this church after the plan of the Grail Temple at Monsalvat,' Ludwig writes to Wagner from near the Ettal Abbey in Thuringia. 'There the figure of Lohengrin revives anew my vision; and there I see in my mind Parzival, the hero of the future, searching for salvation, for the single truth.' Parsifal, the spelling of whose name remains a mystery to this day, became the Grail King, and Lohengrin was his son. Like Venusberg, the Grail is a Teutonic fantasy left over from the Holy Roman Empire: the sacred conjunction between Christ's blood and a cup as foretold by Flegetanis, 'the heathen astrologer who with his own eyes saw secrets hidden in the constellations and spoke of them reverentially.' Through the mystical power of his name and his bloodline, Ludwig II sees in himself the reincarnation of these hidden mysteries: of oaths and chivalry, spiritual ecstasies and holy combat. Work on his castle begins immediately after the mountain peak has been dynamited flat to make a solid foundation and ensure the finished building will fit into the mountain topography.

Ludwig will only ever see his castle as a building site: high walls of brick and cement surrounded by scaffolding slowly being encased in limestone cladding. Steam-powered cranes and locomotive tractors labour at his mediaeval dream, which is known as 'Neuschwanstein' only after his death. The magnificently decorated Throne Room on the second floor of the castle will also remain unfinished – its blue and gold Byzantine interior still lacks a throne for one thing. Originally intended as the castle's Grail Hall, its design is based on the Church of Hagia Sophia, built in Constantinople in 524 AD during the reign of Emperor Justinian. Hagia Sophia was also believed to have been the model for medieval descriptions of the Grail Temple. The Byzantine Emperors all ruled by the divine right of kings, guaranteed by the executioner's arm. In the gilded apse where a throne should be standing are the richly coloured depictions of six holy kings: Casimir of Poland, Stephen I of Hungary, Emperor Heinrich II, Louis IX of France, Ferdinand III of Spain and Edward the Confessor of England. Other paintings on the walls of the Throne Room include 'Landgravine Elisabeth von Thuringen Performing Charitable Works', 'Saint George' and 'Queen Clothilde of France Converts Her Husband to Christianity'. At its centre a huge chandelier of gilded brass hangs down from an iron dome resting upon an iron framework. All outsiders are forbidden entry to this holy shrine.

The Throne Room murals have the look and feel of Sunday School illustrations. The holy kings and queens are nothing more than richly dressed mannequins, faces rendered in bright pastel shades showing no emotion whatsoever, their lifeless expressions conveying a soulless serenity that only the truly blessed can hope to understand or share. Their costumes, gestures and attitudes represent to Ludwig his personal expectations of kingship as one in a chain of absolute rulers by divine right who knew the inner mysteries of the church and drew upon a sacred bloodline that reaches back all the way to the Grail. It seems to him that in exquisite raiment, and to the delicate sound of flutes, the virtues of the world are passing in dumb show before him. Things that he had dimly dreamed of are suddenly made real to him. Things of which he had never dreamed are gradually revealed. 'Parsifal knows his mission and will do everything in his power to help,' Ludwig assures Wagner, identifying himself in the third person with the Grail King, as he frequently does in their correspondence.

In Wagner's opera, Parsifal is an innocent, resisting the magical charms of the Flower Maidens in Klingsor's garden – and also an idiot mindlessly killing a swan, heraldic bird of the knights of mediaeval Schwangau and Ludwig's personal emblem. For those of a nervous disposition, Trash becomes a banquet of poisons; 'where we think we have caught hold of the Grail,' observes Georges Bataille, 'we have only grasped a thing, and what is left in our hands is only a cooking pot...' Ludwig II has allowed himself to be poisoned by a myth.

••• ✝ •••

There are moments when he looks on beauty simply as a mode through which he can realise his conception of divine right.

V

In The Shadow of the Earth

The Second Sphere

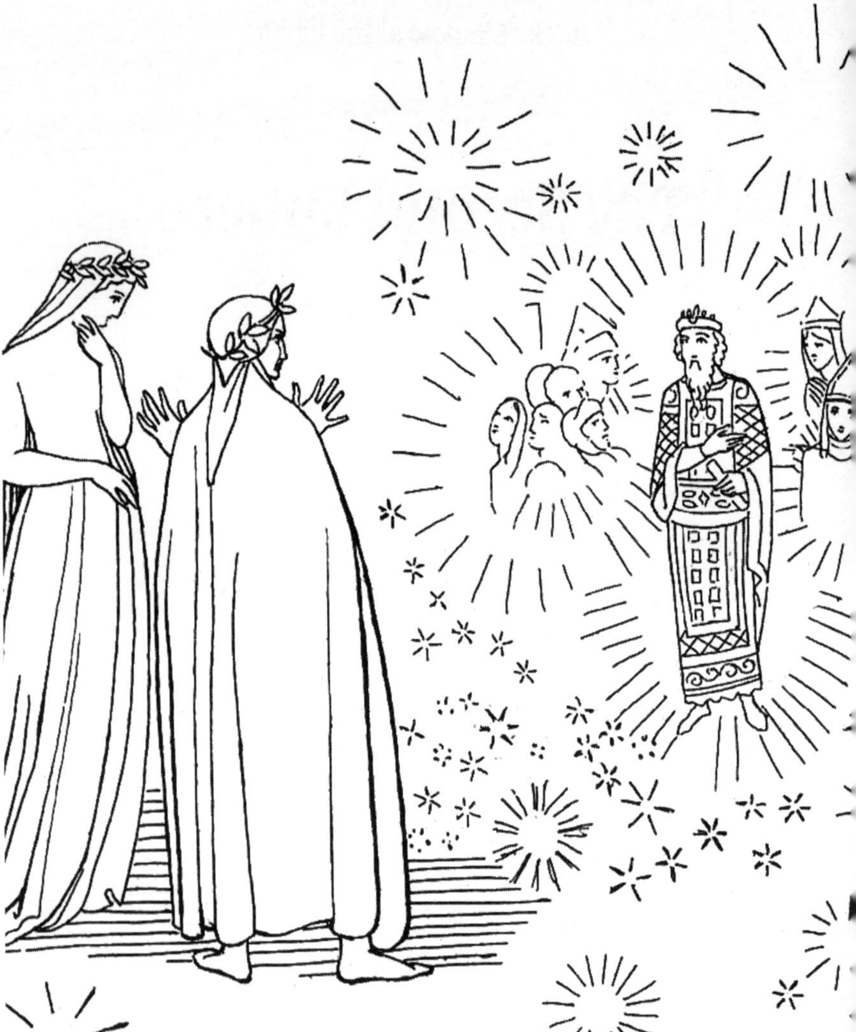

Mercury in Heaven

As Lucifer fell from Heaven, a jewel shook loose from his crown and dropped towards the Earth, where it was transformed into the Holy Grail. You can see it depicted on one of the walls in the Singers' Hall, located above the Throne Room in Neuschwanstein, the smell of fresh polish and lacquer rising from the floor. At the far end of the hall a mural shows the forest that surrounds the Grail Castle: a painted woodland scene from the Parsifal legend presented on a neatly crafted wooden stage, squirrels and old trees forming a theatrical backdrop, the branches reaching up towards the ceiling. Other murals on display include: 'Parzival's first encounter with knighthood', 'Parzival's fight with the Red Knight', 'Parzival's Dream', 'Kundry Summons Parzival', 'Parzival as Grail King' and 'Lohengrin leaves the Castle of the Holy Grail'.

20.8.18 – Neuschwanstein: Overwhelming impact of the castle – too much to take in, which makes it hard to focus on Ludwig's own experience of it – no portraits of him, no mirrors to lose himself or others in. He hides himself instead in the overwhelming richness of the imagery – visual displays and patterns – the colours carvings embroideries furnishings. His name only appears once, in Latin, above the entrance to the Singers' Hall, finished just two days after his death. Hard to take the simpering nobles depicted in the murals after a while – cheap copies of Pre-Raphaelite copies (a lack of maturity in their antiquity) – a king's refuge from the masses – Neuschwanstein: 'a big place to be alone in.'

··· ✠ ···

Parsifal and Lohengrin, Tannhäuser, Siegfried, Tristan and Isolde are represented throughout the castle. Ludwig assures Wagner that Neuschwanstein will be 'a worthy temple for the divine friend who has brought salvation and true blessing to the world' while at the same time commanding his artists and designers to follow closely the original legends and not the composer's interpretation of them. Once they are detached from Wagner's ponderous musical orgies, the importance of these myths to the young king becomes clearer. Ludwig wants 'only painters who make an exact study of medieval poetry': in other words, illustrators who are prepared to stick with a literal interpretation of the text. As for the castle itself, Wagner holds more sway. Christian Jank, who has designed new productions of Wagner's *Lohengrin* and *Tannhäuser* at the Court Theatre in Munich, incorporates elements from the sets for both operas in the Upper Courtyard and the Singers' Hall, inspired by Wartburg castle in Thuringia, which Wagner had urged Ludwig II to visit. One expert in historical restoration later declares that Jank's designs will 'incite the most virulent and bitter criticism'.

⁂

20.8.18 – Neuschwanstein: The Grail as both a blessing and a curse. Ludwig's bedroom a riot of neogothic carving – the washstand has hot and cold running water and is swan-shaped – there is also a private flush toilet, complete with studded green leather seat. Painted scenes here include Tristan on his deathbed with Isolde and, in Ludwig's dressing room, a medieval lord exercising 'droit du cuissage' *on a young woman's wedding night. Still struggling to understand what either is doing in so monastic a room – Ludwig's private chapel has an altar dedicated to Saint Louis IX... The hardest task is to justify Neuschwanstein as Ludwig saw it – not as an outward statement of power but an inward one – a divine passion that was performed not for him but* by *him – to justify all of this economically, because it pays for itself through tourism, is to give a poor account of it.*

··· ✝ ···

Dressed in the ornately embroidered ceremonial robes of the Order of Saint George, of which he is Grand Master, and looking more like a Florentine prince than a young king, Ludwig is in a bad mood. Around his neck are the collar and cross of the Order of Saint Hubertus of which he is also the Grand Master. In the finished sculpture he is shown stepping forward like a dancer, one hand on his sword, the other on his hip. Hair swept back in waves, Ludwig gazes like an eyeless prophet into the unseen distance. He reluctantly agrees to pose for this life-sized portrait in plaster just as planning has started for the creation of Neuschwanstein. The only statue of Ludwig to be completed in his lifetime, this is the work of Elisabet Ney, an artist from Westphalia and a student at the Munich and Berlin academies. It is, according to an account written towards the end of her life, 'a work of rare poetic feeling to which in some mysterious way the artist has contrived to give a tragic prophecy of the doom which even then impended over this unhappily fated monarch.' To keep the king happy during the long sittings, she reads to him from

V
The Second Sphere

Goethe's *Iphigenia in Tauris*. A particular favourite of Ludwig's, this poetic drama concerns the daughter of Agamemnon, a priestess in exile whose fate is in the hands of the gods. *'An unrelenting curse then seiz'd and sever'd me from those I lov'd,'* she laments, *'and wrench'd with iron grasp the beauteous bands.'* Ney and Ludwig talk for hours. She is related by birth to Marshal Ney, who rode to glory with Napoleon, then pledged allegiance to France's newly restored constitutional monarch Louis XVIII, then rode with Napoleon again – for which he was charged with treason and executed by firing squad. As a constitutional monarch who had his crown taken away by Napoleon, Ludwig II understands a little about fate. 'I feel alone and abandoned on this earth, as someone left over from better days, transplanted into the present time, which I hate and in which I shall always feel alien,' Ludwig confides in a letter written around the time he is posing for Elisabet Ney's statue of him. She wears a flowing white gown while she works; and each morning he fills her studio with fresh flowers.

⁂

'But in feasts everlasting, around golden tables still dwell the immortals,' sings Iphigenia in unbearable exile. The visitors' coach park at Neuschwanstein is an

unacknowledged masterpiece of land art created in the wake of Ludwig's grand architectural vision. The castle, its courtyard and its grounds are overrun by tourists from all over the world; none of them know what they're looking at – a place that exists only in guidebooks and postcards. I am struck once again by the garish luminescence of the murals: bright colours painted onto plaster, intended to be seen only by candlelight at night – even though the first electric light in Bavaria was installed at Neuschwanstein. The ban on cameras anywhere inside the castle protects the paintings' mystique. Much of the gold on display is either gilded, painted or plated – the gemstones are coloured glass. You exit Neuschwanstein via a long echoing tunnel that opens onto a path at the foot of the castle and an amazing view of the mountains receding towards a distant blue horizon.

A woman in reception is talking on the phone: 'But it's Neuschwanstein,' she is saying insistently. 'It's very beautiful.'

VI

In The Shadow of the Earth

The Second Sphere Continued

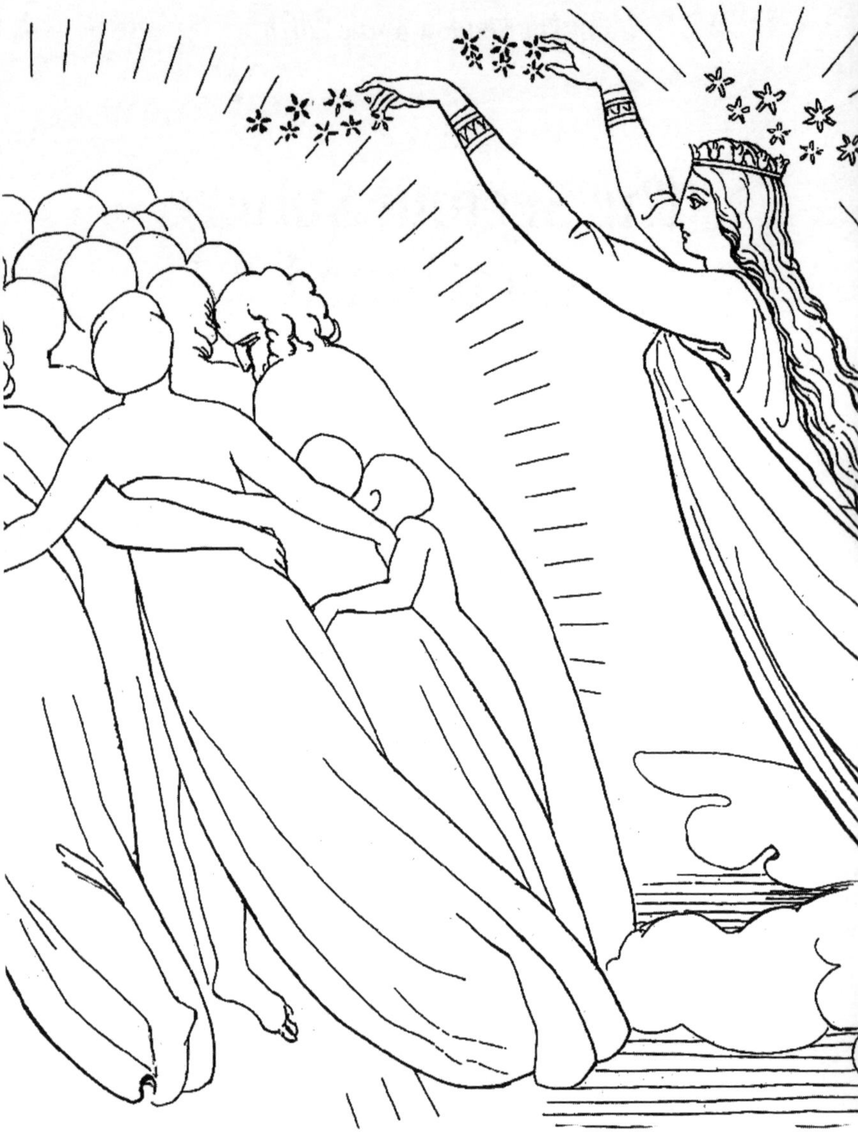

This little star made more beautiful...

From earliest childhood, Ludwig would fix his gaze upon a beautiful painting or object whenever someone plain or ugly entered the room, and remain focussed upon it until they left. As king, he increasingly grows uncomfortable being the centre of everybody's attention. His life becomes one long gallery. Here time does not become space but an uninterrupted sequence of images, faces and associations. Ludwig I famously commanded that a *Gallery of Beauties* be created for the moral education of the public: a set of thirty-six portraits of the most beautiful women in Europe who were also of good character. Included in the series were Ludwig II's mother Marie of Prussia and Ludwig I's mistress, Lola Montez. Ludwig II was only two and a half years old when his grandfather abdicated over his affair with the 'Spanish dancer', leading to the constitutional monarchy his grandson despises so much. Ludwig II comes to believe that his reign can only be justified aesthetically.

Ludwig II meets actresses, dancers and singers and nearly falls in love with them, sending them expensive gifts, but only so long as they remain in character or hidden from view. An innocent fool obliges others to play their part. What happens on the theatre stage, to a self-proclaimed 'shadow king without power', remains more real than anything in everyday life. In the words of Ludwig II's Minister of Justice: 'He placed great value on feeling that his heart was pure and that his soul was chaste and unsullied.' Or as George Bataille will note in a very different context: 'The Maenads would flee in disarray, whereas the object of desire adorns herself with the greatest care and offers a motionless figure to the temptation of a possessor.' Ludwig keeps his mind on higher things, complaining that the sculpted hair on a statue of Venus was 'too much like a cook's'. His bedroom at Hohenschwangau, his family home, boasts an indoor fountain, a 'rainbow machine', plus a ceiling of glittering stars, an artificial moon and the branches of orange trees.

Craving aesthetic sensation above all else, Ludwig II commissions the painter Friedrich Wilhelm Pfeiffer to produce his own *Gallery of Beauties* comprising twenty-six portraits of his favourite riding horses.

VI
The Second Sphere Continued

This includes the dapple-grey mare Cosa Rara, shown standing calmly before a table laden with roast meat, trout and red wine, an overturned glass pitcher and flowers scattered on the ground. Ludwig had once commanded that Cosa Rara dine with him, and a place be set for her in the banqueting hall. Cosa Rara responded by kicking over everything in sight, thereby smashing a costly china dinner service. 'It is necessary,' states Bataille, 'to contrast the courtesan's carefully arranged beauty with the disheveled animality of the Maenads...' Many a lovesick girl, according to one historical account, 'wore in her locket a few hairs of a horse the king had ridden or the petals of a flower that his foot had crushed.'

⁂

Kings and queens are mated like horses. There is an extravagant erotic play to the making of stallions: the imprinting of value upon royal flesh and the transmission of divine right through the blood. Margaret of Provence, one of four daughters to be joined with kings through arranged marriages, weds Louis IX at age thirteen. Ludwig II's love of beauty as a sign of moral perfection transcends all obligation to reproduce. He briefly becomes engaged to marry his cousin, the Duchess Sophie Charlotte in Bayern, sister to Empress

Elisabeth of Austria. Their betrothal being announced, Ludwig and Sophie pose for Joseph Albert's camera: a stiff and reserved young couple. Aside from some informal portraits taken in Switzerland with the actor Josef Kainz, this is the sole occasion when Ludwig allows someone else to share the lens with him. Ludwig orders a magnificent gold carriage for their wedding, but it is never used; 'the gloomy image is dissolving,' he writes, having called off the engagement, dismissing the whole affair as 'a tortuous nightmare'. While Ludwig was having doubts about their relationship, a 'base' rumour alleges Sophie had been exchanging passionate love letters with the son of his court photographer.

Perhaps Sophie noticed that, although he addresses his fiancé as 'Elsa' in their correspondence, identifying her with the woman who becomes Lohengrin's bride in Wagner's opera, Ludwig refers to himself as 'Heinrich', king of Brabant. This character is based upon 'Heinrich der Vogler', who in the tenth century founded the Ottonian Dynasty, which went on to rule the Holy Roman Empire: a destiny that clearly did not involve marrying 'Elsa'. Ludwig would always be Parsifal, Wagner's 'innocent fool', while Lohengrin was a role that had to be played by someone else.

On his eighteenth birthday, Ludwig is presented with his own personal aide-de-camp: a handsome young officer from the 2nd Artillery Regiment called Paul von Thurn und Taxis. He shares Ludwig's love of theatre and his passion for Wagner's *Lohengrin*. In November 1865, according to Hohenschwangau castle records, Thurn und Taxis takes the lead in a *son et lumiere* reconstruction of the arrival of the Swan Knight from Wagner's *Lohengrin* on the shores of the Alpsee. 'A large artificial swan drew across the lake a boat in which stood Lohengrin; the Swan Knight was splendidly lit using electric bulbs. Meanwhile the musicians played the respective pieces from *Lohengrin*. By command of His Majesty, the performance was repeated the following evening.' Lohengrin is not only the son of Parsifal but also a symbol of chivalry and a messenger from God. Ludwig projects this ideal upon his handsome young aide with the precision of a sex fantasy. This explains the horror with which Ludwig watched a production of *Lohengrin* staged in Munich with Wagner's blessing: 'Through his opera glasses,' runs one account, 'he saw not the poetic Knight of the Grail of his boyhood dreams but a sagging face painted and plastered into a simulacrum of youth and an ancient body maintaining its uncertain equilibrium.'

Wagner's failed solemnity always sinks into tired and fleshly pleasures. The bath taken by Amfortas in Act I of *Parsifal* is perhaps the most ponderous ceremonial cleansing to take place since the great days of Queen Cleopatra. Enter Kundry, 'the wild woman' with her gift of balsam to ease the wounded king into the holy lake. Just as Act II replaces Ludwig I's *Gallery of Beauties* with the sultry and languid charms of Wagner's Flower Maidens, so Kundry emerges as a Trash Maenad for the industrial age: the mother of all centrefolds and pinups, flinging her arms around the neck of an enchanted fool. 'The raid of the Maenads has the primary meaning of life limited to the moment,' Bataille observes. Meanwhile Kundry mocks and seduces, rages and grieves. She keeps her distance but is always dangerous when she draws near.

Ludwig II's unused gold wedding coach can still be seen on display in the stables at Nymphenburg – along with Cosa Rara's stuffed remains.

VII

In The Shadow of the Earth

The Second Sphere Concluded

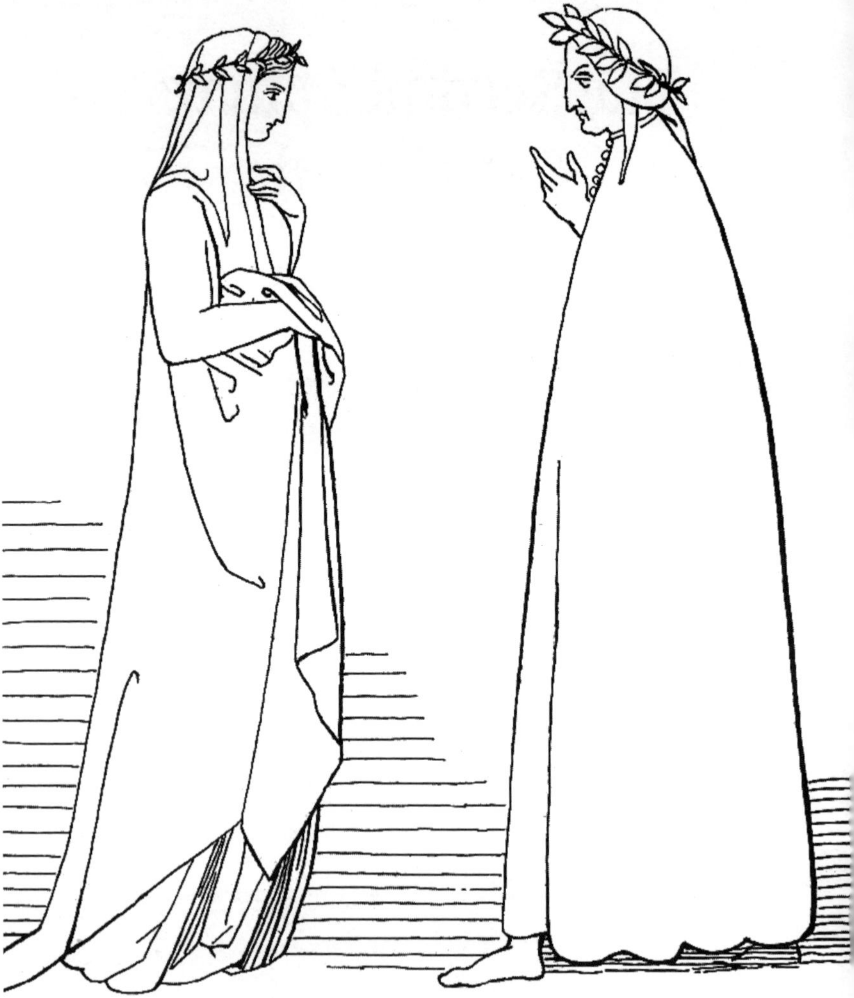

Between the final judgement and creation

The Kingdom of the Grail, the castle and the sacred wood that surrounds it are blighted. There is only pain and sadness here. The evil wizard Klingsor has stolen a precious holy relic: the spear with which the Roman centurion Longinus pierced the Redeemer's side as He hung upon the Cross that first Good Friday. Before taking it back to his magic kingdom, Klingsor uses the spear to wound Amfortas, the Grail King, who remains gravely ill but cannot die. Enter Parsifal: handsome, heroic and dumb as a box of silicone dildos. He doesn't know, for example, that the Spear of Longinus is actually in the possession of the Hapsburgs: rulers for centuries of the Austro-Hungarian Empire, to whom Ludwig II is linked through his cousin Elisabeth's marriage to the Emperor Franz Josef. Furthermore, Parsifal cannot even understand how he got to Monsalvat, the Grail Castle, connected through the Emperors of Byzantium to the Church of Hagia Sophia. The mysteries of the Grail mean nothing to him – but they mean the world to Ludwig, the Parsifal of the modern world and the coming New Age.

The aesthetic tragedy of Ludwig II's existence can only be appreciated once his identification with Parsifal is taken as being both total and literal. He is Parsifal, plain and simple. Everything else is mere imagery: complex, allegorical, open to interpretation but, in the end, seductive and misleading.

'I'm no Lola Montez,' protests Richard Wagner from his elegant new home on Munich's fashionable Brienner-strasse, surrounded by his coloured silks and satins, valences and rosettes, with two peacocks scratching around in the garden. The young king's circle of advisors, as well as many members of polite society and the Bavarian press, beg to differ. To them, Ludwig's obsession with the German composer is another sex scandal waiting to happen. Wagner deals in myths, not allegories. He is referred to derisively as 'Lolus' in public: the next infatuation to bring down a monarch, just like with Ludwig I, the young king's grandfather. Ludwig II showers Wagner with money, paying for music that is renowned for having an unhealthy and unnatural effect upon its listeners. Returning home to his castle in the mountains after a particularly intense performance of *Tristan und Isolde* in Munich, Ludwig orders his private train to stop so that he

can wander around in the dark woods to calm his overwrought nerves. He then spends the rest of the journey in the locomotive's cab, the engine blazing red fire into the night.

As he approaches Klingsor's castle, Parsifal finds himself in a beautiful garden surrounded by Flower Maidens who, adept at luring knights to their destruction, wind themselves around the innocent fool in an effort to seduce him. Wagner, in his own way, is equally adept at elevating sensuality to a form of sublime intoxication – all tawdriness and immorality corrected by high art's equivalent of the 'square-up reel': the unacknowledged Redeemer of exploitation cinema. Confined and cultivated in their magic garden, the Flower Maidens remain safely on the edge of wildness, while the Maenads willingly give themselves up to it in an instant. 'For once I will be open and throw aside my mask, even if in doing so I damage myself in the eyes of the King,' writes the Hungarian actress Lilla von Bulyowsky in a letter to Ludwig II. 'From the moment I saw and greeted Your Majesty as Crown Prince in the English Garden I felt for the first time in my life what the word "love" really means.' Confession, as Parsifal will soon discover, turns guilt into remorse. On a visit to the luxurious Winter Garden installed upon the roof of Ludwig's Munich Residenz, his paradise and refuge in the heart of the city, the operatic soprano Josefine Scheffsky contrives to fall into the artificial lake at its centre, fully expecting His Majesty to rescue her – but the king merely rings for a servant to pull her out again. 'Don't run down dyed hair and painted faces,' Lord Henry Wotton cautions Dorian Gray once again. 'There is an extraordinary charm in them, sometimes.'

··· ✠ ···

In his palace grounds at Linderhof, Ludwig installs not only a reconstruction of the cave where Venus seduced Tannhäuser into a life of sensual pleasure but also a copy of the simple wooden hut where Gurnemanz the hermit joyfully greets Parsifal on the morning of Good Friday: a redeemed Redeemer come to restore the holy rites of the Grail Castle. 'There everything reminds me of that solemn morn of Good Friday in your blissful *Parsifal,* which pierced the depths of my soul with overwhelming force,' Ludwig writes in a letter to Wagner. 'On that holy ground I hear the portentous call of silver trumpets resounding from the Grail Castle; there I hear the holy chants of Monsalvat echoing down from the remote mountains; there I feel so happy, near that fountain where Parsifal was anointed, receiving the consecration of the true and authentic kingship that is achieved through humility and the destruction of all evil inside oneself.'

It is only thanks to Ludwig II's royal patronage that *Parsifal*, Wagner's final opera, is completed – and it is only thanks to Ludwig's help and support that its first performance can take place at the Festspielhaus in Bayreuth, built to Wagner's own specifications exclusively for the staging of his work. Wagner benefitted so much from his relationship with Ludwig that it is all too easy to judge it purely in terms of what he derives from the king, rather than what the king has been able to derive from him. The playacting in Wagner's music dramas, their scenery, costumes and lighting allow Ludwig to embrace what he alone takes to be real. Within the palace grounds at Linderhof there stands a lavish 'Moroccan House' as well as a richly ornate 'Moorish Kiosk', both inspired by Wagner's choice of 'Arabic Spain' as the setting for Klingsor's castle and Monsalvat in *Parsifal*. Ludwig declines Wagner's personal invitation to attend the opera's premiere in 1882 on the grounds of ill health. In fact, the king won't attend a complete performance of *Parsifal* until almost a full year after the composer's death, meaning that the two of them are never to see the work together – but then why would the hero of the future need to? Ludwig will always be Parsifal.

On the journey back from Linderhof, the storm continues to break over the mountains that fringe the valley, violet lightning crackling through the heavy grey sky, the motorway stretching ahead of us. A sudden flash illuminates a medieval fort made out of enormous blocks of yellow foam rubber that appear to be decomposing in the twilight: a play area for children in the middle of a field close to the roadside. The tour guide nods towards the rotting yellow fort, abandoned in the rain – pointing it out to us.

'Another one of Ludwig's castles,' he remarks with an amiable smile, as the coach swings by, and we disappear into the night.

VIII

In The Shadow of the Earth

The Third Sphere

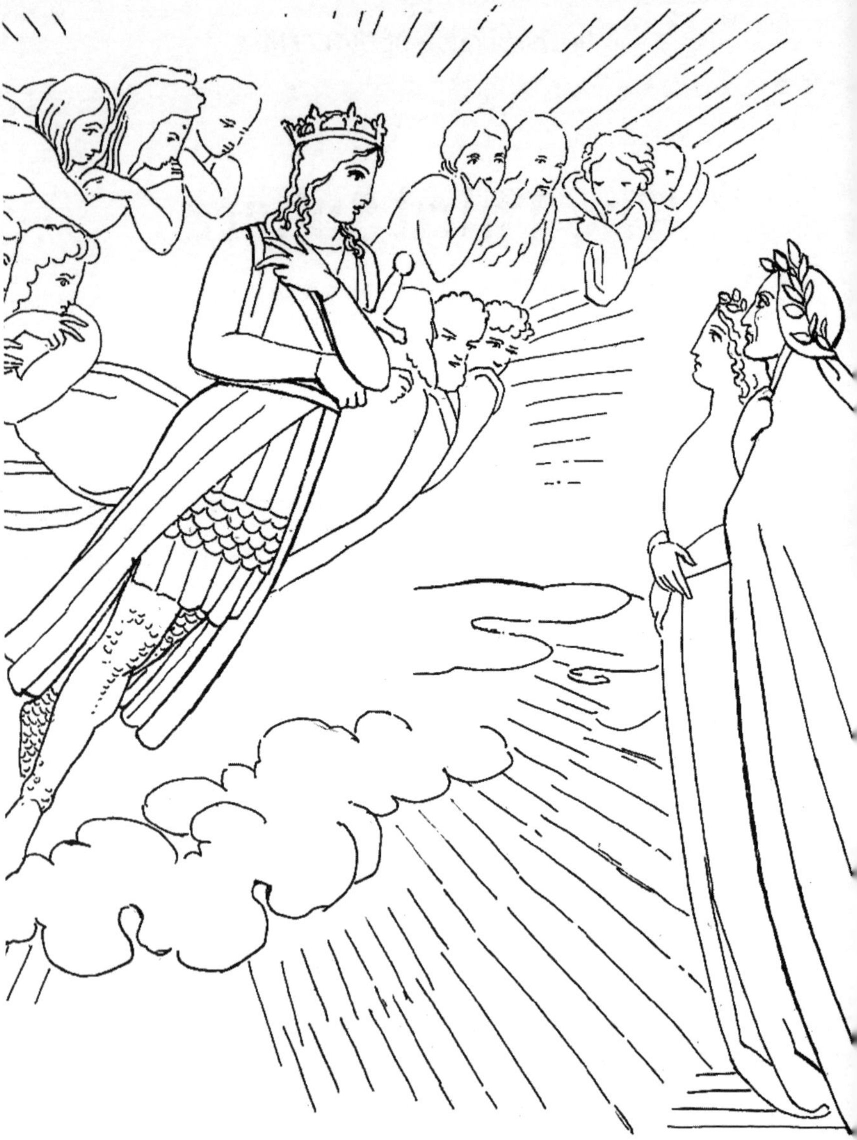

Venus in Heaven

'I saw an enormous garden, lit in the Venetian manner, with palms, a lake, bridges, pavilions, castellated buildings,' wrote the Spanish Infanta, Maria de la Paz. '"Come," said the King, and I followed him fascinated, as Dante followed Virgil to Paradise.' Trapped inside a different book, Virgil would never have been allowed to come this far. The Infanta is describing the interior of Ludwig II's Winter Garden: the vast structure of iron and glass located above the North Wing of the Residenz, filled with tropical plants and exotic creatures. A blue parrot perched on a golden hoop greets the Infanta, while peacocks quietly strut by. A huge painted backdrop by theatrical set designer Christian Jank, depicting a lush green valley and a lake in the shadow of the mighty Himalayas, covers an entire wall. There is a tent of blue silk adorned with roses, a rustic wooden bridge over an illuminated freshwater lagoon, plus a wide range of lighting effects. 'The King invited me to take a centre seat at the table and gently rang a little hand-bell,' the Infanta continues. 'Suddenly a rainbow appeared.'

This rainbow is the work of electrical engineer Max Thomas Edelmann, who has created numerous effects from nature for Ludwig's castles, including sunrises and sunsets, moonlight and stars, thunder, lightning and rushing water. 'I don't wish to know how it works,' Ludwig impatiently informs Edelmann, who is attempting to explain the principle behind one particular illusion. 'I'm only interested in the effect it produces.' How can anyone after Mallarmé not grasp the sensibility behind that statement?

The King has a castle on Lake Starnberg, together with a small private steamship that he christens *Tristan* and uses to visit his cousin the Empress Elisabeth, more familiarly known as 'Sisi', across the water from him. Sisi is slender and glamourous with long beautiful hair. She hates her life in Vienna but loves horseback riding in the mountains and writes bad poetry. Ludwig worships her like a goddess, showering her with flowers and writing equally bad poetry dedicated to her.

Ludwig also uses the *Tristan* to seclude himself on the Roseninsel, a small island in the middle of the lake. Here an Italianate summer house offers him and his aide-de-camp Paul von Thurn und Taxis a refuge from the world. 'Oh! It is essential to create such paradises, such poetical sanctuaries where one can forget for a while the dreaded age in which we live,' Ludwig II writes to his former governess. At night Thurn und Taxis dresses up as Lohengrin, and they organise firework displays together. 'The King sees no one now,' the Prince of Hohenlohe-Schillingsfürst notes gloomily, as war looms between Prussia and Bavaria. Meanwhile, Ludwig and Paul ride around the island setting off so many fireworks that the Starnberg fire brigade has to be called – or for long periods of time Ludwig stays in his room, soothing himself under the light of an artificial moon. On the day hostilities break out with Prussia, he and Thurn und Taxis are too busy celebrating the third anniversary of the first performance of *Tristan und Isolde* to notice. A visit by the Russian Tsarina is marked by evermore fireworks. 'I want to escape this damned, hellish gloom, which is constantly trying to suck me into its miasma... far away from the profane, everyday world, from unholy politics, which tries to wrap me in its tentacles, hoping to suffocate all poetry entirely,' Ludwig complains to Wagner. 'Our royal master is living wholly in the realms of legend, poetry, music and drama,' notes one observer. 'His world is the theatre, which for him is the epitome of all splendour. He wants nothing to do with the rest of the world, with the prose of life, and would like to keep himself as far away from it as possible.'

••• ✝ •••

In September 1898 Sisi is assassinated while boarding a steamer on Lake Geneva, stabbed by an Italian anarchist who later proclaims that 'it did not matter to me who the sovereign was whom I should kill... it was a crown that I had in view.' The previous year, her sister Sophie, formerly affianced to Ludwig II of Bavaria, died in a fire at the annual Bazar de la Charité in Paris, where an unattended Joly-Normandin movie projector had burst into flames.

••• ✝ •••

24.7.17 – Merano: Trauttmansdorff Castle in the South Tyrol, where Empress Elisabeth stayed for her health and to avoid being in Vienna. Rooms dedicated to her visits, views of exotic gardens through the windows. R and I see her bedchamber – also the one occupied by the Emperor Franz Josef on his cold lonely visits to renew their failing marriage. Reliquaries include Sisi's bathrobe and a chocolate cake especially baked for her, of which she only ate a thin slice, the rest being-

preserved as a 'holy relic': flat, dark and brick-hard, so 'even the mice won't touch it'.

··· ✝ ···

'I am suffering terribly,' Ludwig writes. 'I feel completely alone, alone on the royal throne, surrounded by the glow of princely splendour, a fire that gives off no heat.' How close he comes here to the distinguishing characteristic of the dandy's beauty, according to Charles Baudelaire: the 'air of coldness which comes from an unshakeable determination not to be moved; you might call it a latent fire which hints at itself, and which could, but chooses not to burst into flame.' The king is the unmoved eye at the centre of an intense aesthetic storm. The hurried entrances and exits of artists, designers, singers, actors and servants are synchronised around him. He becomes a recluse, spending much of his time reading. 'The main requirement was for books of the seventeenth and eighteenth centuries dealing with the time of Louis XIV and XV,' notes a secretary.

··· ✝ ···

Soon Ludwig is commanding private performances of selected plays, operas and ballets, mostly set in seventeenth and eighteenth-century France, at the

Residenz Theatre. These works are never staged for the public, nor will they ever be. They are for the king's sole pleasure. The elaborate, time-consuming and costly preparations required for these presentations reflect a literal understanding of aesthetics as a form of power. Once again, the innocent fool requires everyone around him to play a part. 'Theatre cannot be an illusion for me as long as I am constantly stared at by the people, my every facial expression followed through their opera glasses,' the king explains. 'I want to watch, not be an object watched by the masses.' For him, the illusion had to be complete. 'The performance was not considered over until the King stood up,' notes one onlooker. Ludwig often leaves the royal box in silence and without applauding. He starts to stay up all night, shunning the hours of daylight.

⁘ ✝ ⁘

He rises at seven in the evening, lunches at midnight and is served dinner in the small hours, going to bed just as the rest of the world is waking.

IX

In The Shadow of the Earth

The Third Sphere Concluded

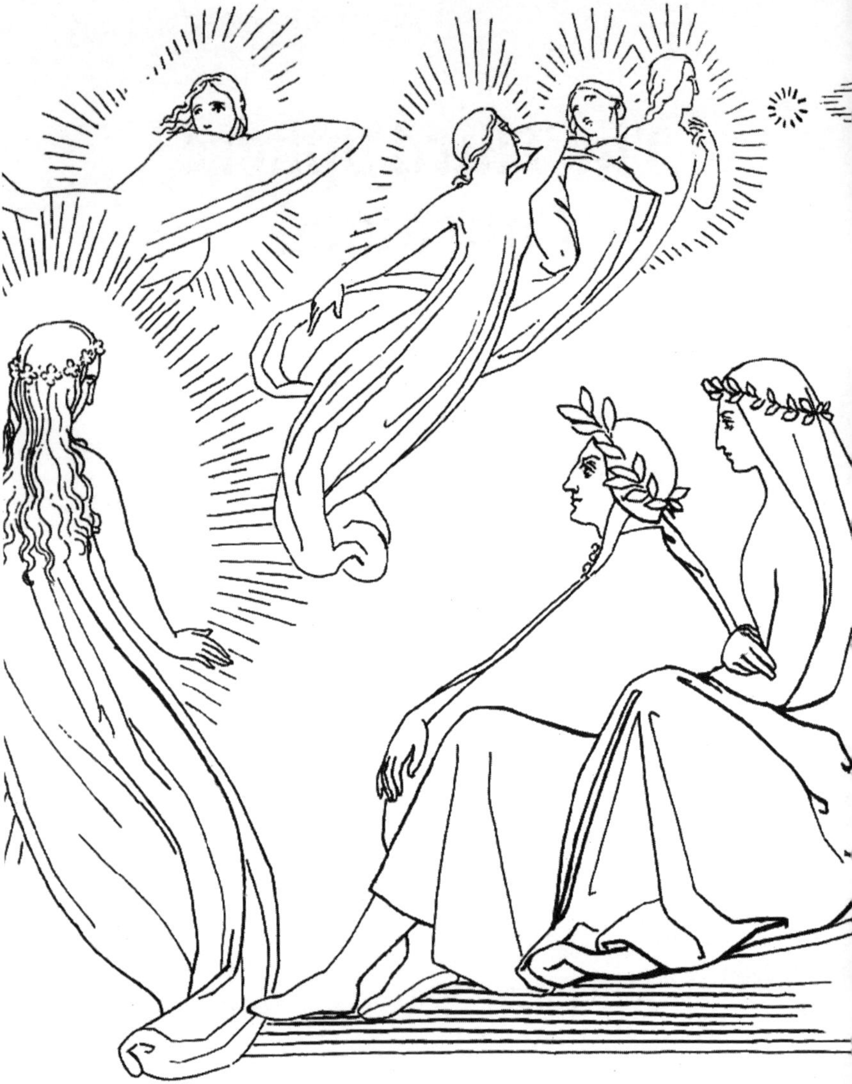

Past halls of mirrors and thrones...

In the late summer of 1901 two English women, on a visit to Versailles, went in search of the Petit Trianon: a small palace within the grounds favoured by Bourbon kings and queens as a retreat since the reign of Louis XIV. They followed what they thought was the correct path but soon found themselves lost in an unfamiliar landscape. 'Everything suddenly looked unnatural and therefore unpleasant,' one of the women recalled, 'even the trees behind the building seemed to have become flat and lifeless, like a wood worked in tapestry.' There were, she revealed, no effects of light and shade and no wind stirred the trees. 'It was intensely still... I was beginning to feel as though we were walking in a dream, – the stillness and oppressiveness were so unnatural.' A sense of great oppression and dreariness dogged them. The isolated figures they encountered in this eerie landscape appeared to have come from another age, presenting a sinister eighteenth-century *tableau vivant* featuring aristocrats and servants caught in brief instances from their lives. A woman in an 'old fashioned' white dress sat sketching the quiet trees. Convinced that they had somehow managed to travel back in time together, the two women published a detailed account of their experiences. What they had witnessed, their book claimed, were the events of 10 August 1792, six weeks before the French monarchy was bloodily abolished. The woman sketching in the white dress, they were now able to reveal, had once been Marie Antoinette.

··· ✝ ···

Ludwig holds annual funeral masses for Louis XIV and Marie Antoinette. 'On 21 January,' a diary entry reveals, 'the day of the murder of King Louis XVI, a day that is forever dark and terrible, at funeral mass I vowed once again before the image of the Holy Virgin and the Christ Child and before the image of Holy King Louis IX… vowing before the image of King Louis XIV the Great to overcome evil…' His palace at Linderhof is intended to be his Petit Trianon: a small retreat from 'a world that always denies me and which I will never, ever be able or desire to befriend.' Everything about its ornate Baroque interior is designed to overwhelm: the visual logic of space and dimension have been delicately but thoroughly overwrought – all the colours blend in with the overall predominance of gold. The elaborate carved and moulded interiors of the Lilac, Rose and Blue Cabinets are home to portraits of Louis XV and his lover Madame de Pompadour, together with prominent members of his court. An intricate Hall of Mirrors and a richly appointed bedchamber pick up the intricate gilding of the stucco, directly evoking the splendour of Versailles. A ceiling fresco depicts the apotheosis of Louis XIV, which is his elevation to the rank of a god. King Ludwig II of Bavaria holds conversations in French with long deceased members of the Bourbon family, occasionally even dining with them. To be dead is to exist solely in the past: to be limited by the dimensions of the past to an image. And how does Parsifal, the innocent fool, the future hero understand this? One technical innovation is the 'wishing table' in the palace's elaborate Dining Room. Based on French eighteenth-century prototypes, this table can be lowered to the ground floor by pulleys then raised back up again, thereby allowing the king to dine undisturbed with his dead guests.

Ludwig had originally wanted to call this personal villa 'Meicost Ettal': an anagram of Louis XIV's absolutist pronouncement: *'L'État, c'est moi.'* Each grand room, each decorated corridor is just another place for the king to hide from his own fall from sovereignty. A king cannot rule by divine right in a constitutional democracy. Ludwig's understanding of absolute power, sovereignty and death remains literal, which means that it takes the form of playacting. It is a role imposed upon him; just as Louis XIV is alive in Louis XV and executed in the body of Louis XVI, so are their former majesties reincarnated in him, Ludwig II. He exerts his will without condition, flying into rages if any of his demands are questioned. *'Must?'* Ludwig declares. 'A king never *"must"* anything...' He builds his castles and palaces as 'holy places' in which he enacts the passion of the royal body as both performer and sole spectator. To atone for the loss of sovereignty that has been handed down to him, he conceives of Herrenchiemsee, a second Versailles standing alone and unfinished on an island in the centre of a very large lake.

••• ✝ •••

Intended as a 'Temple of Glory' for Louis XIV, Herrenchiemsee is not a copy of Versailles but an expanded reconstruction: an overpoweringly rich setting in which Ludwig himself becomes a humble interloper, spending only three nights and ten days there. At its innermost sacred centre is the sumptuous red and gold bedchamber in which the spirit of Louis XIV is once again able to enact the ritual of his *levee* before an audience of favoured courtiers. Elaborately ornate versions of the Hall of Mirrors and the Ambassadors' Staircase overwhelm visitors while providing familiar surroundings to the former King of France.

··· ✠ ···

14.10.11 Herrenchiemsee: Hall of Mirrors kept growing until it finally reached 89 metres, ceiling and upper walls smothered in frescoes and stucco depicting the deeds of Louis XIV – 23 windows and 23 mirrors making the most of all available daylight – illuminated by 2000 candles at night but solely for Ludwig's own contemplation. Rough exposed brickwork of the unfinished North Staircase. Shared leftover chocolate gateau with R in the empty Marble Court flooded with warm sunlight. Walked down a tree-lined avenue to the water's edge before returning to the landing stage for the ferry back to the harbour – grebes among the reeds on the lakeshore – start of a glorious sunset discernible in the sky and the mountains looking magnificent in outline across the horizon.

··· ✠ ···

One possible explanation for the English women's 'time travel' experience at Versailles is that they unknowingly wandered into a *fête galante* organised by dandy and aesthete Robert de Montesquiou, who lived nearby. He was known to throw elaborate parties in the palace grounds that featured his guests dressing in historical costumes and taking part in elaborate *tableaux vivants*. Montesquiou also idolised Ludwig II of Bavaria and had in his possession a framed envelope addressed in the king's own hand.

••• ✠ •••

Herrenchiemsee remains Ludwig's biggest, most ambitious palace; out of its seventy rooms only twenty will be finished. There will be no library here, no theatre and only one working bathroom in the entire building. Most of the rooms are never to be used. The blue nightlight in Ludwig's apartment took his painters an age to perfect. Stranded between dream and reality, it's not a palace for living in but for seeing. To stay too long might ruin the illusion.

••• ✠ •••

Construction on Herrenchiemsee ceases when the money runs out, leaving an orderly set of empty spaces for ghosts to creep into.

X

In the Shadow of the Stars

The Fourth Sphere

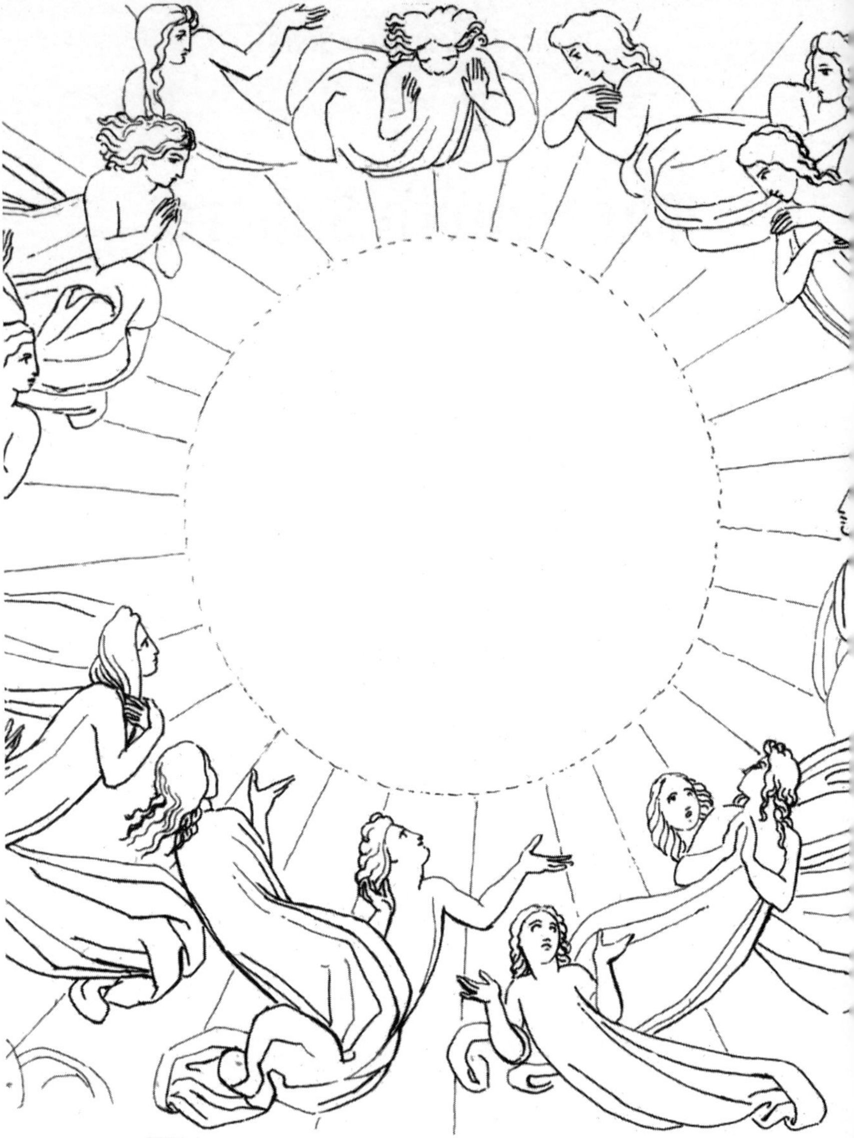

The Sun in Heaven

••• ✝ •••

As it was in the end, so shall it be at the beginning. Louis XIV of France loved to dance from a very early age. A drawing shows the king as a youth of fourteen dressed as Apollo, performing in the *Ballet of the Night*: entrée to the opera *The Wedding of Peleus and Thetis*. His costume is made of richly inlaid gold brocade and silks studded with precious stones, intended to represent the Sun God's radiance. The young king's ankles, knees, waist, wrists, neck, shoulders and head are encircled by shafts of divine light. The sun gazes down serenely from below his chest. His long curling hair is adorned with ostrich feathers and more beams of light. One of Louis XIV's first acts as king is to establish a royal academy of dance – at the same time adopting the sun as his royal emblem. He becomes, in effect, the living embodiment of Apollo, the god of music, poetry and dance. The swan, a symbol of Orpheus and all those associated with death and resurrection, is sacred to him.

⸻ ✝ ⸻

'Always to be misunderstood in one's actions is a sign of distinction,' Nietzsche confides in one of his notebooks. 'It is then necessary, and no reason to become embittered.' People are incapable of fully comprehending actions of which they themselves are incapable – at best they can only appreciate them. Late one March night in 1959, Elvis Presley sweeps into a Munich strip club, high on army-issue amphetamines and looking for fun. He's on a three-day pass from the 1st Medium Tank Battalion, the 32nd Armor Regiment of the 3rd Armored Division, on active duty in Western Germany. 'The Moulin Rouge' can be found at Herzogspitalstraße 6, part of the red-light district nestling close to Munich's main railway station and within walking distance of St Michael's Church where Ludwig II's last remains are laid to rest, in lead-lined splendour, beneath the full weight of a replica Bavarian crown, in the Wittelsbach family crypt. Elvis has his picture taken with some of the club's performers. Not long before he is drafted into the US Army, a Baptist minister denounces Elvis from the pages of *Life* magazine as an apostle of 'degeneracy'.

⸻ ✝ ⸻

One of the Moulin Rouge strippers, the international press reveals, develops a routine featuring nothing, but a 'standard-size Presley record.' Her name is

X
The Fourth Sphere

Marianne. A sequence of photographs, credited to Studio Pavini in Munich, shows Elvis backstage with the Orkowski Twins, another of the club's dance acts. The pictures are playful, trashy and sweet – kisses, knowing looks and smiles are exchanged. The Orkowski twins are in their stage costumes: sateen leotards, fishnet tights, evening gloves and cheap costume jewellery. The only person wearing more make-up is the clown who sneaks into the lower left-hand corner of one photograph: sucking his lips in tightly in a way that suggests you are about to die violently at his hands – once seen, he can never be forgotten. Elvis is in a dark suit and tie over a white shirt. He appears relaxed and happy and to be having a good time.

Like a dream, the strip club is a palace that only exists at night. Those who cannot afford the luxuries of the day indulge themselves in the glittering Trash to be found after dark. Everything looks so good under artificial light. The Sun God's gold brocade hides a filigree of rags and tatters; the king's dainty step becomes a tawdry burlesque. This is all about taste, which has nothing to do with money and everything to do with class. A young blonde at the Moulin Rouge leans in smiling for the camera, her fake pearls, dark lipstick and bad post-war dentistry caught forever in a single moment, a mere breath away from Elvis' sullen stare. Strip clubs, like palaces, are spaces that consume themselves, offered up to a perverse integrated experience of the senses. They are created for dreaming, not practical living, and best suited to short visits. Stay too long, and you risk shattering the illusion.

••• ✝ •••

13.10.11 – *Munich: No insights or reflections – just reactions. So much of the old city under scrim and tarpaulins while its façades are being restored. Our first call, after checking into our hotel in the red-light district, was the Wittelsbach family vault in St Michael's Church, where R and I found Ludwig II: a large heavy sarcophagus with fresh lilies at its foot. There were also flowers and a candle burning on the coffin of his brother Otto who died, hopelessly insane, in 1916, which seems unimaginable now. Impossible to comprehend the changes that had taken place between Ludwig II's death and the middle years of the Great War. Got lost trying to find our way around the squares and side-streets in search of the Residenz – but soon we were sitting in the Cuvilliés Theatre, its sumptuous Rococo curves and patterns making the air itself seem peaceful and hushed – like a suspended moment of ascension – gods and cherubs at play.*

Elaborate, rich and ornate, a palace is a strip club tourists can enjoy during the day. Shortly before going to Germany, Elvis buys the house in which he is to die some twenty years later; and the visitors have been flocking here ever since. 'Colonial Courtliness of Georgian Style Exemplified in Stately "Graceland",' ran a headline in the 27 October 1940 edition of *Commercial Appeal* about a mansion that had only been completed the year before. Located outside Memphis, Graceland stands in fourteen of its own richly wooded acres, give or take. Looking at its elegant neoclassical portico, you can see where Batman got the inspiration for stately Wayne Manor. 'As you roll up the drive,' noted the *Commercial Appeal*, 'you sense the fine heritage of the past in its general feeling of aristocratic kindness and tranquility.' Elvis completes the purchase in 1957 – the same year he is accused of having simulated sex with Nipper, the RCA dog, while onstage at the Pan Pacific Auditorium in Los Angeles. To dissuade Elvis from committing further acts of public indecency, the LAPD place three 16 mm cameras in the audience to film the following night's antics. Like jokes and dreams, wealth and fame allow the repressed to come through, both individually and collectively. Distinction vanishes – together with the order of taste and value upon which it is based. With Ludwig II, it was the repression itself that comes through. Despite its splendour, there are barely 4.5 kilos of gold in the whole of his palace at Linderhof, and the 'tapestries' are painted canvas. The Southern Stairway at Herrenchiemsee is clad with Stucco marble: a mixture of plaster, glue and pigment. A servant restrains Ludwig from smashing *objets d'art* with his umbrella when the king discovers that they have been made of plaster and not marble.

⁂

In an unfinished corner of the palace, sits the red glass Grail fitted with an electric light bulb to make it glow at the end of *Parsifal*.

XI

In the Shadow of the Stars

The Fourth Sphere Continued

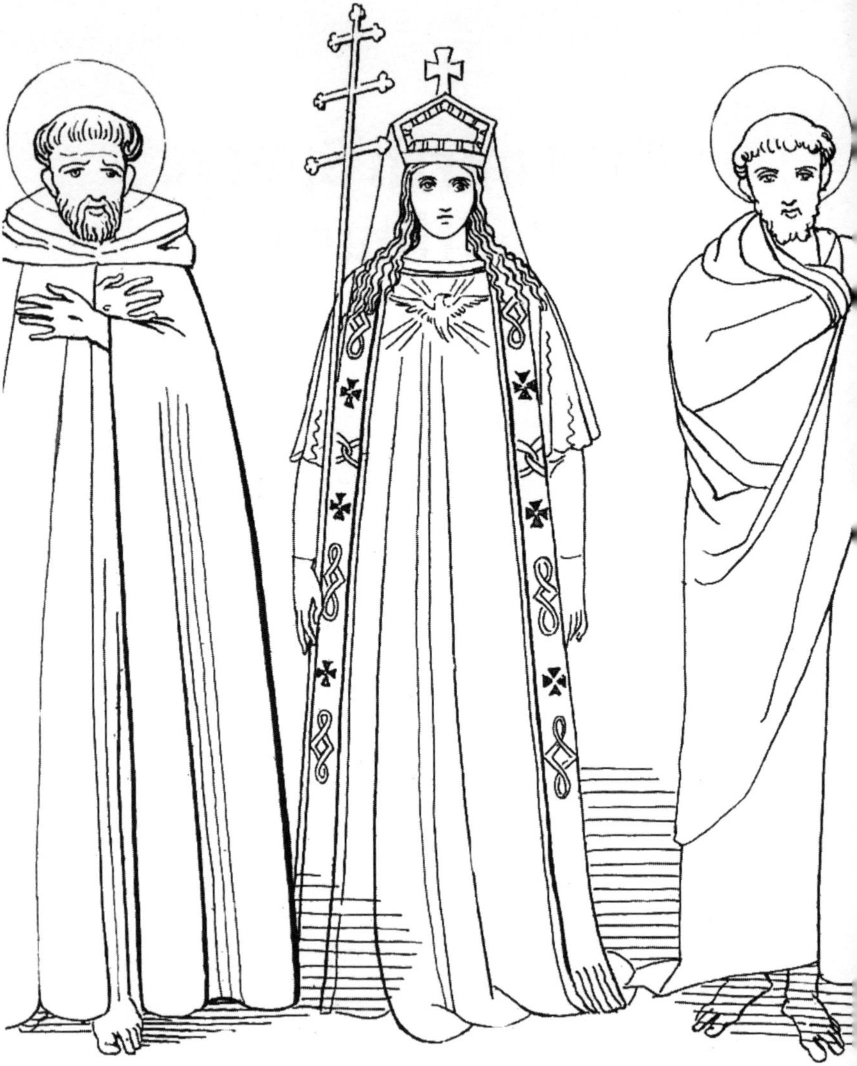

From within the splendid radiance...

••• ✝ •••

'I was really getting used to the Hollywood bit,' Elvis tells an audience upon his return to performing live in 1969. 'I had a Cadillac limousine, I had sunglasses on, sitting in the backseat, saying "I'm a movie star, hot damn, I'm cool." Eating hamburgers and drinking Pepsi Colas, you know.' Once again, darkness is where this other life exists, and only there. The magic of cinema is entirely nocturnal. People, places and things all look brighter in movies, as if illuminated from within by an excess of shadows. 'After all, I am one of the night people,' Elvis discloses to *Parade* magazine at the height of his Hollywood fame. 'The sun's down, and the moon's pretty. It's time to ramble.' Time also to see what's lurking in the background.

••• ✝ •••

'There is no way to describe the pandemonium,' recalls 'hillbilly' comedian Minnie Pearl on being with Elvis in the 1960s. 'I never saw as many women in my life. They were screaming. They were yelling. I was just horrified. I thought, "They're going to kill him." And they would have if they could have gotten loose, I'm afraid.'

Photographs from Presley's early tours show teenage girls bracing their bodies against their seats and screaming as America's Atomic Powered Singer takes the stage. The Maenads are back to tear Orpheus limb from limb again. Some of them swoon, loose-limbed: falling backwards as if invisible arms were there to catch them. Others soil themselves. Elvis gazes at the LAPD cameras trained upon him in the Pan-Pacific Auditorium. 'I wonder if they're gonna release this in the theaters?' he ponders out loud. The painted effigy of Nipper, the RCA dog, stands beside him unmolested, black-eared and white-faced – even after Elvis performs 'Hound Dog'. Nipper was first associated with discs released on the His Master's Voice label at the end of the nineteenth century. The dog looks quizzically into the horn of a wind-up gramophone, head cocked to one side, hearing the voice of his recently departed master. Positioned in front of the gramophone horn, Nipper is the popular embodiment of love, fidelity and death in the age of mechanical reproduction. Without the gramophone, he's just an oversized dog sharing the stage with a future movie star. 'I'm gonna be an angel tonight,' Elvis tells his audience. Pretty soon he will stop performing live altogether and concentrate on making movies instead.

··· ✝ ···

Shortly after his return to Graceland, Elvis Presley is presented by RCA Records with a combined stereo and TV console, a heavy piece of furniture combining twin hi-fi speakers on either side of a black-and-white cathode-ray tube. Affixed to it is a plaque commemorating the fact that Elvis had sold over fifty million records for the company. Photographers capture him standing inside the entrance to his new home, excitedly taking delivery.

··· ✝ ···

Before going into the army, Elvis had played the brother of a Confederate soldier in *Love Me Tender*; driven a beer truck and owned a hot rod in *Loving You;* been a construction worker imprisoned for manslaughter in *Jailhouse Rock* and a high-school dropout singing in a nightclub in *King Creole*. Returning to Hollywood, he becomes a member of a US tank crew serving in West Germany in *GI Blues;* a piece of good-natured White Trash in *Follow That Dream;* a tour guide in *Blue Hawaii;* a struggling young writer in *Wild in the Country;* the son of a white father and a Native American mother in *Flaming Star;* a boxer in *Kid Galahad;* dances with a visible erection in *Girls! Girls! Girls!*; is a freelance pilot in *It Happened at the World's*

Fair; a former trapeze artist with a fear of heights in *Fun in Acapulco*; drives a racing car in *Viva Las Vegas*; is both a hillbilly and an Air Force lieutenant in *Kissin' Cousins*; a singer, Karate expert and carnival handyman in *Roustabout*; a night club singer in *Girl Happy*; a singing cowboy in *Tickle Me*; a motion picture and recording star touring the Middle East in *Harum Scarum*; a singer on a Mississippi showboat in *Frankie and Johnny*; a helicopter pilot in *Paradise, Hawaiian Style*; a singer and a champion race car driver in *Spinout*; a US Navy diver searching for sunken treasure in *Easy Come, Easy Go*; sings at a London discotheque in *Double Trouble*; is the son of an oil millionaire who becomes a water-ski instructor in *Clambake*; a champion motor racer in *Speedway*; a Native American rodeo rider in *Stay Away, Joe*; a successful newspaper photographer in *Live a Little, Love a Little*; an itinerant singer in *The Trouble with Girls*; a former outlaw in *Charro!*; a New York ghetto doctor in *Change of Habit* and Elvis Presley in *Elvis – That's the Way It Is* and *Elvis On Tour.*

Elvis Presley movies are a genre unto themselves; but they share certain features with what is loosely called 'musical comedy', being the kind of movie where an establishing shot will show Big Ben and the word 'LONDON' spelled out in large red letters, while an up-tempo pop arrangement of 'Rule Britannia' trips along on the soundtrack. Elvis becomes the highest paid star in Hollywood simply by making more movies than anybody else, grinding out two or three pictures a year. 'Once you get involved in this business, your life is not your own,' he tells *Parade* magazine. People want to know everything about you. *Ludwig II of Bavaria*, a silent film released in 1913, is the first to convey 'the titanic struggle of this martyr of beauty' as cinema – no copies of the movie survive. This is followed in 1920 by *The Silence in Starnberg Lake* depicting the events leading up to Ludwig's tragic death and then by a final silent movie, *Ludwig II King of Bavaria*, in 1930 – this one featuring a brief appearance by Max Schreck, star of Murnau's *Nosferatu*, as a sanctimonious priest conspiring to overthrow the king, rubbing his hands together with sombre glee. Other versions follow. Meanwhile Elvis acts out endless reincarnations of himself in his movies, reframing them through his unchanging presence, everything contained within the lens of his being. The TV Room at Graceland contains three identical television sets mounted in the wall, each reflected endlessly in the mirrored walls and ceiling: chrome and glass fixtures chopping up and duplicating further details.

A mirror-lined staircase leads from the hall down to the basement and a portrait of Elvis painted just as he had entered the US army. Like it or not, reincarnation is always a form of atonement; you end up paying for the sins of your former lives. In the painting, Elvis appears to be wearing a shirt fashioned from the frilled, white satin lining of a luxury coffin. There must be a moment when he thinks his next movie will not be any better and then makes it anyway.

••• ✝ •••

Received an email the other day after making an online purchase: 'Did "Elvis" meet your expectations?' Still not sure how to answer that.

XII

In the Shadow of the Stars

The Fourth Sphere Continued

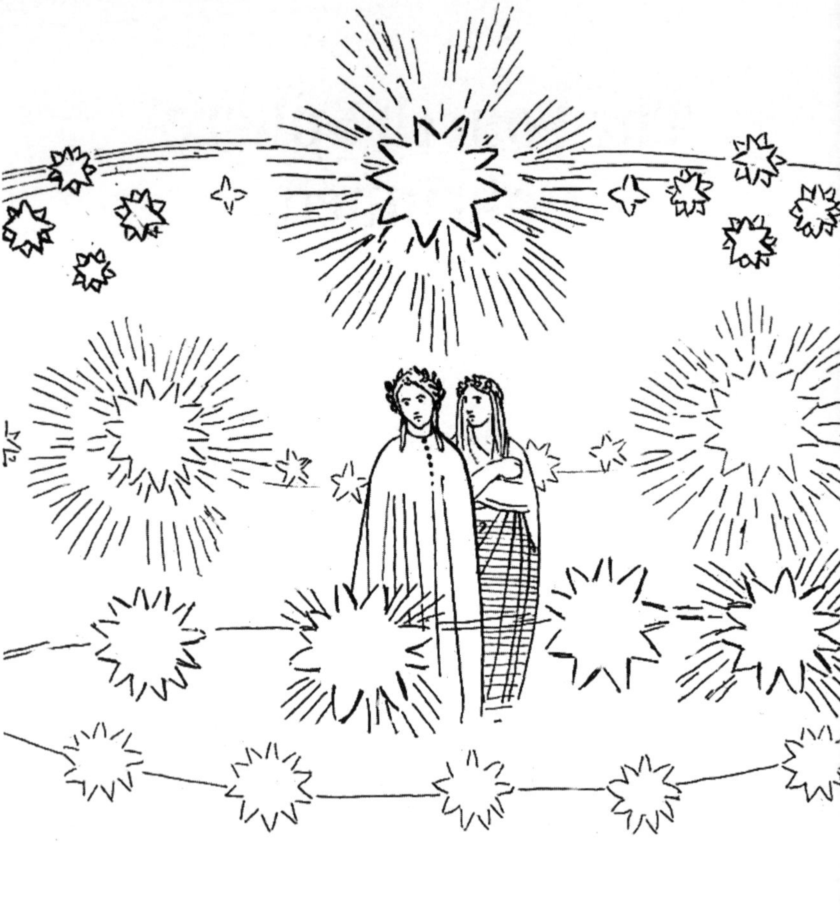

The outer form an echo of the inner...

••• ✝ •••

It's hard to pay for your sins when you don't even know you're committing them. Elvis loves Hollywood – he *believes* in it. Elvis is true to its living ideal, even if the ideal itself is false. You can't blame Elvis for believing what everyone else believes. He is merely the conduit of that belief, not its shaper or modifier. The truth is that 1960s Hollywood churns out absolute garbage, and that isn't Elvis' fault, is it? What do you want from a king? Take the big international co-productions out of the picture, and the typical American movie going into production during this period is unbelievably dumb. Maybe not *Harum Scarum* dumb, but close enough. While Elvis allows himself to be eternally reborn in one movie after the next, the average Hollywood production remains stupefyingly average. It's enough to turn you to drugs.

••• ✝ •••

In the Warner Bros movie release *The Big Cube*, Lana Turner is progressively driven out of her mind when someone starts spiking her prescription sedatives with LSD. 'This is the cube... the big one,' a male voice growls authoritatively on the soundtrack to the trailer over scenes of psychedelic drug orgies. 'The sugar cube they load with LSD... the cube that takes you off on the Trip... the Trip that starts with a giggle and ends with a scream.' After leading roles in such perfumed swill as *Peyton Place* for Twentieth Century Fox and *Imitation of Life* for Universal-International, Lana Turner is yet another Hollywood female star going insane in a 1960s movie production. It's the latest craze. Doris Day is scared out of her wits in *Midnight Lace*, while *Lady in a Cage* pushes Olivia de Havilland over the edge of reason before she warps Bette Davis' sanity in *Hush...Hush, Sweet Charlotte.* 'You take LSD and strange things begin to happen,' a hip young medical student explains in *The Big Cube* before sipping on a dry martini. 'You... uh... see sounds. You hear colours, so they tell me.' Pretty soon Lana Turner is gasping and gnawing on the wildly coloured scenery. Cue night clubs and freaky dancing, nudity, lightshows and acid rock performed by 'The Finks'. None of this is aimed at any of the actual kids taking drugs; it's their parents who are the real target. The sight of LSD-laced sugar cubes being dropped into so many foaming mugs of beer and overflowing glasses of champagne is vaguely nauseating, as indeed are Lana Turner's wildly erratic stabs at acting serious. The message flashed up on the screen is clear enough for everyone to read: 'From the ball to the bad trip, this is the LSD Scene Today, as a Psychedelic Conspiracy takes over the mind.'

Elvis takes regular trips to North Hollywood, where King of the Kustomizers George Barris has his workshop. Barris is responsible for the 'Solid Gold' Cadillac being sent out on tour by RCA to promote the release of *Tickle Me* while Elvis is busy working on his next movie. Sporting gold trim and some forty coats of white gold 'Murano pearl' paint, made from crushed diamonds and fish scales, this Series 75 Fleetwood features gold lamé curtains, two telephones, a record player and TV, all gold plated, plus a refreshment bar, an electric shoe buffer, and 'a golden amenity case with hairbrush, clipper and razor.' Barris Kustom Industries are now turning a forty-foot Greyhound bus, that George 'personally considered a piece of shit', into a 'rolling Graceland.' Its rear engine lined with lead to reduce noise, the former D'Elegance coach is outfitted for long-distance highway cruising, complete with a sophisticated stereo system, galley kitchen and sleeping quarters. The hydraulic driver's seat is moulded to Elvis' own body so he can stay at the wheel all night if he wants to. Once Barris finishes with it, Elvis plans to drive it all the way home: non-stop from Hollywood to Memphis.

⁘ ✠ ⁘

'This is a Pop Art world, baby,' proclaims a well-heeled hippie chick in *The Big Cube* as she dances around Lana's enormous living room. Ludwig II goes on long nocturnal rides across the snowy landscape between Linderhof and Neuschwanstein sitting in the back of his Cherub Sleigh, pulled by six white horses in glittering blue and white harnesses, attended by liveried outriders and grooms. The ornate gilded splendour of its coachwork is visible for miles around, thanks to the illuminated crown mounted at the front. With the battery carefully hidden in a box beneath the footman's station at the rear, Ludwig's Cherub Sleigh is one of the first vehicles in Europe to be lit by electricity.

⁘ ✠ ⁘

Television is Pop Art. America is Pop Art. Elvis is Pop Art. Andy Warhol paints him in a pose from one of his movies, dressed as a gunslinger drawing his pistol, eyes wide and focussed on something nobody else can see. Popping pills is also Pop Art. Warhol does it all the time so he can keep working. Elvis comes alive at night on the highway, driving all the way to Graceland, wired on Dexedrine and gabbing with his hairdresser in the seat next to him about his mission here on earth and about the immortality of the human soul. Larry Geller started out washing, dyeing and styling the King's hair back in LA then quickly becomes his spiritual advisor. He turns Elvis on to Annie Besant, Madame Blavatsky, Alice Bailey, *Cheiro's Book of Numbers*, Joseph Sieber Benner's *The Impersonal Life* and the *Tibetan Book of the Dead*. Motel stops during the day are cut short when the screaming of his fans prevents Elvis from sleeping. He also reads *The Bible* and *The Physician's Desk Reference*.

⁂

As an experiment, Elvis takes LSD one night and ends up watching George Pal's *The Time Machine* on TV and then ordering in a pizza.

XIII

In the Shadow of the Stars

The Fourth Sphere Continued

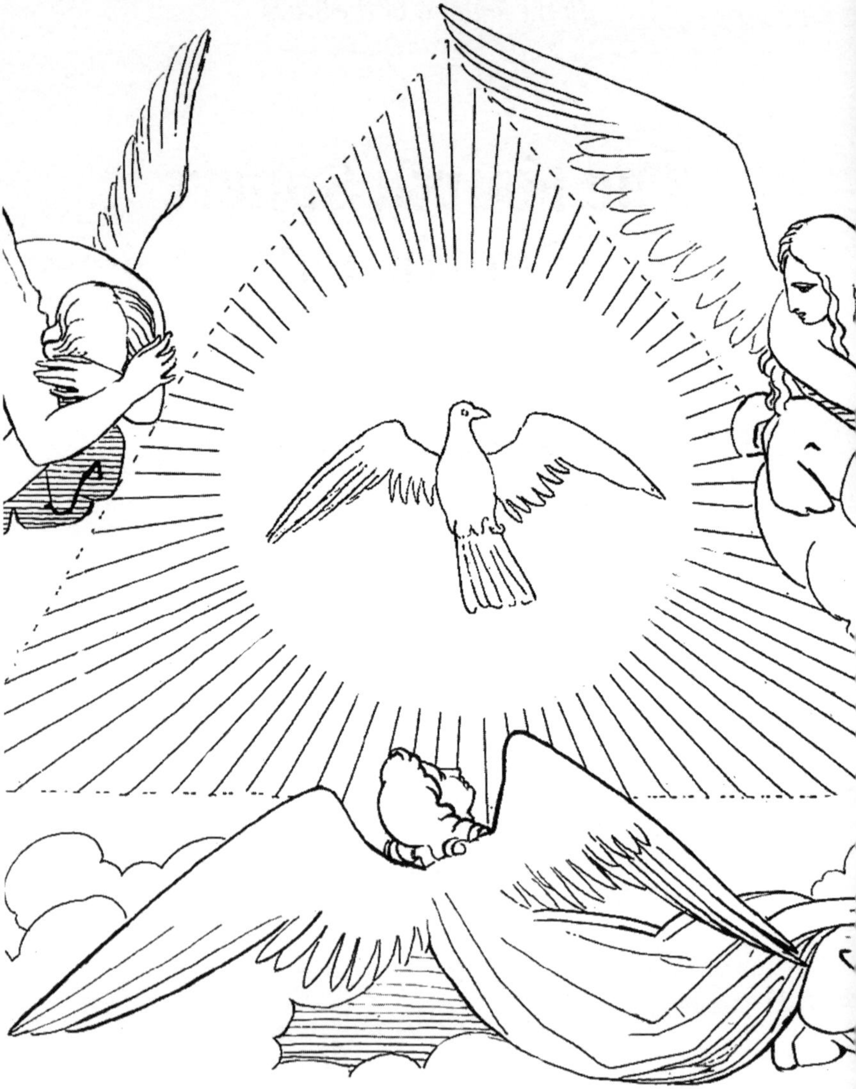

Neither paean nor dithyramb

While filming *Harum Scarum*, Elvis Presley makes frequent visits to the Self-Realization Fellowship's Lake Shrine Retreat at Pacific Palisades, just a few blocks away from the ocean. He has been constantly rereading *Autobiography of a Yogi* by Hindu guru and founder of the Self-Realization Fellowship, Paramahansa Yogananda. Elvis discusses the book at length with his hairdresser, who first introduced it to him. It details the divine teacher's spiritual development and his many encounters with great and remarkable souls. Nothing about Paramahansa Yogananda's life impresses Elvis so much as his leaving of it. Following his death at the Biltmore Hotel in Los Angeles on 7 March 1952, just two years after dedicating the Lake Shrine Retreat, the guru's body is put on display in an open coffin for three weeks. 'The physical appearance of Yogananda on March 27th, just before the bronze cover of the casket was put into position was the same as it had been on March 7th,' the Mortuary Director at Forest Lawn Memorial-Park will attest. 'He looked on March 27th as fresh and as unravaged by decay as he had looked on the night of his death... This state of perfect preservation of the body is, so far as we know from mortuary annals, an unparalleled one.'

••• ✝ •••

No physical disintegration visible on the body after death... no indication of mould on the skin... no odour of decay... Elvis keeps returning to this again and again: that someone this pure and spiritual can withstand the corrosion of time and mortality. Elvis' mother Gladys died in the summer of 1958 just as he was starting in the US Army. Now Elvis makes private visits to the Memphis Funeral Home on Union Avenue and Pasadena Place, where her body was prepared for burial. He takes tours of the place. Surrounded by cadavers and coffins, he asks morticians about what happens to the human body after death. Elvis shows off his knowledge to his new girlfriend Priscilla. 'Elvis believed fervently in reincarnation,' according to Joe Esposito. Autopsies and embalming methods fascinate him. Sometimes Elvis will sneak into the Memphis Funeral Home late at night, taking his friends along with him, to wander among the sheeted dead. Funerary practices offer a way of preserving order, while decay reveals the inherent chaos of the mortal body. 'Weak people can't bring themselves back from the dead,' Elvis tells Sonny West, one his bodyguards. 'Only strong people.'

Based around a former resort hotel, the Spiritual Research Foundation's Lake Shrine Retreat has a Meditation Garden that Elvis immediately duplicates at Graceland. His ideas about the mood he wants to create are very definite. At its centre is a circular pool with a fountain capable of fourteen different spray and underwater light formations. A circular wall encloses it with bricks imported from Mexico, marble statues from Italy and stained glass from Spain. Elvis weeps with joy the first time he sees it. The guys in his entourage chip in and buy a four-foot-high plastic statue of Jesus spreading his arms as part of the Meditation Garden; 'they still think it's marble,' the sculptor admits. Like the kidney-shaped swimming pool at Graceland, the private, highly personalised body of water at its centre is a reinvention of the Venus Grotto. More versions of it will appear – further sites for seclusion and dreaming. The designer of the Meditation Garden is also responsible for reconstructing the artificial waterfall that Elvis has installed in his den at the back of the main building, so it doesn't flood the outside yard anymore.

Fully restored, this indoor waterfall promotes a gradual blurring of the senses: an inevitable by-product of the industrial processes involved. Exotic illusions require the smoothest running machinery. Elvis loves to watch the thin rippling sheet of water as it tumbles over the red flagstones, loves the twinkling play of coloured lights across its surface. The effect goes well with pills. His preferences when it comes to interior decorating have been dismissed over the years as 'seventies hotel' style. Think of the kind of resort bar or reception area where a sudden sense of a fake locale takes over from the endless uniformity of corridors and air-conditioned rooms. These are carefully defined, intimate spaces – like Don the Beachcomber's Dagger Bar in Honolulu, where pianist and arranger Martin Denny develops his 'exotic' sound in 1954. As well as special lighting effects, the bar has hidden loudspeakers to relay recordings of bird calls made by Denny's Hawaiian-born percussionist, Augie Colón. These play while Augie produces the same sounds live onstage, creating the illusion of birds flying around the customers. 'We also set up one of the first echo machines on the market to provide some of Augie's birdcalls with a reverb effect,' Denny discloses. A return to paradise is the literal truth of exoticism.

Exotica combines a wilful rejection of nature, locale and authenticity with an understanding that all three are products of human technology and therefore merely environments to be occupied and enjoyed. Denny's arrangements are a lush audio approximation of the peaceful, stress-free existence considered an essential part of life in a tropical paradise, such as the one on offer at billionaire Henry J Kaiser's Hawaiian Village Hotel complex in Waikiki. Denny moves his quartet to the old Shell Bar, one of the many entertainments in its grounds. 'The Shell Bar had a beautiful, open-air, exotic setting,' Denny will later recall. 'The wall of the bar resembled an ocean floor with sand and various types of shells, starfish and all sorts of aquatic creatures.' Elvis stays at the Hawaiian Village Hotel, swapping locale for location while working on *Blue Hawaii*, his 'latest travelogue' as he now calls each new movie. He is back at the Hawaiian Village for *Girls! Girls! Girls!* and again for *Paradise, Hawaiian Style*. Apart from his time in Germany with the US army, Presley's eternal return to Hawaii is the nearest he ever gets to leaving the United States throughout his entire life.

Hollywood's teens and former teens go abroad in the hope of finding the kind of wild adoration that

Elvis commands simply by staying at home. Frankie Avalon leaves the California beaches for Swinging London in *The Haunted House of Horror*. Sharon Tate comes to witchy old England for *The Eye of the Devil*. In Japan, Elvis' old buddy Nick Adams stars in Toho's *Frankenstein Conquers the World* and *Invasion of Astro-Monster*, while Russ Tamblyn is forever Russ in *The War of the Gargantuas*. Meanwhile, Elvis is 'practically worshipped' in Hawaii, according to one biographer, looking like a Hindu idol garlanded with leis of bright red flowers. Writing on the nature of the sacred, Roger Caillois records that, 'In the Hawaiian islands, the populace, upon learning of the king's death, commits every act ordinarily regarded as criminal. It burns, pillages and kills, and the women are required to prostitute themselves publicly...

••• ✝ •••

'This will continue as the king's body decomposes until finally nothing more is left of the royal remains but a hard, sound and incorruptible skeleton.'

XIV

In the Shadow of the Stars

The Fourth Sphere Concluded

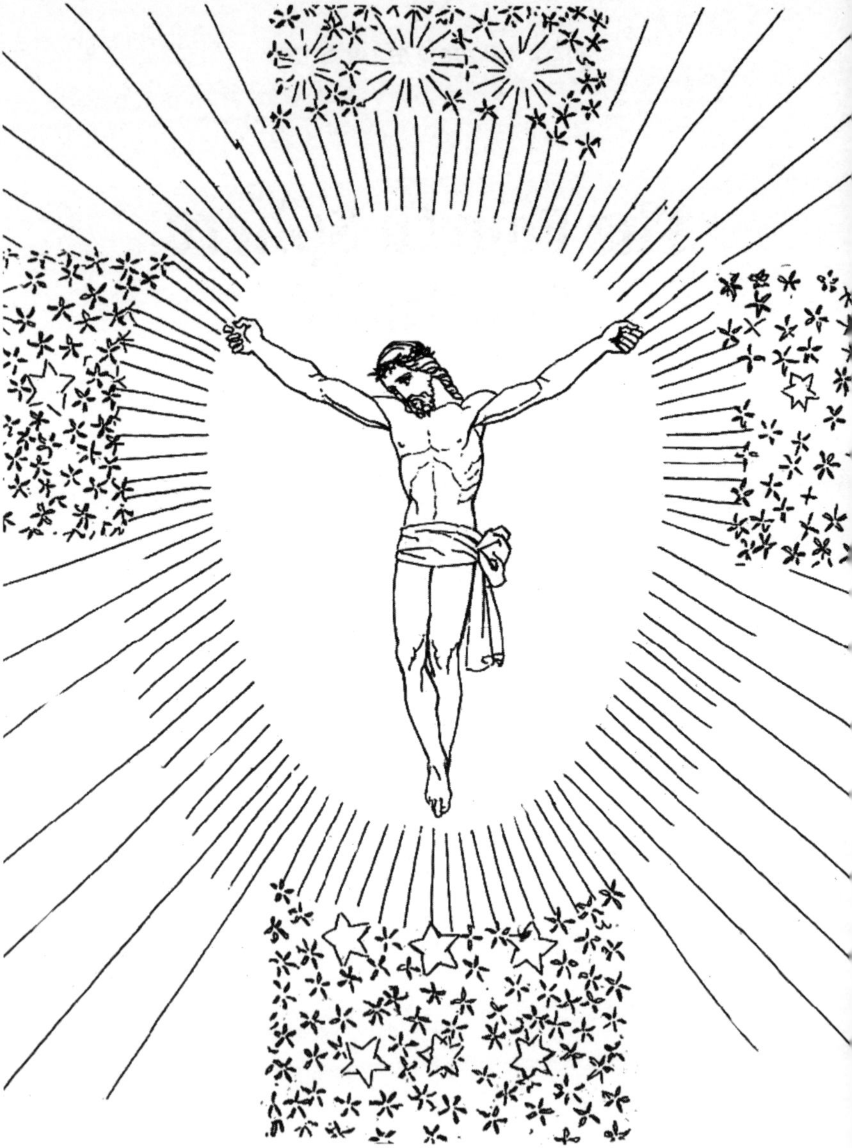

From the centre to the rim, to the centre from the rim

Elvis reads science fiction and believes he has psychic powers. He believes in fate and numerology. Flying saucers are real. 'They will come, but they won't hurt us,' he reassures Sonny West. 'If they make contact, we can't be afraid, because they are not going to hurt us.' It's possible that the weirdest thing ever to have happened to the 1960s will turn out to be the 1950s. 'Stand by!' a voice commands from the soundtrack to a short promotional film made in 1957 for Kaiser Aluminum: *the bright star of metals*. 'You are about to see a miracle in aluminum.' In just twenty hours a shining and segmented alien dome takes shape at the entrance to Henry J Kaiser's Hawaiian Village Hotel on Kalia Road, Waikiki. The Kaiser Aluminum Dome covers an area of 16,500 square feet, is forty-five feet in diameter and nearly fifty feet high. Based on Buckminster Fuller's geodesic design, it 'offers living proof of what the world's most versatile metal combined with imagination can accomplish... free of annoying columns and beams.' The dome's unique location and acoustic properties make it an ideal venue just as exotic easy listening and high-fidelity sound become rising passions. The showroom's opening celebrations include '8 Acts in Symphony-Polynesia', which features George Barati conducting the Honolulu Symphony Orchestra and 'the Golden Voice of Hawaii' Alfred Apaka performing with the Hawaiian Village Serenaders. The Kaiser Aluminum promotional film shows Apaka onstage inside the dome, surrounded by musicians. He looks so serene: a dark lei of flowers around his neck.

'Symphony-Polynesia' offers an indigestible array of musical treats embracing selections from *South Pacific* and 'Stars and Stripes Forever' through to Apaka and his Serenaders performing 'Samoan Knife Dance', 'Beyond the Reef' and 'Hawaiian War Chant' – *Hawaiiana* for the tourist who can afford it. A note in the published programme advises that Alfred Apaka's 'new long-playing album' *Broadway Wears a Lei* is on sale during the intermission. Alfred Apaka has a warm engaging presence. Henry Kaiser loves his rich baritone voice. He installs him in his own venue, the Hawaiian Village Tapa Room, making Apaka entertainment director for the entire resort. It's thanks to him Martin Denny and his quartet find themselves playing the Shell Bar where '"after-the-theatre" cocktails and exotic Polynesian drinks' are served to audience members once 'Symphony-Polynesia' is over. The croaking of frogs in the Shell Bar's ornamental pool blends with Denny's lush trademark arrangements: piano, vibraphone and string bass over exotic sounds and percussion. So much does Denny's presence at the Hawaiian Village chime with the inauguration of the Kaiser Aluminum Dome that it is often assumed that he recorded his first album *Exotica* there. That defining moment takes place at the Honolulu studio of Webley Edwards just as a bitter contractual wrangle develops between Denny and Henry Kaiser. Edwards is a local radio personality and presenter of *Hawaii Calls*, a syndicated show that regularly features the singing of Alfred Apaka. When Martin Denny finally leaves the Hawaiian Village, two key members of his original quartet will remain behind: bassist John Kramer and Hawaiian-born vibraphone virtuoso Arthur Lyman, both of whom Apaka persuades to sign with Kaiser.

⋯ ✝ ⋯

With his own quartet and the financial backing of Henry J Kaiser, Lyman releases a steady stream of albums recorded during late-night sessions in the Kaiser Aluminum Dome, supervised by hi-fi producer Richard Vaughn. Lyman's arrangements tend to be sparser than Denny's; the dome's acoustics, with its three-second delay, gives them a sharp brittle quality that suits his shimmering four-mallet technique on vibes. A photograph of the shining alien dome is reproduced on the back covers of his albums as some form of guarantee for the hi-fi enthusiast. 'Hi Fi sound?' Lyman later complains. 'Yuck! It bounces back.' The late-night sessions often end at sunrise.

··· ✠ ···

While filming *Blue Hawaii*, Elvis stays in the Mahele Suite on the fourteenth floor of the Ocean Tower. When vacationing, he prefers the presidential suite on top of the Rainbow Towers at the Hawaiian Village, according to Joe Esposito – his favourite Hawaiian outfit being 'an aloha shirt and white cotton pants and a yachting cap'. In the grounds of his palace at Linderhof, Ludwig has his 'Moorish Kiosk': decorated with minarets, brightly coloured mosaics, reliefs and vases and containing His Majesty's Peacock Throne, made for him in Paris. The king also has his 'Moroccan House' in the hills, where his guests are invited to recline, drinking coffee and smoking hookahs to establish a suitably oriental mood.

··· ✠ ···

Everywhere becomes a hotel if you travel long enough. Elvis further transforms his Venus Grotto at Graceland with its artificial indoor waterfall: covering the floor and ceiling with green shagpile carpeting to muffle the sound, while thick drapery permanently cloaks the room in shadow. The entire effect is offset by the installation of faux wood panelling, plastic vegetation, coloured lights, fake fur trimming and ceramic tigers. As a finishing touch to what becomes known as 'The Jungle Room', Elvis purchases an exotic set of matching chairs and tables in heavy dark wood. Elvis' father Vernon first sees them on display in Donald's Furniture Company at 405 North Cleveland, Memphis and thinks they look hideous. The armrests and end tables are decorated with crude chainsaw-carved likenesses of sea serpents, native idols and strange beasts. Elvis later goes there and buys them in person, signing the sales receipt for $23,000 himself. By then the national craze for Tiki-style lounges has started to ebb away: hula girls, wooden idols and bamboo curtains being relegated to thrift stores and hotel bars. Elvis loves his new furniture, however, saying it reminds him of Hawaii. The supplier is the Western International Trading Co., better known to the American shopper as Witco. The carved wooden décor made famous by Witco since the late 1950s is not so popular now; but what is freedom of choice without Trash? Elvis knows that throwing stuff away without a second thought is an inalienable right. By refusing to move with the times, Elvis is not staying still but moving backwards, transforming his home into a museum piece even while he is still living in it. According to one of his former bodyguards, 'everything Elvis does, everything that interests him, everything that he takes up, he grabs and strangles and beats it to death.' To be constantly reincarnated is also to condemn yourself to die endlessly, caught forever between sin and atonement.

⁂

Witco offers an industrial variation on exoticism as the unrefined copying of nature – a terrain that is heavily charted but remains forever unknown. The dark carved wood and 'primitive' designs are intended to go with white walls and bright animal prints. It's all a matter of mood. The difference between the fake and the artificial echoes that which exists between the naked and the nude: the distinction in both cases says more about individual taste than it does about understanding.

⁂

'Let's face it – Elvis's taste sucked,' a friend later comments, 'if something wasn't overdone, it was abnormal to Elvis.'

XV

In the Shadow of the Stars

The Fifth Sphere

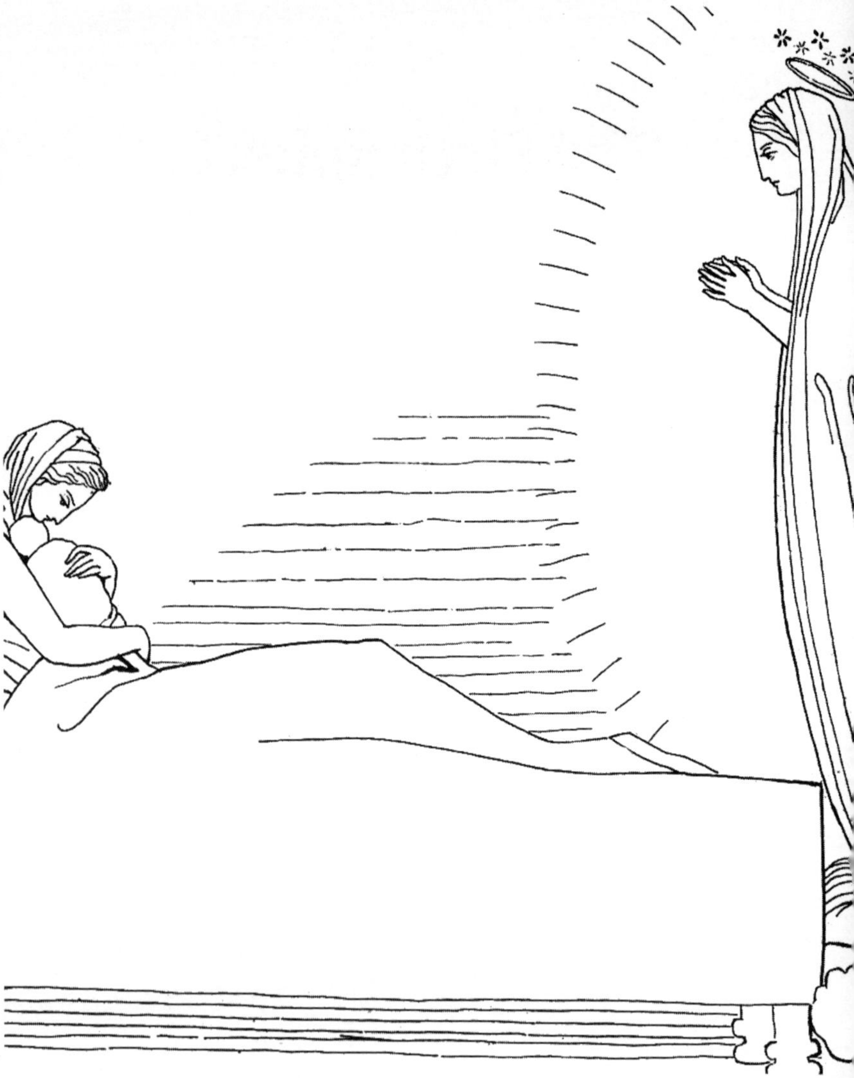

Mars in Heaven

⁂

Elvis is so big that all you can see at times are fragments pulling in different directions. When Priscilla, his teenage crush, first comes to live with Elvis at Graceland, he buys her a handgun to take with her to school – and when she comes out to Los Angeles for the first time, he asks Kustom King George Barris if she can stay with him and his wife so they can be her chaperones. And when he first takes her to Las Vegas, Elvis gives her Dexedrine and sleeping pills so she can stay up all night and sleep through the day. She wears the dresses he buys for her from the Vegas boutiques, slaps on the makeup he likes, and she wears her dark hair in the high beehives he prefers. A sovereign's life can never be understood in its entirety. When Priscilla's mother first sees her at the airport after spending all that time alone with Elvis, she holds a pocket mirror up to her daughter's face, so she can see for herself what he's done to her.

⁂

Elvis knows how to indulge himself in Vegas. Always. He dresses his entourage in identical black mohair suits and dark glasses. They are his 'Memphis Mafia': a pill-popping Rat Pack here to party in between movies and recording sessions. During the 1960s he likes to stay at the Sahara, which is owned by Milton Prell: a close personal friend of his manager, the Colonel. 'We'd stay there and never sleep,' Joe Esposito recalls, 'we were all taking pills, just so we could keep up with each other.' Nothing here makes sense without pills. Regulating your body to go all night and then sleep all day makes time a meaningless concept, especially in a city where the distractions never stop. In the lounges and showrooms, Elvis and his Memphis Mafia are shown to the best tables in the house. They catch some his favourite acts: Jackie Wilson, Della Reese, Fats Domino, Dinah Washington, Nat King Cole, The Dominoes. 'Everything was yours. Anything you wanted. All of that was exciting,' remembers Joe's wife Joanie, a dancer at the Sands at the time.

In Vegas the Colonel lives off the fat of the land: dropping thousands of dollars at a time at roulette and sending sumptuous, half-finished meals back to the hotel kitchen. 'We need to give away, lose or destroy,' Georges Bataille states quite simply in *The Accursed Share*. A surplus becomes an excess only when it is being wasted. Sardanapalus, the mythical 'last king' of the Assyrians, turns his palace into a funeral pyre that consumes 'all his gold, silver and royal apparel', his horses, his servants and his male and female concubines. Roulette, slot machines and the all-day breakfast buffet offer exciting new ways to squander resources. One time, Elvis comes to Vegas for a two-week vacation and ends up staying for six. It's like being in Paradise.

••• ✝ •••

Back in Memphis, Priscilla says she wants a horse, so Elvis buys her one. Then he starts buying horses for everyone, including a golden palomino for himself called Rising Sun and keeps them in the stables at Graceland, where he and Priscilla can go riding in the grounds. The King's fans stand at the gates in the hope of seeing them. Being that close to nature appeals to his spiritual side. Out riding his motorcycle along a country road late one night, Elvis sees a sixty-foot-high illuminated cross of white concrete standing over a small ornamental lake on a wide parcel of farmland. Within days Elvis has bought the wide parcel of land, together with all the buildings, animals and farm equipment it contains, plus the huge concrete cross and the ornamental lake. Elvis puts Graceland up as collateral on the deal. He needs somewhere to keep all his horses. He needs somewhere to keep himself. That's why he needs a ranch.

It's like being in Paradise. The 'Flying Circle G', as Elvis decides to call his home away from Graceland, is the most perfect place on Earth. Elvis wants to live here with Priscilla. He also wants the Memphis Mafia to live here with them. To set everyone up and put them back in touch with nature, Elvis buys over two dozen vehicles, including 100,000 dollars' worth of El Caminos and Rancheros and a '63 Cadillac, plus half a dozen house trailers and six horse vans, 'not to mention numerous tractors, miscellaneous ranch equipment, septic tanks and water lines' according to one account. Everyone is given a horse, a car and a trailer as the bills start to pile up. 'Gift-giving,' as Bataille points out, 'has the virtue of a surpassing of the subject who gives, but in exchange for the object given, the subject appropriates the surpassing: He regards his virtue, that which he had the capacity for, as an asset, as a power that he now possesses. He enriches himself with a contempt for riches, and what he proves to be miserly of is in fact his generosity.'

15.10.11 – Nymphenburg: Palace stables as public gallery, organising excess – the gilded regalia and royal coaches – the ornamental harnesses lined up in tall glass cases suggesting the outline of phantom horses. The portrait of Ludwig II at the end of his life, overweight and dressed in the robes of the Order of St George, stern and majestic, in a side room amongst the carriages and sleighs. R and I outside the Palmenhaus, sitting on a weathered green bench feeling the autumnal warmth on our faces.

Extravagance is not simply about giving or receiving, but expenditure. 'Too much money has been going out,' the Colonel rages as he sees the huge amounts Elvis is prepared to waste on the rural commune that he is setting up at the Flying Circle G. The Colonel blames the good ole boys of the Memphis Mafia for this; and he's not entirely wrong. Excessive giving becomes a form of splendour. It requires an audience: spectators as well as recipients. Under such circumstances, gratitude is exposed as the humble soliciting of further favours, which has as much to do with insecurity as it does with greed. Elvis is estimated to have spent over a million dollars buying new cars for bodyguards, maids, nurses, friends and strangers. In fact, he has given them away to so many people that the recipients must begin to wonder what they themselves are actually worth to him. 'Some of you think maybe he's Jesus Christ, who should wear robes and walk down the street helping people. But that's not who he is,' the Colonel insists, not being entirely right this time, while Elvis looks on, dazed and sullen, at his side. Trash is more than what we are prepared to throw away, to waste and discard – it's a sign of what ultimately owns us. There will have to be cut-backs, the Colonel announces.

••• ✝ •••

Elvis' golden palomino Rising Sun outlives the King by nine years before finally dying of kidney failure in 1986.

XVI

In the Shadow of the Stars

The Fifth Sphere Continued

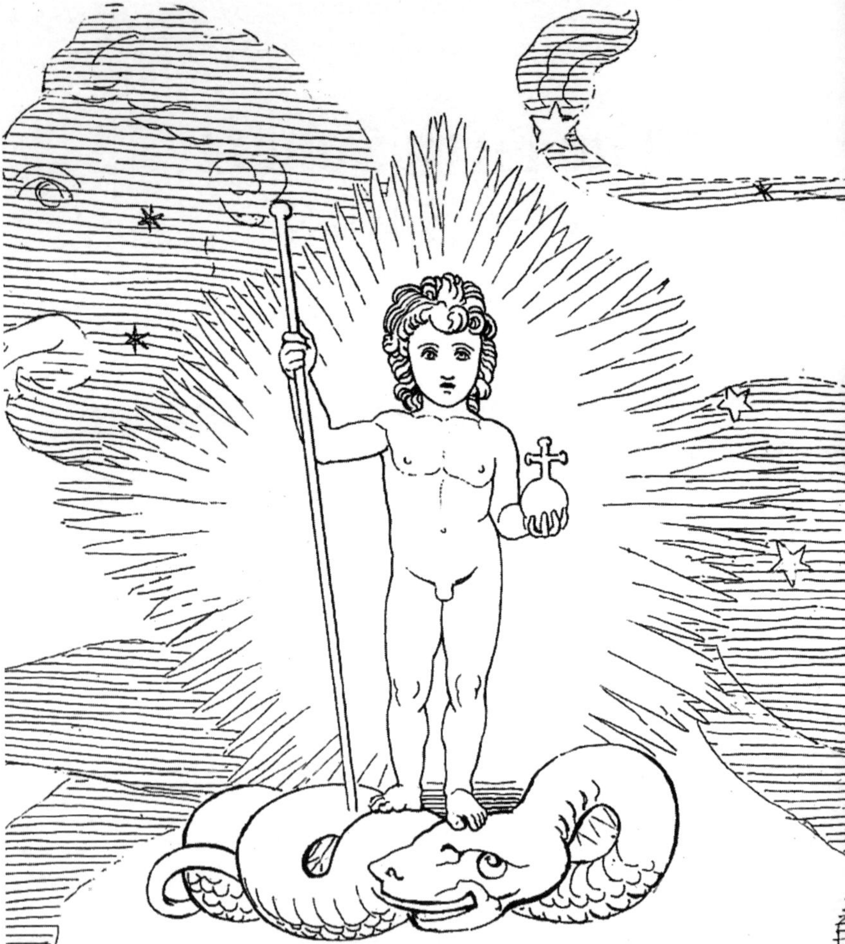

This fiery star once more returning...

'Welcome to the big freaky International Hotel, with those weirdo dolls on the walls and those little funky angels on the ceiling and, man, you ain't seen nothing until you've seen a funky angel.' Elvis is addressing a capacity audience at the Showroom Internationale in the summer of 1969. The Las Vegas International Hotel has only recently opened. A colossal thirty-storey structure situated off the Strip, it is the ultimate in leisure concepts. Hailed as the 1,500-room future of high-rise resort entertainment, everything about it is big, new and ground-breaking. There is a shopping concourse with dozens of boutiques, a casino with over 1,000 slot machines and a wide range of restaurants offering a variety of cuisines from all over the world. Its 'ocean-sized' swimming pool is the second largest manmade body of water in the entire state of Nevada. The International also has Elvis coming back, night after night, one of its biggest attractions, wowing a showroom that holds 2,000 guests packed together inside its vast interior horizon.

⁂ ✝ ⁂

What happened to the Las Vegas Elvis used to know – before he became the main attraction here? The man who signed him to appear regularly at the Showroom Internationale is Alex Shoofey, who formerly worked for Colonel Parker's old pal, Milton Prell, running the Sahara for him. Elvis and the boys regularly stayed there whenever they were in town to party. Shoofey leaves the Sahara for the Flamingo, where he starts recruiting staff for the International. Meanwhile, Milton Prell sets up the Aladdin across the Strip from Caesars Palace. In early 1966, his application to operate 351 slot machines and 29 table games is approved. The Aladdin also acquires gambling and liqueur licenses. This is when the Colonel decides that Elvis has to drop all that spiritual stuff he's been fooling with recently and get himself married to Priscilla – at the Aladdin. A brief civil ceremony will be held in Milton Prell's personal suite of rooms. 'I had nothing to do with that,' Elvis will later confess. 'That was railroaded through. I didn't even know who was there in that little old room the size of a bathroom with a Supreme Court Justice. It was in there over and done so quick I didn't realize I was married.' Elvis and Priscilla then sneak through the pool area to the Aladdin Room for the press conference followed by a champagne breakfast. They honeymoon together in one of the trailers Elvis has on his Flying Circle G ranch. Just before he commences his first residency at the International Hotel, Elvis sells off the Circle G and everything on it.

··· ✠ ···

Las Vegas exists in a perpetual state of déjà vu: a nervous erotic cabaret made up of repetitive acts. Trashy excess utters truths that would otherwise remain hidden away inside. Private life erupts as public presence. 'I never did fit in that scene, and I never will,' Elvis says about marriage. 'I'm not your average American male, and I don't aim to be that sucker.' Pills turn everything into a non-stop fantasy, an indefinitely extended twilight – otherwise, the whole Vegas experience is apt to go hard on chemically dilated eyeballs. The ruched golden curtain at the Showroom Internationale gathers and raises itself once more. Elvis is now part of the Vegas entertainment package. Over the next seven years he will come back from Graceland to give over six hundred sold-out performances here.

··· ✠ ···

Elvis likes to tell his Vegas audiences how he started out training to be an electrician, how he drove a truck for Crown Electric in Memphis – 'but I was wired the wrong way.' The company's logo is an ornate king's crown with lightning emanating symmetrically from it. Like Ludwig II before him, Elvis sees electricity as a divine spark, capable of working magic. Its most primal form is the lightning bolt, connecting Heaven with Earth. Add the magic word 'Shazam', and it marks the sudden and dramatic transformation of young Billy Batson into Captain Marvel, Elvis' favourite superhero. 'When I was a child, ladies and gentlemen, I was a dreamer,' Elvis reveals in a rare public speech. 'I read comic books and I was the hero of the comic book. I saw the movie, and I was the hero in the movie.' The lightning bolt emblazoned across Captain Marvel's chest echoes the insignia of the US Armored Corps in which Elvis served his time in Germany. Framed by the letters 'TCB' it stands for 'Taking Care of Business'. This is his own personal 'Shazam': a device worked into fourteen-karat gold necklaces that Elvis is constantly giving away to followers, family members and friends. 'TCB' means doing something fast and getting it right first time. It means Elvis is electricity – he is lightning. The stage at the Showroom Internationale overflows with it.

Elvis knows that there is nothing average about being a superhero. The transformation involved requires a change of image simply to survive and contain the disaster of no longer being human. Being a superhero is consequently a fantasy divided against itself. Costume plays a defining role in this. Elvis has all his stage outfits designed by the same man: Bill Belew, who also created costumes for Josephine Baker, Lena Horne, Ella Fitzgerald, Dionne Warwick and Gladys Knight. Belew creates multiple versions of the dazzling white jumpsuit Elvis likes to wear on his return to live performing. It's impossible to picture him wearing anything else. Thanks to Belew, Elvis is changed permanently into a Trash icon.

⁂

Las Vegas disappears, concealed from time, continually rebuilding itself. Everything is temporary. Everything stays the same. Elvis will always return.

XVII

In the Shadow of the Stars

The Fifth Sphere Concluded

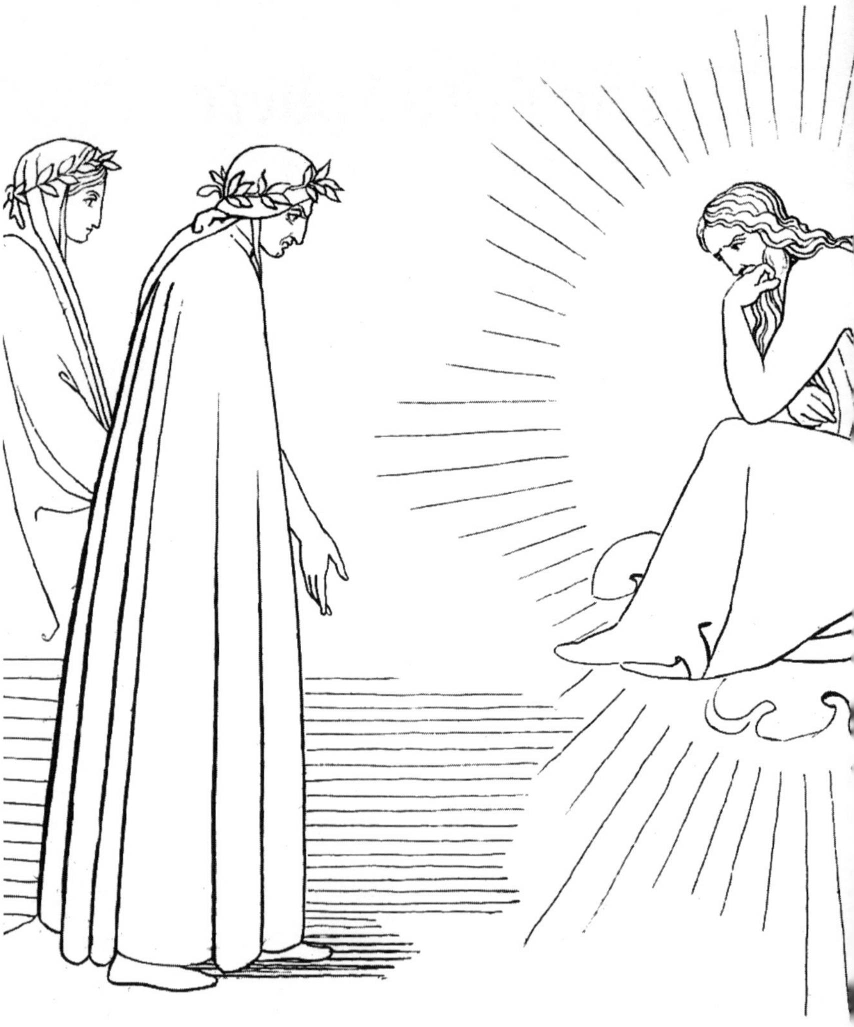

A golden dancer descending and ascending...

Nobody respects the one who gives them everything; they only expect more instead. Sacrifice is a form of rational disgrace: a going under or submersion beneath the order of things. Elvis gives to the point of suffocation – both his own and other people's. 'Anybody that wants something that bad, should have it,' Bill Belew recalls him saying. The sacrificial victim challenges all our safe assumptions. Their actions are troubling and suspect, possibly even criminal, but certainly beyond taste and decency. Belew dresses him in black leather for his 1968 TV Christmas special, making him 'a human truck tire', according to one biographer. The more elaborate the robing, the more splendid the sacrifice. 'At 9:15,' *The New York Times* records, 'Elvis appeared, materi-alized, in a white suit of lights, shining with golden appliques, the shirt front slashed to show his chest. Around his shoulders was a cape lined in cloth of gold, its collar faced with scarlet. It was anything you wanted to call it, gaudy, vulgar, magnificent...'

••• ✝ •••

In 1664 the painter Joseph Werner completes *Allegory of Louis XIV as Apollo on the Chariot of the Sun, preceded by Aurora and accompanied by the Hours*. It shows the Sun King skilfully driving the Sun God's chariot, pulled by four horses while also managing to show off his dancer's legs. What a terrible fate for any artist – to be good enough to paint royalty requires a distinct lack of talent.

••• ✝ •••

Elvis comes across a little jowly in *Viva Las Vegas*. His new look will leave all of that behind. The white jumpsuits reflect the showroom lights better, highlighting his presence onstage. Bill Belew tricks them out with macramé belts, silver fastenings, shiny rivets, studs and clasps. He uses high Napoleonic collars to frame Elvis' face. 'Of course,' Belew adds, 'you want the star to be the person, you know, and not the wardrobe.' Elvis brings his own moves to each costume, his passion for buying and giving away jewellery – more importantly he brings his own physical exertion. We see silver chains swinging unfastened and loose across his bare chest, dripping with his righteous sweat. Glistening in the intense blue light of a thousand instamatic flashcubes, perspiration becomes an outer, almost cinematic sign of some powerful internal process. The sweat has its own visual build-up. There are over fifty individual musicians and singers behind Elvis onstage. Priscilla suggests adding a cape to his outfits, further strengthening the connection with Captain Marvel. After opening in Lake Tahoe with a lush supper-club version of the 'Sunrise' from Richard Strauss' *Also Sprach Zarathustra*, its swelling climax precedes Elvis' entrance at the start of every show. He becomes, like the white-suited astronauts of the Apollo mission who find themselves walking out to the same Strauss tone poem at every public appearance, a modern form of sacrificial offering: one perfectly suited to the age of mass consumption and mass communication.

··· ✝ ···

'By nature,' Bataille observes, 'the object of desire has nothing to do in this world except to respond to desire.' Elvis bumps and grinds before an audience already seated at their tables, eating and drinking their way through the dinner show. 'I feel like an old stripper,' he admits from the stage one night in Las Vegas. His musicians follow every move his body makes. As a stage performer, Elvis has more in common with Jayne Mansfield and Mamie Van Doren, who offer an update on the sacrificial image of the gilded woman: the blonde bombshell. Alluringly dressed solely to be undressed, the blonde bombshell embodies a contained state of controlled chaos – it's all about the anticipation of what *might* happen. Striptease, and the bodily decoration that precedes it, remains an exposure of the spirit. 'Well, I know he liked the dragon suit,' Bill Belew recalls of Elvis' costume choices. 'I know he liked the peacock. He liked the leopard.' Belew creates stage outfits for the Jacksons, Pia Zadora and Gloria Swanson. He also styles the Osmonds, turning them into a young posse of Elvis impersonators before their time, wearing the same white flares, fringes, collars, macramé belts and rhinestones. In many ways, the stage costumes Belew designs for Elvis anticipate the glam and teenybop look of the 1970s. 'Bob Mackie had Cher,' Belew observes. 'I had Elvis Presley.'

Like Elvis, Liberace becomes a regular fixture at the Showroom Internationale after it becomes the Las Vegas Hilton in 1971. The flamboyant pianist and singer brings even more glitz and camp to each performance, being driven onstage in a glittering Rolls Royce. Elvis hates the cherubs and the 'Louis XIV ladies and gentlemen decorating the walls in cold marble splendour,' according to one account. 'You know, I've never liked the way this showroom's looked, the interior decorating,' the King announces during one of his shows then tells the audience how he and his boys painted one of the 'fat angels' on high to make them look black. So far, the management hasn't said anything. Meanwhile, Liberace believes that he's the King Ludwig of Las Vegas, and that Ludwig was the Liberace of Bavaria – but only one of them can play the piano.

••• ✝ •••

Like Liberace, Elvis wears the showroom décor as part of his costume. The gaudy Trash Palaces in which they perform are reproduced upon their person; they have fully absorbed the resort hotel aesthetic. The old Vegas of Sinatra and his Rat Pack is on its way out. In the end, it's not the costume but the building that communicates. Old Vegas first met what will be the New Vegas back in 1960 during the taping of Frank Sinatra's *Welcome Home Elvis* television special at Florida's Fontainebleau Hotel: 'the showpiece of Miami Beach's fabled Collins Avenue,' according to Joe Esposito. Its architect and designer, Morris Lapidus, is responsible during the 1950s for a fantastic line in resort hotels, the Fontainebleau being his crowning achievement. 'Lapidus has elevated a kind of taste to a kind of art, even if it is made of plastic, mirrors and spit – it is still uninspired super-schlock,' sniffs *The New York*

Times as the hotel opens in 1954. Mixing styles, materials and functions, Lapidus piles excess upon excess, shaping the Fontainebleau experience into a series of cinematic illusions: for example, the spectacular 'staircase to nowhere' in the lobby. It's at the Fountainebleau that James Bond discovers the body of the dead blonde covered in gold paint draped across his bed.

••• ✝ •••

Sinatra, in his simple black tuxedo, is the medium through which the hotel experience communicates itself. In his bright, shimmering costumes, Elvis *becomes* the experience. Like Pat Barringer, transformed into a golden statue in *Orgy of the Dead*, or Nancy Kovack covered in gold paint as Medea dancing before the altar of Hecate in the 1960s Trash classic *Jason and the Argonauts,* Elvis is a sacrificial object of desire. It's something he will always share with Jayne Mansfield and Mamie van Doren.

••• ✝ •••

The two blonde bombshells appear together in *The Las Vegas Hillbillys*: that most abject of things – an Elvis Presley movie without Elvis in it.

XVIII

In the Shadow of the Stars

The Sixth Sphere

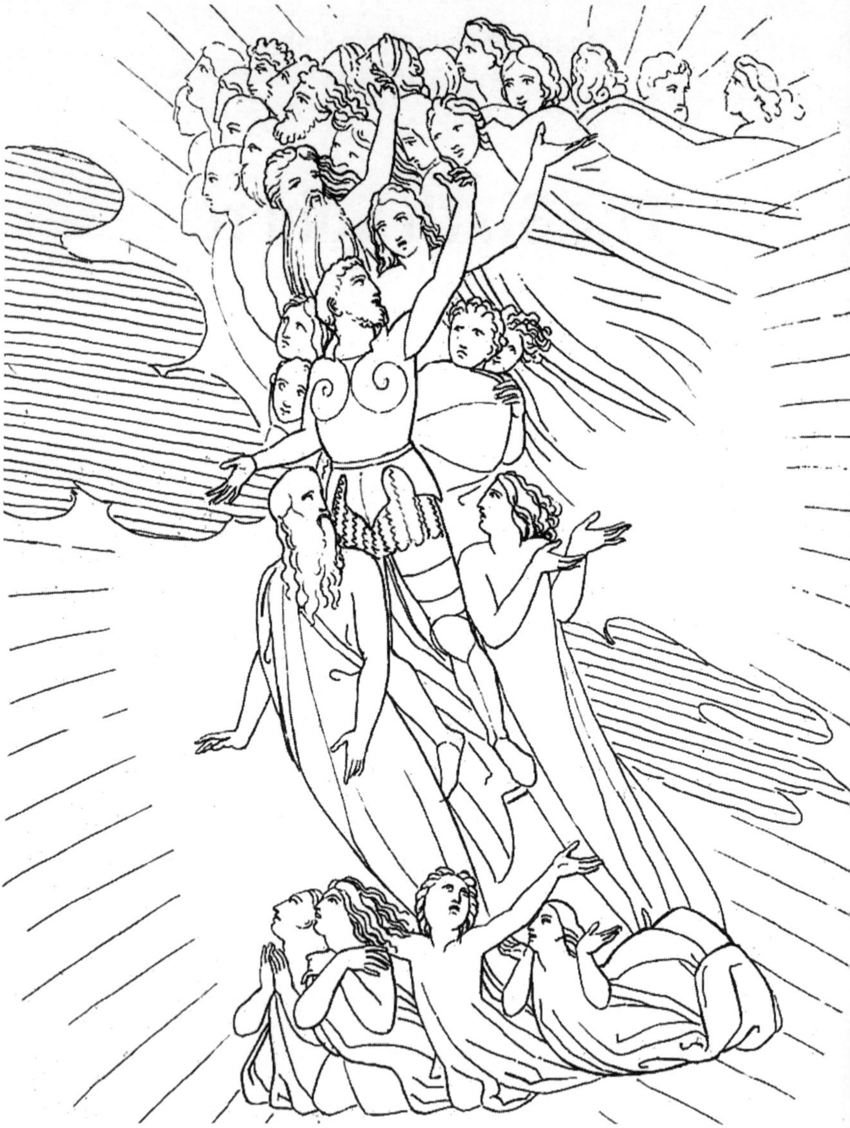

Jupiter in Heaven

According to Ovid, Medea worships Hecate 'the threefold goddess' and rides through the sky in a golden chariot pulled by dragons. She is the daughter of King Aeëtes, who is brother to the semi-divine Circe. According to Trash Movie legend, Jason slays the Hydra so he can steal the Golden Fleece then uses it to bring Medea back to life after she is mortally wounded by an arrow. A vengeful Aeëtes sows the Hydra's teeth in a field of dry soil overlooking the sea, and an army of skeletons rises up to kill Jason. Kings unleash monsters, while the business of entertainers is to put them on display. Occasionally Frank Sinatra gets to make better movies than Elvis – *From Here to Eternity*, for example, is his *Paradise, Hawaiian Style* – but this doesn't stop him denouncing Presley's whole act as 'a rancid-smelling aphrodisiac.' Elvis is nothing but White Trash, and parts of Hollywood will forever remain closed to him. *Harum Scarum* is released on a double bill with Toho studio's *Ghidra the Three-Headed Monster* under the promotional banner: 'The Beat & the Beast make a holiday feast!' Movies are so great. No wonder the King goes back to performing live again.

••• ✝ •••

In 1972 two movies based on the life of Ludwig II are in production. An Italian version, directed by the aristocratic Luchino Visconti and starring the fabulous Helmut Berger, is filmed in Ludwig's actual castles and palaces and looks expensive. The German version is shot on cheap Bavarian soundstages by Hans-Jürgen Syberberg using back-projected slides and clandestine video footage recorded 'on the run' in and around selected historical locations. Both are destined to be released within six months of each other. Meanwhile, *Elvis on Tour*, the King's last real movie, goes on general release in the US. Forever finding its own level, like any material lacking all form or distinction, Trash finally goes mainstream by the early 1970s.

••• ✝ •••

The first movie Elvis ever saw is thought to be *Abbott and Costello meet Frankenstein*, which showed at a Tupelo theatre when he was fourteen. It features Bela Lugosi playing Dracula for only the second time in his screen career. At seventeen Elvis works as a cinema usher at Loew's State Theater in downtown Memphis but is immediately fired when he gets into a fist fight with one of the other ushers. Originally built in 1920, Loew's is closed by 1970 and demolished in 1972. Now Elvis rents The Memphian, a 1940s Art Deco picture house just fifteen minutes from Graceland, for private all-night movie screenings. He sits 'enthroned in front of all the other guests', mostly friends or fans who are allowed into his presence just so long as they leave him alone to watch the screen in peace. Sodas, snacks and popcorn are all free. If Elvis doesn't like the movie, he'll signal the projectionist to show something else. If Elvis really likes the movie, he may demand that it be shown again. He loves watching Kung Fu and action flicks like *Five Fingers of Death, Across 110th Street* and *The Chinese Connection*. Between screenings, a guest disturbs Elvis while he is in one of the Memphian's bathroom stalls, so he pulls a gun on him.

Falling asleep is too much like dying. Elvis suffers from insomnia and sometimes walks in his sleep. He cannot relax in the dark, his heart beats too loud. Instead, Elvis rents fairgrounds and roller rinks for entire nights and invites all his friends along. That way he never has to be alone. Or he has big firework parties round the back of Graceland, watching hundreds of dollars at a time going up in smoke and sparks. Sometimes he cannot wait until 4 July to play 'War': a game Elvis and the boys devise in which a 'Red team' and a 'Blue team' pad themselves up in protective gear, including helmets and goggles, then blaze away at each other with bottle rockets, handheld roman candles and firecrackers. Waste is, after all, as American as the Fourth of July. Confounding space and order, people see and feel the effects of waste more immediately than those of extravagance. Waste exists economically as a more violent form of extravagance – except that nobody in the King's circle can afford to push back against Elvis. Nobody.

Guns, like pills, are a dream that fits right into your hand – they consume themselves in an instant, taking you with them. In the run-up to Christmas 1970 Elvis drops close to $20,000 on guns while shopping at Kerr's Sporting Goods on Wilshire Boulevard in Beverly Hills. Among the thirty-two handguns purchased are a gold-inlaid .375 Colt python revolver, costing $1950, and a .44 Ruger Blackhawk revolver, also gold-plated, at $1850. The rest of his haul ranges in price from over $1000 down to $66 for a Derringer, plus a shotgun and a rifle. 'Now because, coming from the South, all of us have been pretty close to guns, you grow up with them,' explains Red West, another of his bodyguards. 'But Elvis is absolutely kinky about them. He would buy an armoury if he had the chance. He is kinky about guns, and I mean kinky, man.' To prove a point, Elvis will shoot out the dashboard of his yellow Ford Pantera and any television set within range showing a programme he doesn't like.

Elvis and the boys set up police silhouette targets in an old smokehouse standing next to Vernon Presley's office in the grounds at Graceland – during the day the place is littered with discarded junk and spent shell cases. At night it becomes a firing range. On one occasion, Elvis manages to set the smokehouse on fire with a prolonged burst from his M16. 'Oh, Daddy, let it burn,' he laughs as Vernon tries to smother the flames with his jacket. 'It's only money.' There's plenty more where that came from. The Colonel is always working on some new deal. With Elvis back on tour, breaking all records at halls and casinos throughout America, the Colonel starts to think in global terms: a single concert beamed around the world via satellite, with WE LOVE ELVIS translated into every language, flashing in bright lights behind him. Elvis asks Bill Belew to design a new costume for the occasion. 'I just want the suit to say America,' he says. And who, in his appetite for cars and guns and pills, is more American than Elvis? The first time one of his Memphis jewellers meets him, Elvis is kneeling in the mud, wearing a full-length mink coat, blasting away at a target pinned to the outside wall of his father's office – it is two o'clock in the morning. Elvis tells Belew he wants an Imperial American Eagle tricked out in jewels on his chest and back. The design must include a broad white leather belt inlaid with the Great Seal of the United States.

⁂

'I think possibly his favourite was always the Aloha Hawaii suit,' Belew remembers, 'the American Eagle, you know.'

XIX

In the Shadow of the Stars

The Sixth Sphere Continued

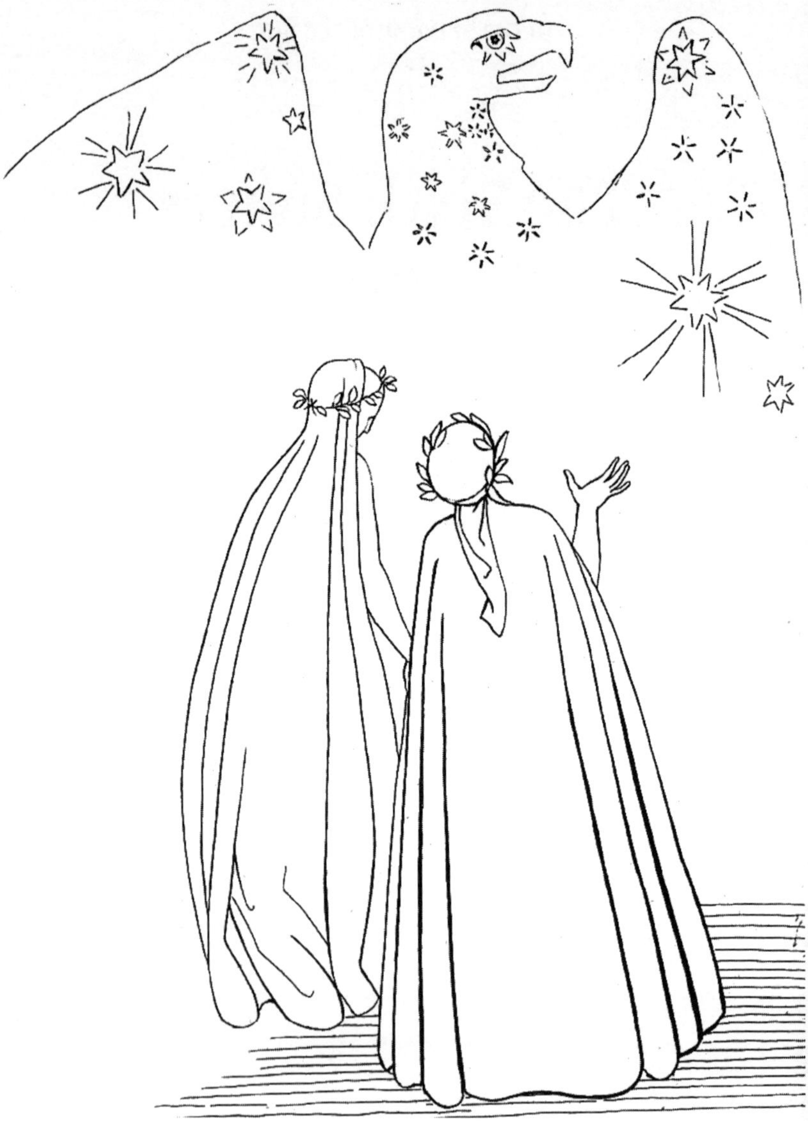

Before eyes and wings spread wide

Like a diamond hanging in the darkness of space, Intelsat IV F-4 follows a circular geosynchronous orbit in line with the Earth's equator. The satellite is equipped with twelve broadband communication channels capable of handling up to 6,000 two-way phone calls or twelve colour-television broadcasts or a combination of the two, along with fax and data transmission. Intelsat IV F-4 was successfully launched into space from Florida just after midnight on 23 January 1972. Almost a year to the day later, on 14 January 1973, just after midnight, Intelsat IV F-4 relays a live concert performance given by Elvis Presley from the Honolulu International Center in Waikiki. Everything passes through this one point of light. *Aloha from Hawaii* will provide prime-time television viewing in Japan, Korea, Australia, New Zealand, the Philippines, Thailand and South Vietnam. A Eurovision simulcast will then pass the show on to twenty-eight more countries that same night. US audiences finally get to see it in April, giving Elvis a combined worldwide audience of 1.5 *billion* viewers. Rehearsals take place in secret under the protective cover of Henry Kaiser's Aluminum Dome on the front lawn of the Hilton Hawaiian Village, where the hotel's entire thirtieth floor has been set aside for Elvis and his entourage. *Aloha from Hawaii* includes footage of Elvis arriving by helicopter, plus travelogue shots of Diamond Head, mountain ridges, ocean waves and flowers. Bubble-headed robots in colourful leis, marching bands and dancing geishas are shown performing to the crowds outside the auditorium at the Honolulu International Center. Just days before the actual performance, Elvis gives away the ruby-encrusted 'Great Seal' belt from his stage costume to the wife of *Hawaii Five-O* star Jack Lord, obliging Bill Belew to ship in more of the precious stones to fashion a replacement. With eagles rendered in rubies on its front and back, the gleaming white jumpsuit is fitted with a high collar and a cape also decorated with rubies, making Elvis look more like Captain Marvel than ever. At the end of the show's dress rehearsal, Elvis sends the cape sailing into the outstretched arms of his audience.

Our collective desire for fame is defined by taboos about what it means to be loved by the masses – to be simultaneously held high above them and abjectly below them. For one night only and before the entire world, Elvis is a bejewelled and decorated god, hung with garlands of red flowers. In his entire career he has never looked more gorgeous than he does at the Honolulu International Center, and he never will again. It's as if in this one moment he has been able to stop the destructive flow of time from moving through his body. On his recent tours, Elvis had appeared bloated and overweight, his performance displaying signs of a sluggish deceleration and loss of energy. To prepare for *Aloha from Hawaii,* Elvis withdraws inside Graceland, where he submits himself to a punishing regime of dieting and exercise. There are regular Karate workouts, protein drinks, diet pills and mineral water. Meals now come in freeze-dried portions totalling 500 calories per day, supplemented by daily injections of vitamins and 'a hormone extracted from the urine of pregnant women', according to one account. Elvis loses twenty-five pounds in this way but then piles it back on again right after the show as he reverts to his former self, bingeing to excess on pills and food. Ed Parker, his Karate instructor, describes Elvis banqueting like a Roman emperor on 'cheeseburgers, french fries, pizza, ice cream, popsicles by the box, banana and peanut butter sandwiches, Pepsi-Cola and a stomach-wrenching assortment of junk food.' The increase in bodyweight is accompanied by violent mood swings. Elvis starts alternating his favourite uppers with larger and larger doses of Placidyl, Valium, Percodan and Demerol. Red

West reports that 'toward about 1970 he started taking the downers – got heavier into them in 1972 and continued through to 1976, when it got ridiculous.' Dilaudid, known familiarly as 'drugstore heroin', soon becomes his favourite. 'I've tried them all,' Elvis tells Pat West, Red's wife, 'and Dilaudid is the best.'

••• ✝ •••

Underneath this violent oblivion of excess, Elvis asserts himself by maintaining a state of wilful helplessness, nodding out over his food in the predawn hours of the night, forcing those around him to watch over the King to make sure he doesn't choke to death. Downers and junk food are ways of staying in one place: of leaving Elvis unmoved and unmoving – overloaded and at the centre of his own world. The Graceland colour scheme changes over this period, the familiar blues and whites being replaced by the deepest shades of red. Black marble and black tile merge with balustrades and doorways shrouded in heavy red velvet, tied back with gold tassels. Floor-to-ceiling red drapes hang from push-button electric traverse rods. Overstuffed Louis XV chairs are reupholstered in red satin and rhinestones. Chandeliers sparkle above surfaces encrusted with fake rubies and sequins. A nocturnal stillness surrounds him. Elvis needs to slow everything down.

XIX
The Sixth Sphere Continued

He habitually eats with his fingers, making it easier still to stuff his face. And he no longer goes out riding in the grounds of Graceland; like an overweight Ludwig II of later years, he is unable to find a horse stout enough to carry him.

••• ✝ •••

In the stay-hungry world of twentieth-century capitalism, consuming what you want when you want represents a state of blissful stasis. Squandered upon drugs, guns and unconstrained gluttony, money becomes a perpetual flow channelled specifically through Elvis. None of his fabulous fees, including the one million dollars he receives for *Aloha from Hawaii*, are conserved or rerouted into investment schemes, production companies or any other project that might retain them. There are no tax shelters, and Elvis covers his own overheads. Within the confines of a political economy, finance has never been so fluid, but its constant movement is designed to keep Elvis static. There's something almost karmic, Elvis tells Ed Parker, about the way money comes in one door just as it's heading out the other. Money, for him, has the same basic exchange value as love, but money can never buy love or even express it. Business and love always obscure each other, the one rendering the other motionless and frozen; but the two are never separate. Money regulates and maintains the identity of love for Elvis by creating a space in which self-assertion through wilful helplessness can exist untroubled by any of the contradictions it throws up. Elvis remains a fixed centre through which the fabulous sales figures and performance fees pour in from one side, while gifts, extravagances and indulgences flood out of the other. Love generates small bubbles of ease and excess, which must be consumed in the moment. Once these have passed, people, places and things start to erode until entropy and decay become new sources of life.

Something recalled from one of my dreams: 'Decrepitude is the degree of truculence displayed by objects towards the action of time.'

XX

In the Shadow of the Stars

The Sixth Sphere Concluded

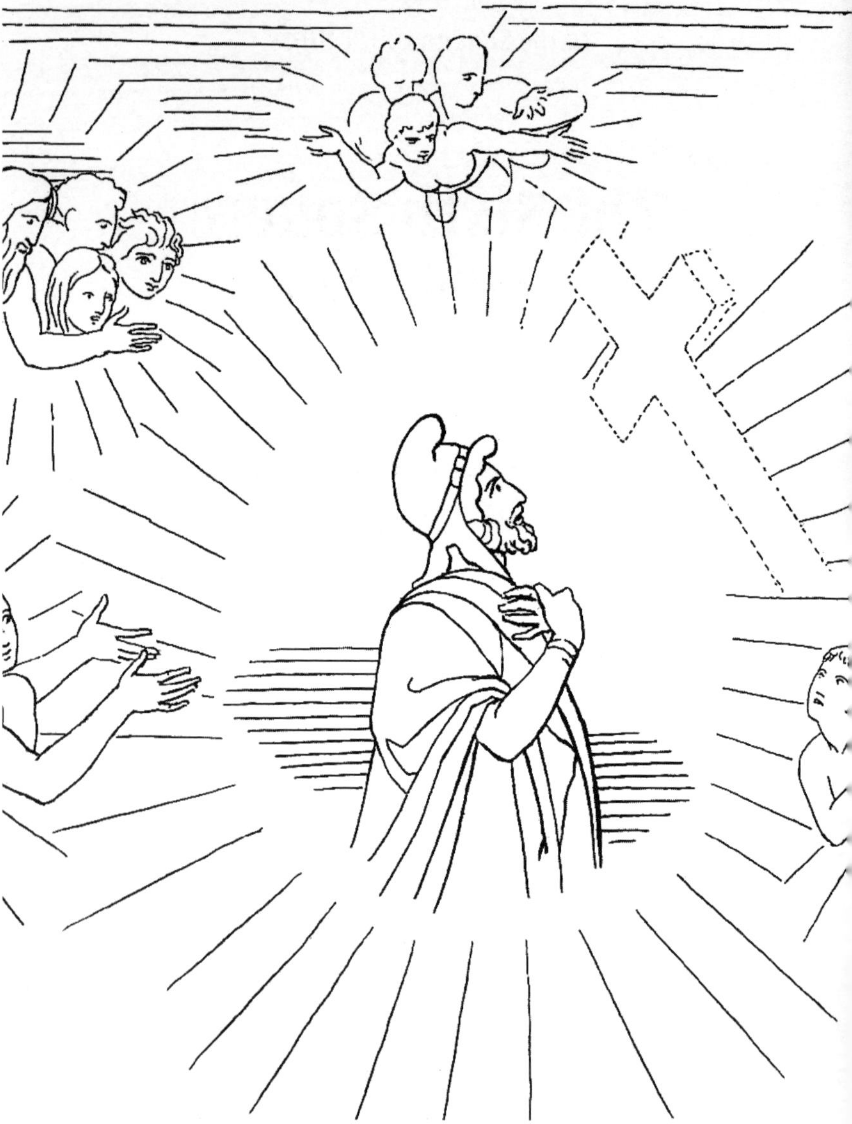

Snake in the eagle's shadow

And Elvis now knows that he has been right all along. Bruce Lee in *Enter the Dragon* just saw to that. Kung Fu is a national craze in the United States. Karate has become the next big thing. It's everywhere – in movies and magazines, on sweatshirts and television. Ads offering Kung Fu training and equipment appear alongside more traditional ones for body building courses in the back of comic books. 'I have been involved in the art of karate – most people don't know to what extent,' Elvis confides in a rambling onstage monologue. 'It's become to me like a way of life.' He first became interested back in 1959 while he was in the Army. *Enter the Dragon* merely confirmed what he already knew. 'I see your talents have gone beyond the mere physical level,' the head of the monastery solemnly informs Bruce Lee at the start of the movie. 'Your skills are now at the point of spiritual insight.' That which is popular quickly loses all definition – its value and meaning metastasise, getting blurred around the edges. 'Kung Fu and karate are two different things,' Elvis tells his audience. 'Kung Fu is slower – like sand blowing in your face. Karate is quicker – karate gets on with it.' Following Bruce Lee's death, the producer and director of *Enter the*

Dragon come up with *Golden Needles*. Elvis watches it repeatedly in all-night screenings at the Memphian cinema. The story concerns the epic search for a butt-ugly gold statuette on the mean streets of Hong Kong and Los Angeles. Very little actual Kung Fu is involved, the emphasis being upon acupuncture, Daoist magic and flamethrowers. Retained from *Enter the Dragon*, Lalo Schifrin is once again doing the music; and *Black Belt Jones* star Jim Kelly makes a brief reappearance staging his own fight sequences. Neck-deep in wide lapels and safari suits, the star of *Golden Needles* is Joe Don Baker, a chunkier Texas-born version of Elvis in his prime – his Kung Fu style is little more than Hollywood roughhousing with some martial-arts sounds dubbed on for effect. The villain is played by Burgess Meredith, better known as the Penguin from ABC's *Batman* television series.

••• ✠ •••

And Elvis now knows that Karate is a thing of the spirit even when he's too stoned to move or even see straight. It helps his self-control: body discipline, mind discipline, in his stage work, diet and breathing techniques. It involves yoga. It involves meditation. It combines violence with eroticism. Bruce Lee features as sidekick Kato in *The Green Hornet*: an unsuccessful attempt by ABC to extend the success of *Batman* with another series based on a comic-book character. 'We forge our bodies in the fire of our will,' proclaims the villain in *Enter the Dragon*. His life on a private island is devoted to martial art tournaments, face painting and powerful narcotics administered by nurses, which must seem like hog heaven to Elvis. Bruce Lee winds up doing 'fight choreography' for *The Wrecking Crew*, the fourth and last movie in the Matt Helm series of spy spoofs starring Dean Martin. Ed Parker, Karate instructor and personal bodyguard to Elvis Presley, has a walk-on part. Parker's former pupil and future action star Chuck Norris also makes his onscreen debut. Norris fights Bruce Lee in the Roman Colosseum at the end of *The Way of the Dragon*, watched only by a rather startled-looking kitten. For months Priscilla Presley has been studying at the Chuck Norris martial arts studio, where she starts hanging out with Karate expert Mike Stone, the man for whom she will leave Elvis.

✝

And Elvis now knows only hurt and betrayal. Mike Stone, aka 'The Animal', is an International Karate Champion with 91 consecutive wins to his name; and Priscilla has fallen under his manly spell. Elvis breaks down in tears in front of Ed Parker. This is not a world in which women feature much. It seems more like a movie – or a conspiracy, which amounts to the same thing. Parker has never seen Elvis cry before. All the pieces fit together. Mike Stone is from Hawaii, and so is Ed Parker. One night Elvis is attacked during a performance at the Showroom Internationale by four Hawaiian assassins trained in martial arts. One of them has adhesive tape across his knuckles. Elvis and his bodyguards chase them offstage and out of town. According to one account, the four Karate killers are in fact 'South American porno and go-go hustlers from Lima, Peru.' Elvis keeps a four-shot derringer in his boot onstage and expects his bodyguards to drop anyone who tries anything like that again. 'If some sonofabitch tries to kill me,' he tells them, 'I want you guys to get him. I want you to rip his goddamn eyes out. I don't want him sitting around like Charles Manson with a grin on his face, saying "I killed Elvis Presley."'

••• ✝ •••

And Elvis now knows that Mike Stone has to die. He climbs the walls of his penthouse suite in the MGM Grand, drenched in sweat and pinned to the eyeballs. 'The man has to die,' Elvis tells Sonny West, thrusting an M16 into his arms. Red West is ordered to contact a Mafia hitman, who agrees to do the job at a reasonably low fee out of professional courtesy. Elvis holds Karate displays in hotel rooms strewn with his books and guns. Elvis disappears into a black hole of vengeance and retribution, desire and rage. He'll see to it that Priscilla watches helplessly while Stone begs for his life.

••• ✝ •••

And Elvis now knows that he is alone in his weakness and his anger. He is a slurring dead-eyed innocent in the violent order of men. Nobody will strike back at him. 'I want to be the baddest motherfucker there is,' he says and starts making plans to produce his own martial arts movie with Ed Parker. One screenplay sees him as a former CIA agent running a Karate school while avenging the death of a friend. It will feature actual documentary footage of martial arts tournaments and training sessions. Ed Parker will see to that. 'We don't want to talk about *From Here to Eternity* and Frank Sinatra,' he tells a scriptwriter. There is no story and no structure. Elvis wants Bill Belew to design the costumes. Some footage is shot in Memphis at the Tennessee Karate Institute, a school financed by Elvis and run by Red West. Featured fighters include World Full-Contact Champion Bill 'Superfoot' Wallace and Ed Parker student Dave Hebler – another bodyguard working for Elvis. 'We intend it to become an Americanization of the art,' Elvis says of the Institute in his onstage monologue. Caught between a violent action movie and a factual documentary, between the vengeful drama running inside his head and the anaesthetised reality of his daily life, he lets planning and production drag on for months.

••• ✝ •••

And Elvis now knows that his Karate movie will never be made; the money he has pumped into the project is already gone.

XXI

In the Shadow of the Stars

The Seventh Sphere

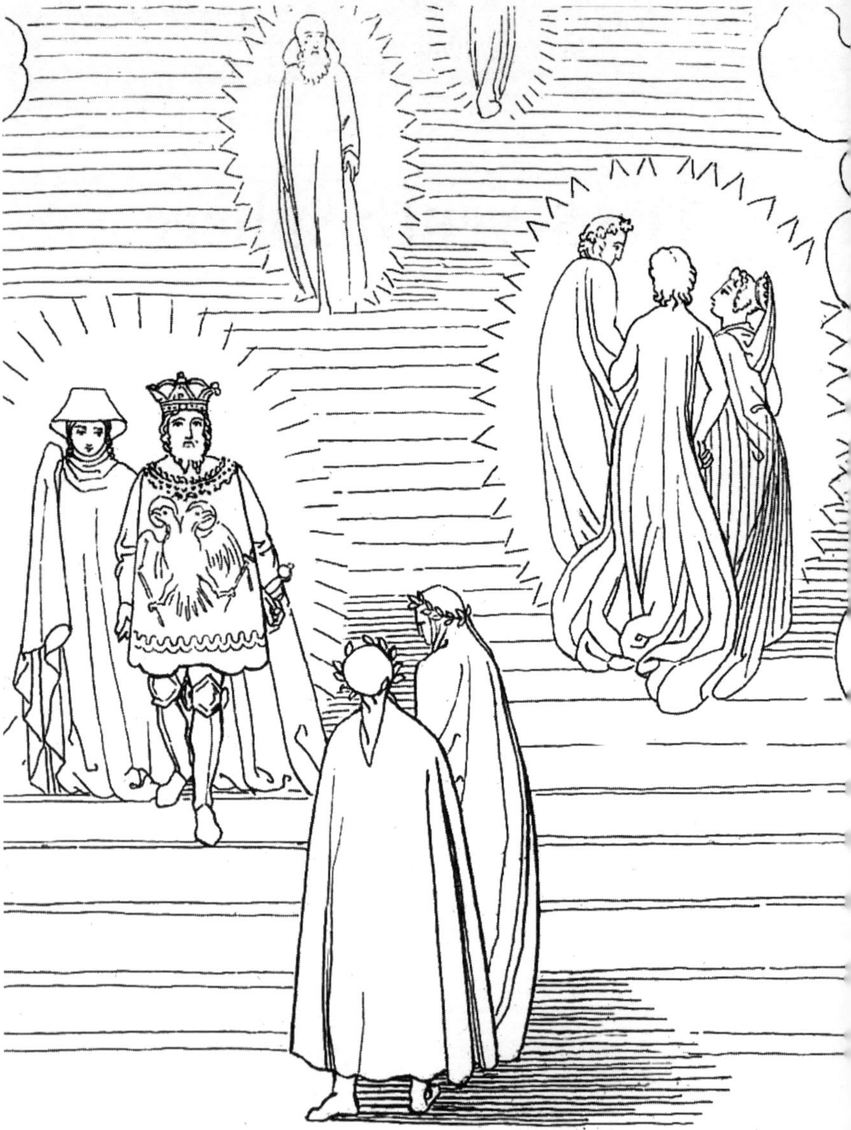

Saturn in Heaven

Like falling dust, everything eventually settles into a routine. The four-shot derringer Elvis wears stuck in his boot when he's onstage starts chafing his ankle. In front of an astonished audience, he whips it out mid-performance, laying the gun aside for one of his musicians to scoop up and put in their pocket. Numb on sleeping pills, Elvis steps down from his private jet one rainy night at Dallas/ Fort Worth International Airport. He is wearing pyjamas with his favourite magnum handgun stuck in the waistband, a coat pulled around him. The magnum tumbles out and skitters across the dark wet tarmac. Red West grabs a flashlight and starts searching for it, while Elvis keeps on walking, not even stopping to look back.

Elvis continues to project his own action movie into his darkest innermost depths. 'Destroy the image and you will break the enemy,' Bruce Lee is advised in *Enter the Dragon* – but this is the one thing Elvis cannot do. 'The opponent' is an illusion produced by the ego – but Elvis cannot see that either. 'He believes he is a law unto himself,' according to Dave Hebler. 'He is an industry, making a lot of money for a lot of people. That can be, to some degree, understood. But he loses sight of reality. Because when he gets out into the real world – your world, my world – he can't differentiate between the two.' This is one of the reasons why those charged with looking after Elvis take such care to ensure that there is never a bullet in the chamber of any gun within his reach. He is far too fond of showing his displeasure by shooting out hotel TV sets or firing at penthouse ceilings just for the hell of it.

••• ✠ •••

On a personal level, sovereignty plays itself out in a state of endless immaturity. 'Like a little boy who picks up a rock and throws it through a window for no real reason apart from the fact it was there, Elvis will pick up a gun and blast away with it,' Dave Hebler maintains. But there are always other reasons – play can be the expression of violence, frustration and other wildly self-destructive urges.

••• ✠ •••

'In this day and time, you can't even get sick,' Elvis rages. 'You are *strung out*!' He's onstage at the Las Vegas Hilton

Hotel talking to the audience. 'From three different sources I heard I was *strung out on heroin!* I swear to God...hotel employees, Jack... bellboys, freaks that carry your luggage up to the room, people working around, you know, talking... maids. And I was sick. I was getting... I had the doctor and had the flu and got over it in one day, but all across this town... *STRUNG OUT*!' Elvis likes to talk to his audiences during his live appearances. 'If I find or hear the individual that has said that about me,' he continues, 'I'm going to break their goddamn neck, you sonofabitch. That is *dangerous*. That is damaging to myself, to my little daughter, to my father, to my friends, to my doctor... It's *DANGEROUS!* I will pull your goddam tongue out by the *ROOTS!*' By now his audience is cheering, so Elvis thanks them and asks how many of them saw the movie *Blue Hawaii*.

When forced to operate within certain social limits, sovereignty can express itself as an uncontrollable rage. Elvis has never let his anger show on stage before, but now it's starting to come through. Ludwig II of Bavaria flies into a fury whenever one of his commands is not met with immediate obedience, lashing out and throwing things at those who have displeased him. Ludwig's treatment of his servants becomes increasingly tyrannical; they are ordered to bow low whenever they meet him, and on no account should they look him directly in the face or make eye contact. One servant at Neuschwanstein who fails to comply is sentenced to wear a black mask for an entire year, just so Ludwig doesn't have to see 'his criminal countenance.' Those who live around Elvis are in constant fear of what he *might* do. He has been known to strike his bodyguards and pull guns on them, but no one ever dares to raise a hand against him. Elvis remains alone and isolated at the heart of his own entourage. 'He still believes he's in charge,' Hebler remarks. 'He is like isolated royalty, like the Emperor of Japan or the Queen of England.'

'I can no longer bear to be stared at by thousands of people, to smile and wave a thousand times, direct questions at people I have nothing to do with and hear answers that I am not interested in,' Ludwig writes to his Court Secretary. 'No! No! I can no longer give up my solitude.' At a show in North Carolina a strung out and bored Elvis Presley gives away individually selected items of jewellery valued at over $35,000 to the first two rows of his audience. 'Once the resources are dissipated,' Bataille remarks of sovereignty's relationship to limit and waste, 'there remains the prestige acquired by the one who wastes. The waste is an ostentatious squandering to this end, with a view to superiority over others that he attributes to himself by this means.' For Elvis, the live stage has become his one true medium; he will no longer appear in films and will never guest on any television chat shows – the Colonel sees to that. How else can Elvis communicate his anger and disdain to the outside world? Sovereignty imposes itself as a form of boredom: yet another routine that is increasingly hard to bear. Any excess that repeats itself simply ends by becoming too much. Ludwig complains in a letter to his former governess that 'so many misunderstand and continue to misunderstand me, so that I naturally felt more and more rejected by the world and withdrew into myself.' Elvis lowers a black ladder down into an endless well of silence, inertia and oblivion: a physiological tarpit in which all his senses are suspended. 'I felt sorry for Elvis and at the same time, I hated him for being drugged and out of control and wasting his wonderful gifts,' Joe Esposito confesses long after his death. The chemical hydraulics required to maintain Elvis in body and soul are prodigious and deeply repetitive. He is shot full of uppers before each show, both the early and the late, then given something to level him out once Elvis climbs down from the stage, descending from rung to rung into narcotised darkness. Finally heavy sleep medication is administered at dawn so he can close his eyes before having to climb back up again. One afternoon Elvis finds himself caught up in traffic on the freeway heading home. He looks at the daylight – at the crowded world of cars and faces all around him.

⁂

'Isn't it fun to get up before dark, E?' a voice says from somewhere close by. 'Everywhere you look, man, there are real people.'

XXII

In the Shadow of the Stars

The Seventh Sphere Concluded

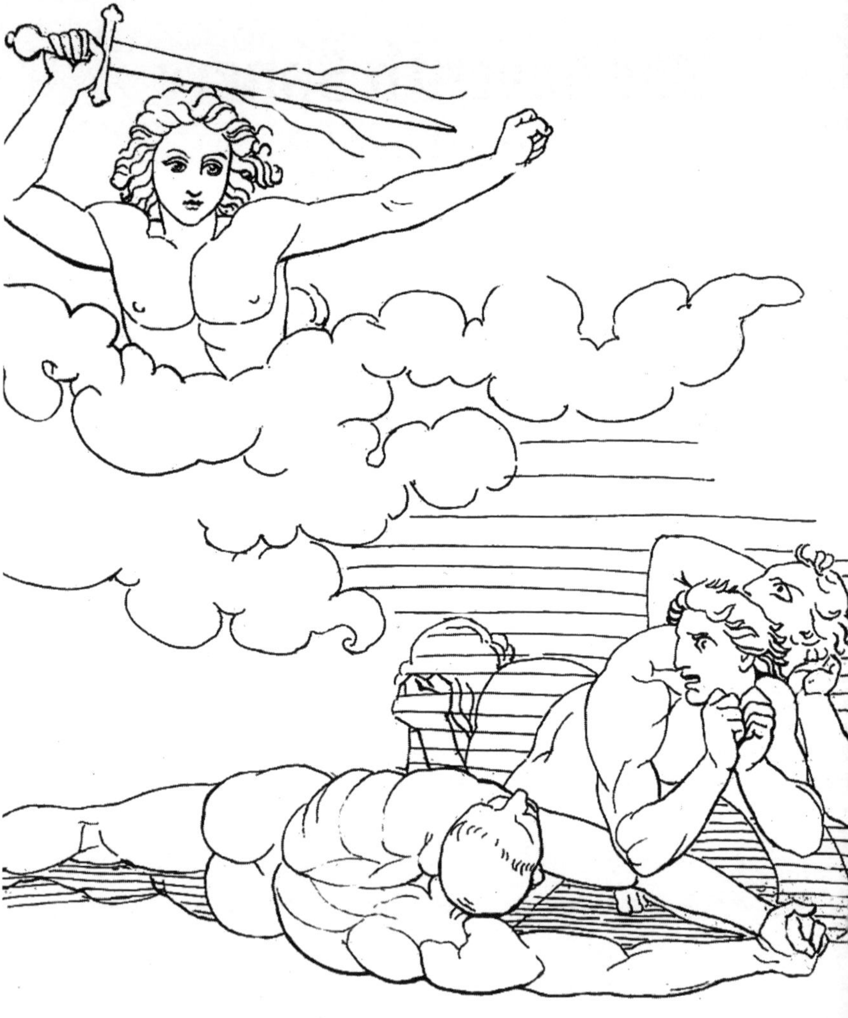

Down through the depths of all seven solitudes

••• ✝ •••

When Elvis was a little boy, he couldn't sleep. He was afraid of the dark because he didn't know what was going to happen to him. 'I know in the daytime when I go to sleep that it's dark in my room, and I pretend like it's night, but I know it's daytime, and I'm not afraid to fall asleep,' Elvis tells a Denver police officer. That's why he stays up all night with his friends so he can feel comfortable. 'In the morning, when everybody is up and going to work,' Elvis tells the same detective, 'I feel safe because it's daytime – and then I can go to sleep.' Staying awake all night allows him to remain a child: mothered by the darkness. Elvis will hole up in his Graceland bedroom for days at a time. The windows are covered with aluminium foil to keep out the light of day. Two ceiling-mounted televisions are permanently on, while a third murmurs softly at the foot of the bed. Candles burn on the television stand in a room filled with books. Elvis spends endless hours reading, writing notes in the margins, poring over numerological formulae, gazing at astrological charts and pondering his fate. He never learns how to give up the needs of the present, however. That's why Elvis is so rarely alone.

••• ✝ •••

A lot of young models and beauty pageant winners, from a Miss Tennessee and a Queen of the Memphis Southmen to a former Miss Traffic Safety and a Miss Mid-South, ascend the stairs at Graceland and pass through the big gold doors that lead to his bedroom, where Elvis is awaiting them, already attired in his dark-blue pyjamas. He tells them he will be the perfect gentleman and asks them to read to him. He also asks them to fetch him Jell-O and watch over him while he takes his pills. 'Will you stay here and hold my hand?' he asks one young beauty queen. 'It was the strangest thing,' she remembers. 'He would sit there in bed, silent with his eyes closed for the longest time, and I would think he was sound asleep, but when I got up to leave, he'd claw my arm saying, "Don't go!" He wouldn't let go of my hand until he was really sound asleep.' The next morning Elvis buys her a new car – a white Pontiac Grand Prix at a time when cars really looked like cars.

••• ✝ •••

Sex isn't really a thing here. 'It was adolescent,' one companion recalls of her nights spent with Elvis, 'until all of a sudden you graduated into Mother.' The King regresses to a condition of contented infancy, but only in the presence of someone young, caring and beautiful like the smiling female co-stars of his

Hollywood movies. He says he feels more comfortable if they're wearing pyjamas too. Elvis sinks deeper into the private world of a little boy, with his mother still close at hand. The face smiling down at him may change, but in the illuminated darkness of his bedroom the maternal return is a limitless reality. Nothing has the immediacy of a mother's love – after all, how can anyone think of the future in the presence of one whose needs and wants are so desperate, so urgent? 'Whatever Elvis wanted to do, he did. Whatever he wanted to buy he bought,' Joe Esposito observes about the King's nocturnal activities. During the night, the child's uncontrolled consumption and total dominance are united in a complete rejection of the values inherent in the order of things. In an eternal sovereign moment, Elvis turns his back on the future by wasting everything that the present has to offer him. Nobody can say 'no' to him. He becomes a child who can only be obeyed to the point where he loses himself.

It is worth remembering that Elvis came into this world foreshadowed by the simultaneous birth and death of his stillborn twin, Jesse Garon: a sovereign being who had used up his entire future before he had even drawn his first breath. Elvis and Jesse Garon were both born under Capricorn and therefore ruled by Saturn, a planet whose influence is associated with constraint and limitation. In classical mythology, Saturn devours his children so that they cannot rise up and kill him. What a sovereign being like Jesse Garon experienced directly, and Elvis only understands in the deep darkness of his extended childhood, is that stasis can never be confused with conservation. Sovereignty maintains itself as an irreversible squandering: an all-out consuming and wrecking of the self. It opposes the identifiable and constraining order of things with the unknowable and unstable limits of Trash – and whatever else is left at the end of the night.

··· ✝ ···

The sovereign surrounds himself with a court where the darkness emanating from him shines most on those who are nearest to him. Sometimes Elvis calls his favourite beauty queen 'Mommy' and sometimes 'Ariadne', which is the name by which Nietzsche addressed Cosima Wagner as his mind consumed itself in madness. And sometimes, on the wasted edge of oblivion, Elvis takes his beauty queen by the hand and asks her to tell him about her life – her childhood, her family, her friends. And it is perhaps then that Elvis is at his happiest.

··· ✠ ···

'Sometimes when I am tired of reading and everything is silent as the grave,' Ludwig confides to his Court Secretary, 'I feel the irresistible need to hear a human voice. Then I summon a servant or a postillion and get him to tell me about his home and his family.' Elvis insists that his beauty queen keep on talking to him. Doesn't the King know that he's already descending into Heaven? Lying in his bed, her voice in his ears, Elvis eats his cheeseburger at dawn, ready at last to fall asleep.

··· ✠ ···

Reader, always remember that Elvis can be found at the deepest end of all our dreams, no matter how public or private they might be. To paraphrase and inevitably to betray Georges Bataille: no one can step down a single rung on this ladder without having first proved that the ladder itself had not the slightest meaning in their eyes. Elvis can't even see the ladder anymore. 'You kids be good,' Elvis tells Michael Jackson and his brothers when they come backstage after seeing him perform at the Sahara Hotel and Casino in Lake Tahoe. This is in 1974 when the Jacksons are playing the MGM Grand in Las Vegas. Sweating and bloated, drugged to the eyeballs, having entered the final stage of his steady decline, Elvis grabs hold of Michael's hand as the young entertainer turns to leave.

'You started so young,' he says. Lisa Marie, the King's six-year-old daughter, is present at this moment and will remember it long into her adult life. She loves to watch Michael dance.

Elvis buys a new private jet, a Delta Airlines Convair 880, refurbished with gold faucets in his private bathroom, and names it *The Lisa Marie.*

XXIII

In the Shadow of Heaven

The Eighth Sphere

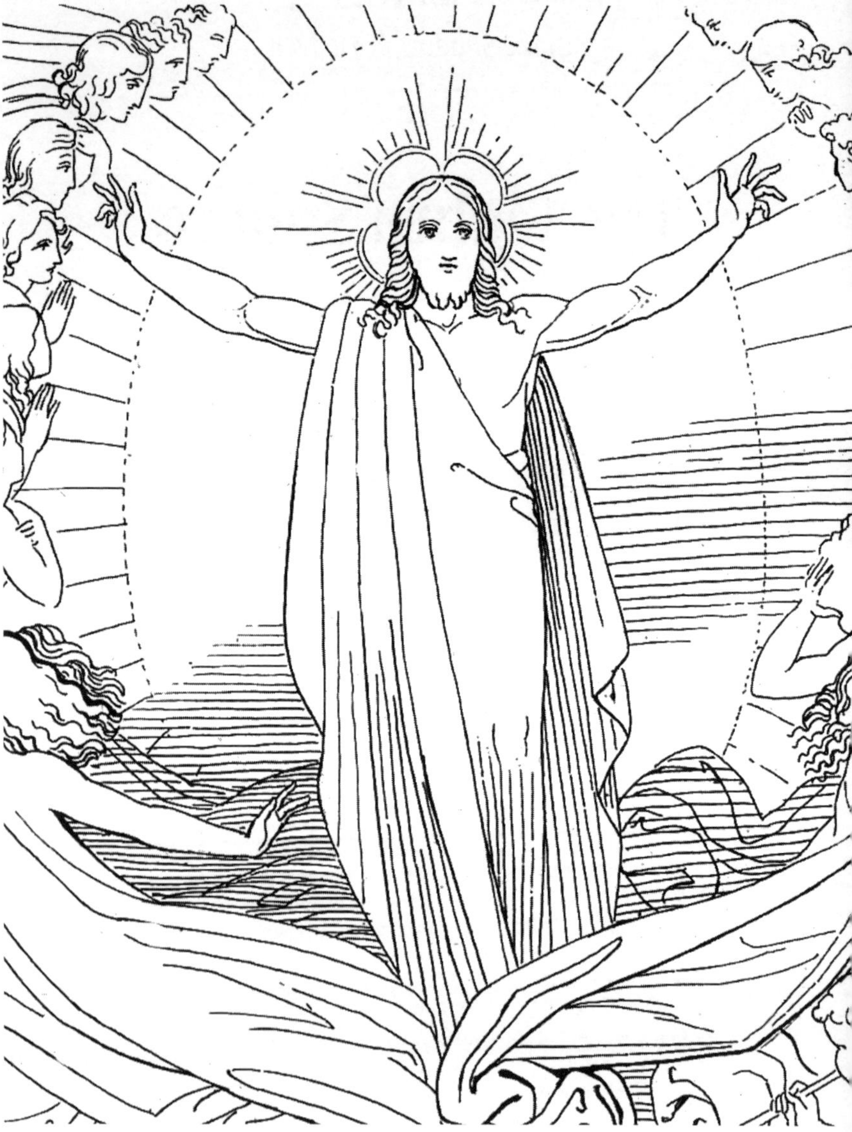

The Fixed Stars Under Heaven

··· ✝ ···

As was prophesied in ancient Scripture, Jesus has been ruling Heaven as its King since as far back as October 1914. Satan, once God's favourite, was then deposed at His command and sent down, along with the rest of the wicked angels, to reign over the Earth. This marks the beginning of End Times and is a sign of Christ's Final Judgement upon humanity – for it was Satan who deceived Adam and Eve into disobeying God's Laws. Such Knowledge can only increase as we approach the Last Days and the Eventual Collapse in the Order of Things. For God has ordained that those who follow this teaching shall be His chosen people. While stationed in Germany with the US Army, Elvis Presley frequently receives letters from those who claim that he is the Messiah. Panics, pandemics, wars and terrors will follow upon each other until Christ Himself shall finally come back down to reclaim the Earth.

··· ✝ ···

Crowned with fire, Michael Jackson descends a staircase to the main stage at the Shrine Auditorium in Los Angeles in front of an audience of thousands at approximately

18.30 on 27 January 1984. A mistimed magnesium flash has just ignited his hair, turning Michael's head into a flaming torch. Surrounded on all sides by exploding pyrotechnics, he continues his triumphant downward dance, from step to step, unaware that his head is still burning. Michael is filming a Pepsi commercial with his brothers. 'You're a whole new generation,' they sing. 'You're loving what you do.' Michael is wrapped in a billowing cloud of smoke. The cameras are still turning, catching everything that's happening. According to a conspiracy theory circulating at the time, many fans believe that Michael is the second coming of Christ. They firewalk to his music, exclaiming that the 'power is in the music'. A photo of Michael Jackson haloed in flames is distributed by the Associated Press, making the front page of every newspaper. Michael wants footage of the incident released to the public. 'After my fans see the tape, Pepsi will be history,' he tells his lawyer. Michael doesn't drink Pepsi because he doesn't *believe* in it. 'Did the press reports say his hair was on fire?' comments Pepsi president Roger Enrico. 'To me it looked like his whole head. Like a human torch. No way can *anyone* see this footage.'

••• ✝ •••

In exchange for two commercials starring Michael and his brothers, Pepsi agrees to put up the money for their epic nationwide 'Victory' tour, which starts on Friday 6 July 1984 in Kansas City, Missouri. Running the show is flamboyant boxing promoter Don King. 'Michael has transcended all earthly bounds,' King tells the press. 'Every race, colour and creed is waiting for this tour. The way he shall lift the despairing and the despondent enthrals me.' 'Can't someone shut the man up?' Michael asks his entourage. Imagine some stern order of experience outside of the banal compromises of everyday life – a chance to exist in a world of angels and demons with no negotiation, no softening of purpose, no bargaining to exist. There are those who claim that the Archangel Michael and Jesus are One and the Same, leading some to believe that Michael Jackson is the actual Messiah – a Special Messenger put here on Earth for this purpose.

••• ✝ •••

At the start of each concert on the 'Victory' tour, in place of the actual Jackson brothers, a lumbering, clunking line of giant muppets lurches across the darkened stage. 'Long, long ago, the Kreeton people walked this Earth,' a disembodied voice announces in Godlike tones. 'They held the people captive as slaves in bondage, bringing evil and ruin to what was good.' The multi-part Kreetons consist of chain-draped blue canvas bodies, shoulder-carried frame heads with matching blue covering, giant blue canvas boots and glowing-stone-topped staffs. Only a king can defend the Earth from such monsters. 'For years and years, it was prophesied that a mighty one would come and pull the sword from the stone and destroy the Kreeton people,' the Godlike voice continues. 'This one would be called "great", "most holy" and "powerful". His kingdom will be a kingdom that will never be brought to ruin – it will last from time indefinite till time indefinite.' In a chainmail facemask illuminated by green lasers, Marlon Jackson finally pulls the sword from the stone. 'Arise all the world and behold the Kingdom!' he declares, as the entire stage is plunged into stormy darkness, illuminated by lightning flashes.

··· ✝ ···

At the end of the Great Tribulation, God's Kingdom will eventually be extended to the Earth, transforming it once again into Paradise. Michael Jackson starts calling himself the King of Pop and is treated like royalty everywhere he goes. He will become the first commoner ever to enter Guildhall Great Hall, the centre of City government in London for over a thousand years, via the Royal Entrance. This will be a unique privilege that requires Her Majesty the Queen's personal approval. Dressed like Ludwig II in a blue military uniform embellished in red, Michael will be guest of honour at a Guildhall banquet: a distinction usually reserved for visiting royalty and world leaders. His arrival will be heralded by trumpeters of the Household Cavalry. Michael will giggle and grin. At the £75,000 banquet, the roast beef of Old England will be paraded through the room by the Corps of Drums of the Honourable Artillery Company, while dancers in Old English costume will scatter rose petals at Michael's feet. One after the other, King Henry VIII, Queen Elizabeth I, Lord Nelson, Nell Gwyn, Robin Hood, Maid Marian and Dick Whittington pay their respects to the first and only King of Pop. Ballerinas and fire-eaters, jugglers and jesters will entertain him, while knights in armour bow before him. Merlin the magician will suddenly appear in a puff of smoke.

Everything that is made will be unmade in this new Earthly Paradise. Everything that is made will be remade and perfected here: revealed in the mirror of its own destiny as something bright, shiny and hollow. Out of the darkness of this Final Revelation will come a Final Redeemer: one who has the beauty and innocence of a reflective surface, reducing everything that touches it to a flat outline. In the courtyard Michael will take the salute, as the Band of the Corps of Royal Engineers beat the retreat: walking up and down a line of Life Guards in dress uniform, inspecting them as if he were a general. A knight in shining armour will gallop across the courtyard. Leaping from his saddle and pulling a sword from a stone, he will go down on one knee before Michael. 'Do you realise,' he will be asked, 'that you've just become the King of England? That's supposed to be the sword King Arthur pulled from the stone before he recruited the Knights of the Round Table.'

✦✦✦ ✝ ✦✦✦

'Gee,' Michael replies delightedly. 'A king? I never knew. I love your traditions. You have so much history here in England.'

XXIV

In the Shadow of Heaven

The Eighth Sphere Continued

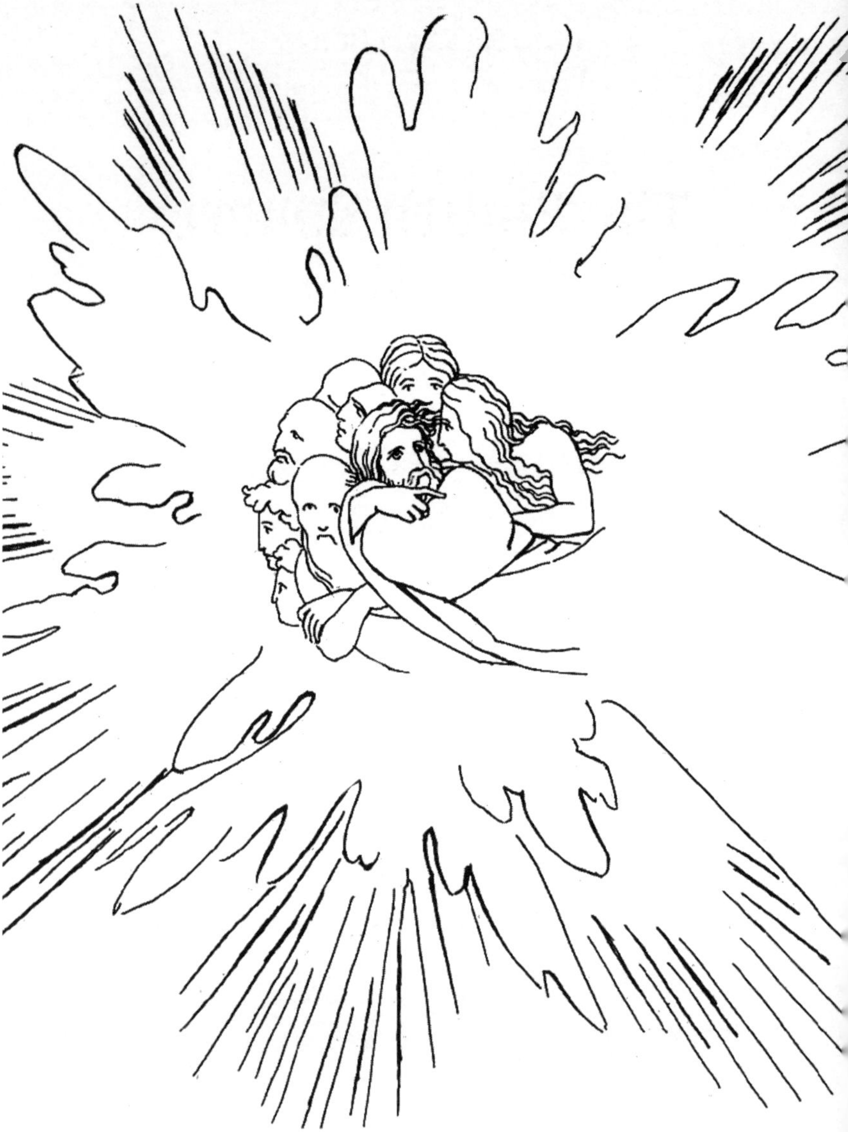

The violence of faith

One afternoon during the Austro-Prussian War, the doors of the officers' mess burst open, and a young man in blue military uniform sweeps into the room. He is, according to an eyewitness, 'of such unearthly beauty that my heartbeat positively faltered'. A feeling of anxiety creeps over the eyewitness: this divine youth is too perfect for this world – he asks a Bavarian comrade who the young man is. 'Our young King Ludwig II,' comes the reply. Few of us can afford to live with beauty on its own terms. Beauty is devastation. Beauty is waste and emptiness. It illuminates everything darkly – like the first moment of an apocalypse. Ludwig opened up beauty's empty wasteland, Elvis stretched its limits, while Michael Jackson gazes at it, enrapt and terrified. He seeks flawless perfection with nothing behind it. Whatever power Nietzsche had discovered in the great stimulants of brutality, artificiality and innocence, Michael has gone beyond far beyond it. Michael now sees that sentiment, naivety and horror are truly his.

What is horror? An oasis in a desert of boredom, according to Charles Baudelaire, who never set foot in an American city. 'The wealthiest, most affluent girl in the world runs away and hides in the Bronx. That's sheer insanity!' the president of the Manhattan Corporation fumes in Enzo G Castellari's *The Bronx Warriors*, a movie with a premise that absolutely guarantees you will stop caring about the plot long before it ends. Released in 1982, this is the American Apocalypse seen from an Italian perspective: low-budget and driven to noisy annihilation by cheap second-hand pop imagery. Its exposition is laid out in a single onscreen title: '1990. THE BRONX IS OFFICIALLY DECLARED "NO MAN'S LAND". THE AUTHORITIES GIVE UP ALL ATTEMPTS TO RESTORE LAW AND ORDER. FROM THEN ON, THE AREA IS RULED BY THE RIDERS.' A message spray-canned across a tenement stairwell proclaims: 'THIS SHIT HEAP IS RIDERS HOME.' The Riders are bikers with glowing skulls on their handlebars and skull decals covering their license plates. They fight for control over the derelict streets of the Bronx with rival gangs such as the Zombies, the Jackals, the Scavengers and the Sharks – the movie's budget doesn't stretch to showing them all onscreen. Leader of the Riders is a teenage pretty boy known simply as 'Trash'. Trash looks vaguely hurt and surprised by everything he sees. Like Michael Jackson, he follows his own dress code, going in for wide studded belts and chokers, one silver earring and leather wristbands. He wears biker boots with silver chains hanging from them and struts around bare-chested in a black leather waistcoat zipped tight like a corset and fastened with shiny silver buckles. Overall, his costume is a muscle-bound, semi-nude reminder of the outfits Michael likes to wear onstage. He gives emptiness an inner depth it never had before.

··· ✝ ···

Can horror be possessed? A dead Rider lies splayed out on the desolate banks of the East River, the Twin Towers of the World Trade Center in the background, a bloodied wooden stake pushed through his chest. Some random extra plays drums in the foreground. Pimps ride around in a fleet of custom cars. *The Bronx Warriors* owes more than a little to Walter Hill's *The Warriors* and John Carpenter's *Escape from New York*, offering the same mix of fantasy and fetishism: the science fiction of a tagged and graffiti-strewn world. Trash is played by seventeen-year-old gym rat Marco De Gregorio, billed in the credits as Mark Gregory. This is his first movie. A local chapter of the Hells Angels is on hand to handle security and add a little authentic menace to some of his scenes. The Manhattan Corporation send Hammer, a psychotic cop played by Vic

Morrow, into the Bronx on a secret mission that could not make less sense. 'He has his own axe to grind, and he's a killer at heart,' says the President of the Manhattan Corporation. 'He's just an asshole who thinks he's God,' remarks his second-in-command. 'I hope you're right,' the President inexplicably replies. After crazed gunman Patrick Purdy attacked Cleveland Elementary School in Stockton, California, killing five children and wounding a further twenty-nine plus a teacher, Michael Jackson turns up wearing a blue military uniform and flanked by armed guards to hand out gifts. Purdy had the misspelled mission statement 'Death to the Great Satin' on his flak jacket and the words 'victory' and 'Earthman' carved into his assault rifle. In *The Bronx Warriors* a solitary biker roars by a playground where kids innocently jump around behind a chain-link fence. Busses ease past in the distance. This is day-to-day life in the wilderness.

••• ✝ •••

What is the source of horror, and how can its validity be established? 'Look at them! Scum of the earth! Enough to make you vomit!' spits a cop from a helicopter flying low over the street gangs and abandoned tenement blocks of the Bronx. At the time of filming, the entire area was being demolished for redevelopment. All spaces are a source of horror until Michael Jackson dances through them; alleyways, prison cells, subway stations and warehouses have no power over his carefully choreographed body. Michael dances to the point of exhaustion; he collapses sobbing and laughing, feeling utterly free. 'I love to forget who I am,' he says. Fred Astaire describes Michael as 'an angry dancer'. Michael agrees – he never smiles when he moves. In *The Bronx Warriors* Trash comes up against the Iron Men, a high-stepping kickline of painted streetfighters, staring impassively through masks of gold and silver eye makeup. Like a Bob Fosse dance troop, they overpower their enemies in perfectly co-ordinated tap routines, swinging their canes and lifting their armour-plated derbies. Michael's perfect eyes flash when he's watching scenes of violence and horror onscreen in the 'Thriller' video. 'No,' he protests when his onscreen girlfriend says she wants to leave the cinema. 'I'm enjoying this.' They burn an ominous amber when he tells her a space is safe even when he knows it isn't. At Hammer's command, apocalyptic horsemen in black uniforms and helmets with visors down ride through the Bronx wielding flamethrowers, clearing out the warring gangs once and for all. Trash knows they're dead already. 'We were born dead,' he says. 'Life means nothing. We live with death every single day. Death walks with us. Death rides and sleeps with us. We carry its smell under our skin.' Michael Jackson arrives in Los Angeles, capitol city of the twentieth century and entertainment success, on 9 August 1969: the same night as the Manson Family slayings take place on Cielo Drive. As Michael recalls in *Moonwalk*, the book he authored about his own life and dedicated to Fred Astaire, 'to land in Southern California was like having the world transformed into a wonderful dream... everyday was special.' Following news of the killings, security is stepped up at the houses of the rich and famous.

Or to quote the shout line on international posters for *The Bronx Warriors*: 'The first to die were the lucky ones.'

XXV

In the Shadow of Heaven

The Eighth Sphere Continued

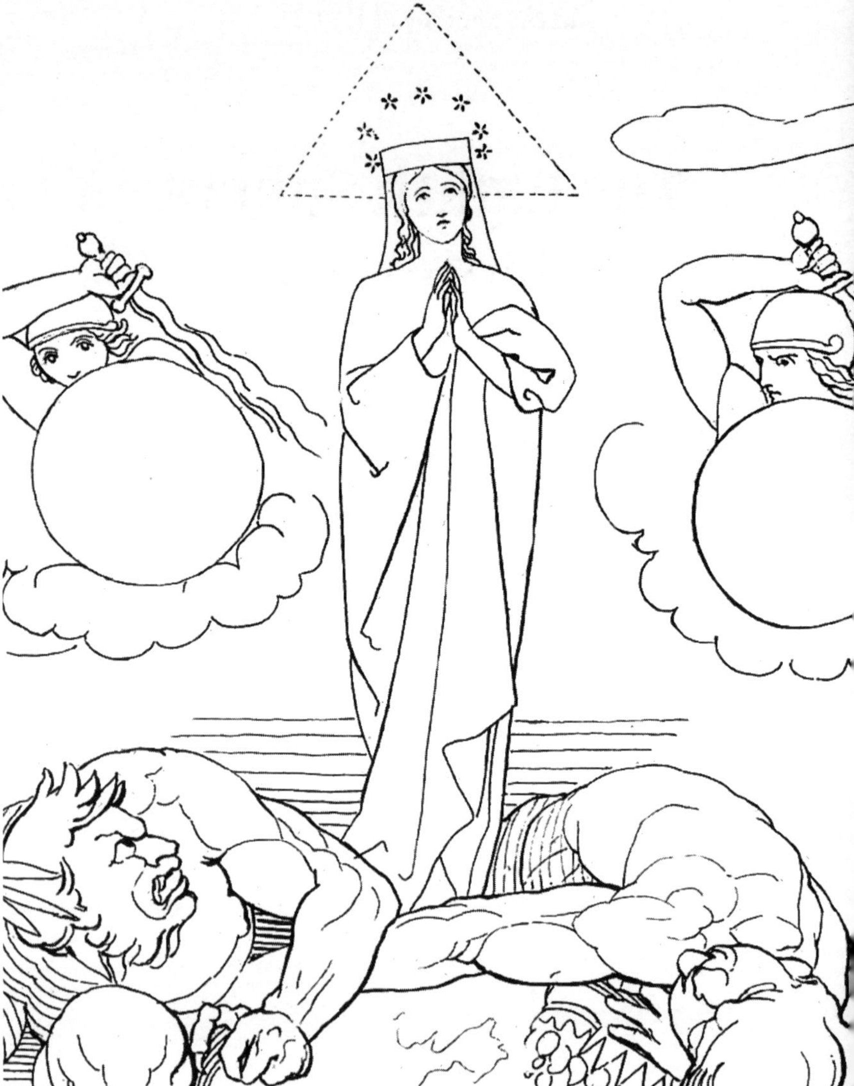

The violence of hope

Like a creature without a God, Michael Jackson is capable of committing unlimited violence against himself. He wants the beauty and perfection of Heaven on Earth right now. And like a creature without a God, he creates himself in his own image through endless bouts of plastic surgery. Michael's face is his continually unfolding masterpiece: something that starts to obsess him after his head catches fire. It becomes a work in progress: eventually overrefined, overworked and perfected to the point where the face appears to consume itself in a single wasteful act. His nose has been slimmed down over so many rhinoplasties that it finally collapses; experts can no longer tell if it is made of bone, cartilage or latex. Permanent eyeliner is injected into the eyelids, and a plastic cleft inserted into his chin, attached to the jaw through two small holes. Michael has several facelifts to smooth out his skin and raise his eyebrows; he has his upper lip thinned and the fat sucked from his cheeks, bone grafts plus several eye jobs to remove wrinkles and bags. Sometimes surgeons anaesthetise him then simply bandage his face, leaving Michael to believe that the work has been done when he awakens.

What is true naivety? 'I want to turn into a monster – can I do that?' Michael Jackson asks John Landis, director of *An American Werewolf in London*, as they embark on Michael's 'Thriller' video together. Meanwhile, Enzo Castellari shoots his next movie, *The New Barbarians*, using as sets the quarries, slip roads and highways outside Rome. The camera picks out skeletons sprawled on the ground in ripped protective suits, gaping mouths showing through the shattered visors of their helmets; '2019 AD: The nuclear holocaust is over,' announces an onscreen title. Filming commences right after *1990: The Bronx Warriors*. The Apocalypse is still happening. Not even Satan himself rules the Earth anymore. Michael Jackson has himself photographed lying in a Secrist hyperbaric chamber, used for the treatment of serious burn victims. A story is leaked to the *National Enquirer*; Michael believes sleeping in its oxygen-rich artificial atmosphere will extend his life expectancy by 120 years. Some interpret this as further evidence that he is the Messiah. Expensive makeup effects used in 'Thriller' transform Michael into a werewolf. His church demands that he disown the tape. Michael announces that the film 'in no way endorses a belief in the occult.' *The New Barbarians* takes place in a devastated landscape. In the future, everything happens in or around cars. Explosions throw people high into the air. The sets and costumes look really cheap – the budget is much lower than for *The Bronx Warriors*. The new movie recycles a metal skull and a music clip from the earlier production. The guns come from a local toyshop; and the futuristic vehicles are mostly dune buggies painted silver or black, plus the occasional dirt bike. 'What difference does it make?' asks Castellari, making a cameo in his own movie as a dying man trapped in an abandoned car. 'Survival means nothing anymore. The end is already here. Maybe it's just as well.'

••• ✝ •••

What is the source of true naivety? Extermination squads of white-clad Templars roam the postapocalyptic landscape. Sworn to rid this world of every last trace of humanity, they carry out search-and-destroy missions in their silver dune buggies, sporting elaborate hairdos. 'We are the Templars: the high priests of death,' declares one of their leaders. 'We have been chosen to make others pay for the crime of being alive.' Michael Jackson hangs out with zombies on empty streets – dances with the Living Dead. The Templars' king smokes weed and listens to tapes of inspirational poetry, dreaming of the day when 'the seed of man will be cancelled from the face of the Earth.' The movie is a scrapheap of references and repetitions taken from old spaghetti westerns and box office hits like

Mad Max 2: The Road Warrior – each piece worn out and easy to comprehend. Only a creature without a God can reproduce itself. Cheap copies represent a new line of discourse. Recognising the already familiar is just another form of distraction. 'Thriller' is not so much a zombie film as a reanimated corpse that has been taught to dance. 'The world is dead!' the Templar king rages. 'It raped itself, but I'll purify it with blood. No one is innocent.' Horror is tightly enfolded with feelings of naivety and sentimentality – it is always a matter of belief. John Landis is charged with involuntary manslaughter following the deaths of Vic Morrow and child extras Myca Dinh Le and Renee Shin-Yi Chen while filming a movie sequence he is directing. A pyrotechnic effect goes wrong, causing a helicopter to spin out of control and crash. Morrow and Le are decapitated by the rotor blades, while Chen is crushed by the right landing skid. All three are killed instantly. *The Bronx Warriors* is the last movie Morrow ever sees to completion.

What does naivety promise with categorical certainty? Its own end, of course – nothing has a shorter or more fragile existence. The Templars punish humanity not just for existing but for believing in anything other than the nuclear wasteland they inhabit. 'Even the heavens are silent!' the Templar king rages at a besieged and huddled mass of believers. 'You are walking dead! Living corpses! There is nothing left – nothing!' Emerging from the barren landscape to defend them against the Templars' onslaught is a piece of existential beefcake named Scorpion in a customised muscle car and 1960s NFL legend Fred 'The Hammer' Williamson, star of such blaxploitation classics as *Hell Up in Harlem* and *Black Caesar*. 'They believe in something called "God",' Williamson explains to Scorpion. 'Oh,' Scorpion replies. To the Templars, believers are 'the Trash of Mankind.' There is a lot of violence and explosions. 'I enjoyed watching your little game of war,' Williamson tells Scorpion. Who knew the end of the world would be this bloody, this boring? Michael Jackson's father used to traumatise him as a child by leaping out suddenly in a werewolf mask, pretending to be a monster. Michael now sees himself as the 'loneliest person on the planet.' Like Ludwig II, Michael is born under Virgo and lives his life behind impenetrable walls of impossible ideals. 'Can't you believe there's something better where we're headed?' Anna Kanakis, the female lead in *The New Barbarians*, asks Scorpion. She is a former beauty queen: crowned Miss Volcano at the age of fifteen and Miss Italy in 1977. 'Heaven is dead – along with all the rest,' Scorpion replies. Imagine asserting your sovereignty to the point where everything is erased. 'It is the glory of God to conceal a thing: but the honour of kings is to search out a matter,' according to *Proverbs* 25:2. A Templar chief tears a King James Bible in half, declaring that 'books are what started the Apocalypse.' Satan always knows what he's doing.

*** ✝ ***

The New Barbarians is eventually released in the United States as *Warriors of the Wasteland*.

XXVI

In the Shadow of Heaven

The Eighth Sphere Continued

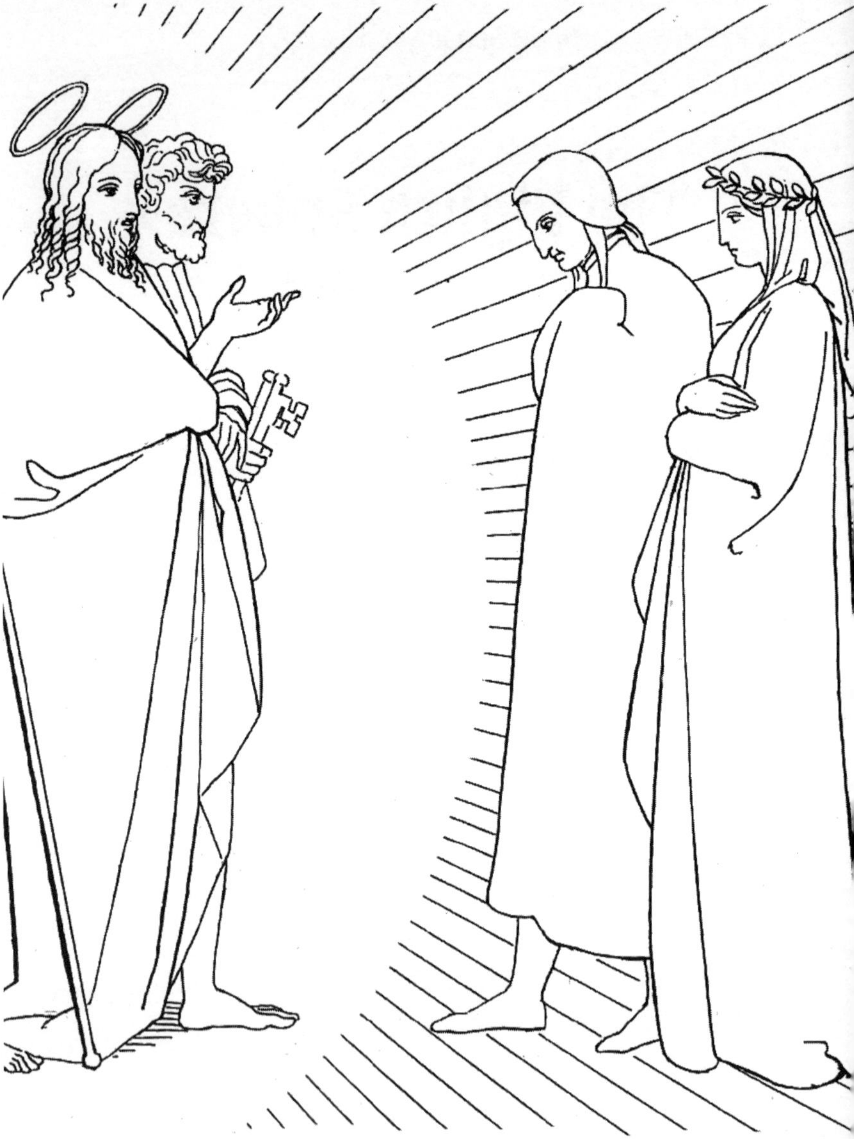

The violence of love

Plastic surgery for Michael Jackson is like a trip to Disneyland; he keeps a piece of nose cartilage from his first rhinoplasty as a souvenir – a holy relic. It represents a first step in eradicating any resemblance to his father from the face he sees staring back at him in the mirror. Joe Jackson terrorised his most gifted son, calling Michael 'his golden child' then beating him with a strap. Michael becomes obsessed with erasing his father's features one by one. 'That's how much he hates Joe,' observes a Jackson family member. Behind Ludwig II's building projects is the desire to remove all memory of his cold and distant father from the landscape. Maximilian II of Bavaria establishes a family home at Hohenschwangau, which is then rebuilt by Ludwig, who originally conceives of Neuschwanstein as a 'New Hohenschwangau' to look down on it from above. The finest view of Neuschwanstein is from the Marienbrucke, a filigreed iron bridge Ludwig commissions in 1886 to replace the wooden structure his father had constructed across the same steep ravine years before. Ludwig's Rococo palace at Linderhof is built over the rustic hunting lodge

Maximilian had set up there. When Michael Jackson wrests majority ownership of Hayvenhurst, the Jackson family home in Encino, from his father, he immediately demolishes the place, replacing it with a mock Tudor mansion, complete with a four-car Tudor-style garage.

What is the main purpose of sentiment? The purification of troubling and inconvenient emotions. Following hard on *The New Barbarians*, Enzo Castellari returns to New York to shoot exteriors for his 1983 release *Escape from the Bronx*. The General Construction Corporation under President Henry Clark is carrying out a social cleansing of No Man's Land, breaking up the surviving street gangs and forcing them underground. GC's policy is to drive out the remaining population either by deporting or killing them. 'Who the hell wants to live in New Mexico?' complains one Bronx resident before being burned alive by members of the Disinfestation Annihilation Squad, who park their silver-painted van close to a smoke-blackened ice-cream stand. Plain text posters cover every wall. Some say: LEAVE THE BRONX. Others: LET'S BUILD A BETTER BRONX. It's the same message but for two entirely different sets of people. Rebuilding something is the best way of obliterating it forever. Where devastated tenements once stood,

XXVI
The Eighth Sphere Continued

Henry Clark plans to place an urban paradise safe enough for the rich to inhabit. 'It's easy to make people who don't officially exist disappear,' remarks GC's vice-president. The brick drive at Hayvenhurst leads to a three-tier fountain in the courtyard and a private version of Disneyland's Main Street USA, including animatronic figures, whom Michael thinks are just like real people – 'except they don't grab at you or ask you for favours.' During the day, swans and other animals from Michael's private menagerie wander the redbrick paths and ornamental gardens of his private theme park. The twinkling 'Tivoli lights', the stained and leaded glass windows, circular staircases, marble floors, Louis XIV interiors and the collection of life-size plastic mannequins in Michael's bedroom establish Hayvenhurst as a defence against the outside world. It has everything Michael needs 'so I will never need to go out there again.' It even has a soda fountain like the one Elvis kept at Graceland. 'Everything seemed to be splashed with gold,' comments one visitor.

••• ✠ •••

What is the essential attraction of sentiment? Any and all emotion is merely the repetition of that emotion. Sentiment expresses the nostalgia for feeling behind each feeling. A lot has changed since Kurt

Russell aimed his military glider at the World Trade Center in John Carpenter's *Escape from New York*. Castellari's new movie may be called *Escape from the Bronx*; but everyone seems grimly determined to stay exactly where they are for as long as possible. One inhabitant who has never left is Mark Gregory, returning as 'that delinquent Trash person'. Looking less shredded this time round, Trash hides his upper torso under a jacket and T-shirt for most of the movie – not so much acting as doing things with his face as dictated by the script. Last seen adorning the hood of Scorpion's muscle car in *The New Barbarians*, the skull from *The Bronx Warriors* is also back. Scorpion himself resurfaces as Strike: an explosives expert who dwells in the Manhattan sewer system. 'There are more ways to die down here than in a Bruce Lee film,' Strike warns. Seen practising their Bob Fosse street-fighting routines in the background, even the Iron Men have gone underground. At the head of the Disinfestation Annihilation Squad is veteran psycho Henry Silva. Described as 'a torturer, an expelled prison warden' and a 'hired killer', he strides around with purposeful intensity, saying things like 'That building! Dynamite it! You! Move that truck!' and 'Fuck Headquarters. I'm doing this my way!' He's a GC employee, charged with eradicating the last of the Bronx's gangs. 'You're worse than they are,' GC's President observes. 'Allow me to correct you, Mr Clark,' Silva smoothly replies. 'I'm worse than anybody.' Playing Henry Clark is Castellari's brother, Ennio Girolami, who also appears in *The Bronx Warriors* and *The New Barbarians.*

··· ✠ ···

At the back of the shot and slightly out of focus, New York city life goes on while the cast of *Escape from the Bronx* slink and prowl through their postapocalyptic drama. Cars, trains and ships pass by – even a line of schoolchildren. Sentiment creates its own world with such a conviction that no one questions it. Castellari's movie shows 1980s Manhattan going about its routines as if Armageddon were a daily fact of everybody's existence. Sentiment, innocence and horror conspire to create fantasy. They will always form a background to each other. The Maenads chase the object of their wild lusts across a desolate landscape. The LAPD receives a constant stream of 'fifty-one fifties' from Hayvenhurst, meaning that a cop car will be sent to remove yet another 'mentally unbalanced person' who has wandered onto Michael Jackson's property. At Graceland, staff keep an eye out for 'the elegant woman in the party dress who gets her kicks urinating on Elvis' driveway'. What has Paradise ever been but a defence against being human? Without telling his family, Michael moves from Hayvenhurst to the Neverland Ranch in Santa Barbara County. When does he make it his new home? In 1992 – four years after first buying it. Neverland is recreated according to Michael's wishes – including hundreds of CCTV cameras distributed across the estate disguised as birdboxes. 'If any one of the thirty full-time gardeners and ten ranch hands didn't smile enough, or seemed otherwise unhappy, he would be dismissed,' notes one of Michael Jackson's more authoritative biographies. 'After all, this was supposed to be a happy place.' Is it possible for a landscape to bear the imprint of a single personality? And can it ever be anything more than a theme park devoted to sovereignty?

More than one hundred loudspeakers hidden among the flowerbeds play back music from selected Walt Disney movies, shows and rides.

XXVII

In the Shadow of Heaven

The Eighth Sphere Concluded

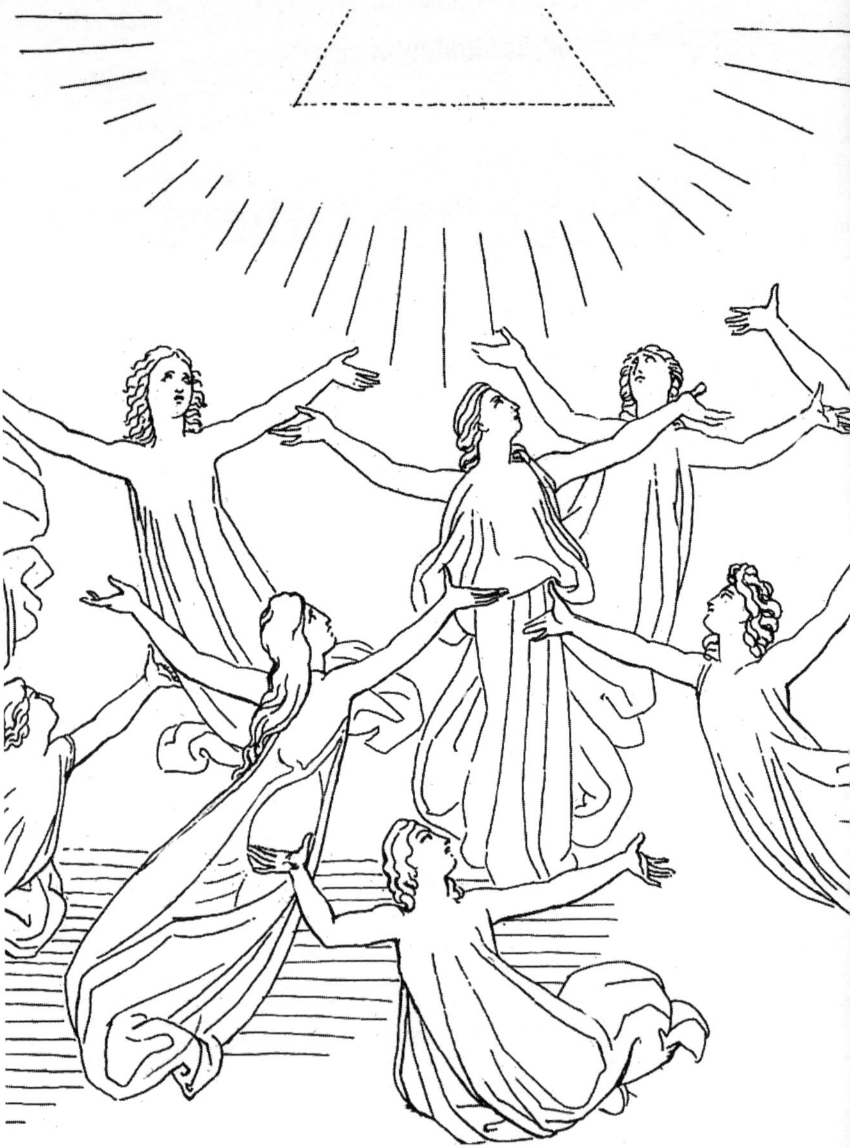

Down through the depths of all eight solitudes

Everything about Neverland is lavish and spectacular. Michael Jackson spends $300,000 a year on planting new bulbs because he cries whenever a flower dies. Neverland's gardeners have strict instructions to replace each one as soon as it starts to wither. 'I hate to see pretty things dying,' Michael says. 'I wished they lived forever, like in the movies.' John Landis refers to Neverland as 'Michael's very own Xanadu'. Everything is geared towards childhood pleasures here. 'What is sovereign in fact is to enjoy the present time without having anything else in view but this present time,' observes Bataille. There is a manmade lake with its arched stone bridge, artificial waterfall and swan boat, a private zoo containing over two hundred animals, a Ferris wheel that plays 'Like A Virgin', candy-striped popcorn stands, children's playgrounds, a swimming pool, basketball courts, a trampoline and a two-storey video arcade. This is Paradise on Earth – the restoration of the Garden of Eden. Michael has already left his church. On the other side of Armageddon, he sees an endless children's party taking place, the trees and paths of Neverland glittering with fairy lights.

⁂ ✝ ⁂

Having dispensed with Father and Church, Michael grants himself the privilege of never growing up, never going to business meetings, never having to see his lawyers again. Fantasy becomes a major part of his life: dressing up, playing make-believe, having water fights, sitting up all night with his young friends watching Disney movies on video – enjoying everything in the moment. 'It's all magic,' Michael says. Imagine what it must be like cleaning up after him. When Elizabeth Taylor marries Larry Fortensky in the gazebo at Neverland, Michael orders his gardeners to dig up thousands of coloured flowers and replace them with all-white ones.

⁂ ✝ ⁂

Flashback to footage of Michael Jackson running through a perfect summer's day captured on film. Michael's playing catch with a couple of young boys, plus a girl and a dog called Skipper. The camera follows them through fields so fresh and perfect you half expect to find a severed ear hidden amongst the yellow flowers and green grass. 'The film must be too good true to be true, like a fairy tale,' Michael once specified. Based on a story by Michael Jackson with a script by David Newman, whose writing credits include the first three Superman movies, this turns out to be *Moonwalker*, which is undoubtedly every single movie Elvis ever put his name to rolled into one. Skipper helps Michael uncover a criminal plot to get the children of the world hooked on drugs. Frank Lideo, AKA 'Mr Big', is behind the plan. 'Stop those kids praying in school,' Lideo orders his unseen henchmen, contemplating a blue globe crawling with spiders. He'll see to it that the drugs will be injected into children through big syringes. This makes Michael cry. Lideo insists his name is spelled right to distinguish him from Frank Dileo, Michael Jackson's current manager, whom Michael is thinking of firing.

Lideo orders a squadron of troopers in black paramilitary outfits, their faces hidden behind visors and helmets, to kill Michael Jackson. They catch him one night in a hail of bullets, shell casings rattling on the dark cobblestones; but Michael manages to sidestep their ambush, spending the rest of *Moonwalker* either running away or weeping. It's only through displays of unhappiness that he can stay in touch with his inner child. Suffering and evasion help bring him to his perfect world. Michael Jackson's sovereignty lies in his willingness to be hurt. Acting for him is about being permanently on the verge of tears, torn apart by the moment. 'I had a terrible childhood,'

Michael claims, surrounded by adoring crowds, living in a big Encino mansion, with brass swans for faucets in his private bathroom. Michael says he was happiest as a child watching himself as a character in the Rankin/Bass *Jackson 5ive* cartoon show. The animated figure that stops moving is reduced to a static arrangement of lines, however. Michael's dancing is a form of flight in both senses of the word – the body that is never at rest also escapes definition. By staying in constant motion, Michael Jackson manages to disappear from view while keeping the camera on him at all times – and it will always be that way.

Monsters take on their fullest moral dimensions once they become cartoons – this is particularly true when dealing with the immense demands of fame. 'When you have people that, from the time you're a little kid, want you, they want pieces of you, they want your clothes, they want your hair,' John Landis says of Michael, 'you're going to get nervous around people.' Michael Jackson evades the Maenads by becoming even more lost in the moment than they are. The sovereignty of fame is glimpsed primarily as a contagious subjectivity: an intimate tidal wave sweeping through the crowd. It prefigures the aesthetic disappearance of the absolutely self-involved, always threatening to withdraw from the gaze of the audience into a state of self-absorbed self-cancellation.

••• ✝ •••

The only thing that remains a constant presence throughout most of *Moonwalker* is Michael Jackson's nose, which closely resembles that of child star Bobby Driscoll, one of the first human actors signed up by Walt Disney to appear in his movies. Freckleface Driscoll's boyish good looks seem to arrange themselves around a pert upturned nose that became his trademark. If Bobby Driscoll's eyes are bright, his expression lively and his smile open and guileless, it is plain which part of his face is responsible. Disney uses Bobby's voice and likeness for the hero of his animated feature *Peter Pan*, linking Driscoll forever with the image of the Boy Who Never Grew Up. No wonder Michael tells *Life* magazine that his favourite toys are 'anything Peter Pan' and that Macaulay Culkin 'spends all his vacations' at Neverland.

••• ✝ •••

Uncle Walt summarily dumps Bobby Driscoll, cancelling his Disney contract, once he hits puberty. He claims the kid has lost his looks. Bobby starts playing around with drugs, getting busted for marijuana possession and experimenting with heroin by the age of seventeen. Film offers dry up, and Bobby spends time in prison. 'I was brought out on a silver platter,' he says of this period in his life, 'and then dumped into the trash.' Bobby moves to New York, where he joins the underground movie scene with Andy Warhol and Jack Smith – writing poetry, making collages and doing more drugs. His last movie appearance is a brief cameo dressed as a nun in Piero Heliczer's *Dirt*. His face looks bloated, but his nose is still recognisably the same. Driscoll is found dead at the age of thirty-one in March 1968, lying in a burned-out tenement building surrounded by empty bottles. He is buried in an unmarked grave on Hart Island in the northeast Bronx; 'our sacrifice must seem sublime' runs a line from one of his poems.

Behind the mahogany double doors of his Neverland bedroom, Michael covers the walls with drawings of Peter Pan.

XXVIII

In the Shadow of Heaven

The Ninth Sphere

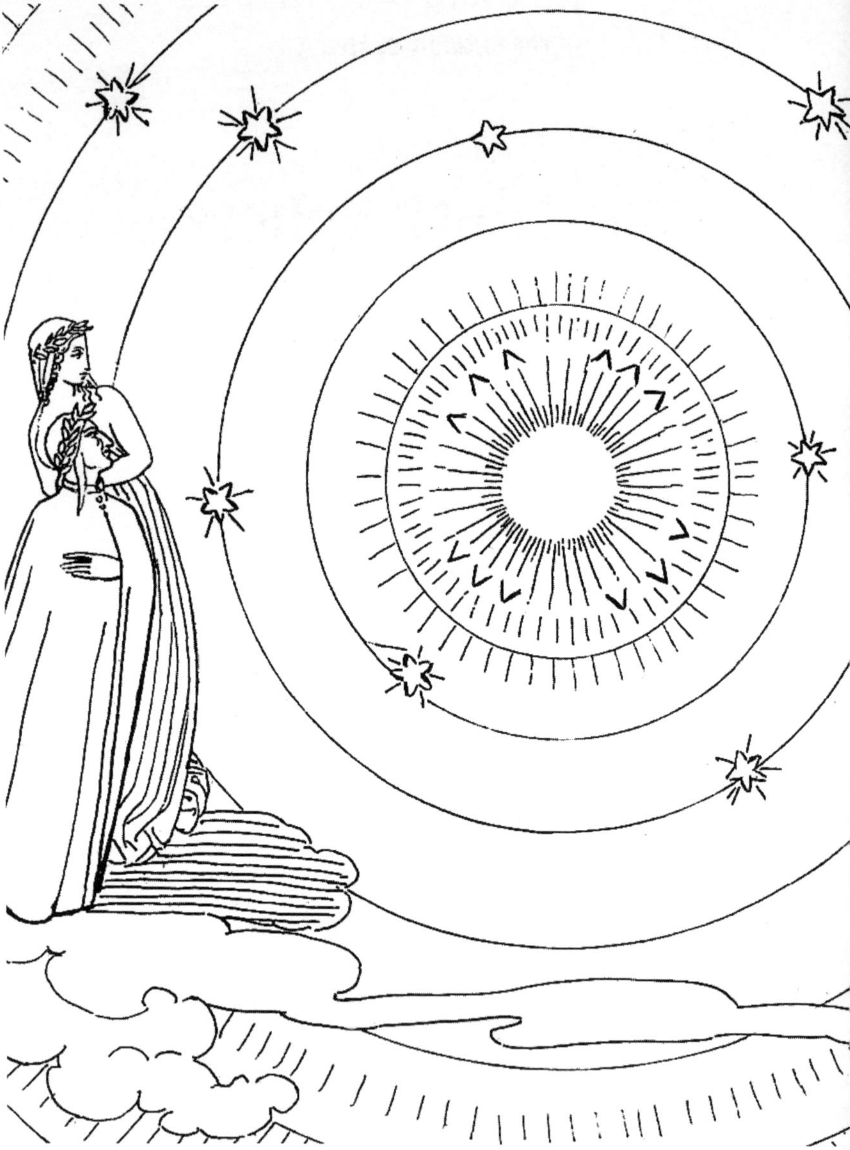

The Primum Mobile in Heaven

Flash forward to the End of Time and the beginning of the movie. *Moonwalker* starts with footage of Michael Jackson's 'Bad' tour. Delirious scenes showing his adoring fans are intercut with a nuclear blast, starving children and the familiar faces of dead pop stars and even deader politicians – visual fragments that exist solely to be cut together with each other. Meanwhile Michael is onstage, offering crowds of ecstatic followers his own personal message of change.

Stirring deep within every New Messiah is the innocent assumption that they are the centre of everything and always will be. This is the prime mover; and the Trash Palace is the material expression of this self-imposed sense of destiny. Ludwig had Neuschwanstein, Linderhof and Herrenchiemsee; Elvis had Graceland; and Michael has his Neverland. The Trash Palace marks a return to the sensory freedoms of the undeveloped child: the extravagant unregulated play of all the senses where everything and anything can bring pleasure. This appeal to childhood is little more than an idealised fetish, however – something fondly misremembered. It's part of the bric-a-brac filling Michael's rooms at Neverland. Visitors report seeing countless dolls, colouring books and crayons, a gun that shoots soap bubbles, tables full of trucks and cars and spaceships. A slow pan during an early sequence in *Moonwalker* reveals a room cluttered with ornaments, ceramic gimcracks, medals and sequinned gloves. The camera lingers over a tiny replica of King Arthur's sword embedded in a crystal paperweight. Sovereignty is a value traditionally attributed to kings and aristocrats, gods and priests; but there are also those who trade exclusively in fame – as Bataille remarks: 'they display that value with an ostentation that sometimes goes with a profound baseness.' Just as Trash overturns the socially ordered regulation of our senses, so the polymorphous perverse displays itself once more as a monstruous innocence.

Michael's Second Coming cannot be understood in purely material terms. An aura of sacred and conspicuous waste surrounds him. Like King Ludwig, another 'redeemed Redeemer', Michael's innocence reveals itself as blank nothingness – an endless denial. It wasn't too long before *Moonwalker* came out that

XXVIII
The Ninth Sphere

Frank Dileo appeared at a West Hollywood press conference arranged by Michael Jackson to counter 'the many false accusations that have been spread about me'. On behalf of his client, who refused to appear before the assembled reporters, Dileo read out a statement from Michael. 'To this end, and I do mean END: NO! I've never taken hormones to maintain my high voice; NO! I've never had my cheekbones altered in any way; NO! I've never had cosmetic surgery on my eyes.' With his heavy build, gruff voice and a cigar wedged in the corner of his mouth, Dileo is a bizarre stand-in for the absent Messiah. Now Michael thinks that Frank is getting too much media attention.

With Michael, everything is up there on the screen; there is nothing perceivable behind it. Animated sequences in *Moonwalker* present his fans as menacing idiots and the media as avaricious liars spreading their 'false accusations'. Michael holds Frank Dileo responsible for planting all those stories in the *National Enquirer* about his sleeping in the Hyperbaric chamber, his Neverland shrine to Elizabeth Taylor and his offer to buy the Elephant Man's bones. They make him look like such a freak. An expensive sequence shows Michael in his trademark military uniform decorated with gold braid, just like the one he wore to the White House, trapped under a fairground rollercoaster. Dog-faced newshounds are busily pinning him to the ground with spikes and ropes. Like a cartoon Gulliver among the Lilliputians, Michael slowly rises to his feet, snapping his bonds, breaking up the rollercoaster and destroying the rides and sideshows that are spread around him. It looks as though Michael were breaking apart his own Neverland. At the end of his life Elvis was going to marry a girl he had met one night at the fairground; and a week before his death he had taken his daughter Lisa Marie and her friends there for one last night of fun.

••• ✝ •••

Breaking free of the fairground rides turns Michael Jackson into a giant – or rather transforming himself into a giant frees Michael from the fairground's restraints – and he is somehow trying to evade the fact that he's in a movie. It's as if *Moonwalker* itself were chasing him. To ensure that he never actually has to do any acting, Michael Jackson is transformed into a high-performance car, an android and finally a spaceship that fires a death ray at Lideo before disappearing into the night sky. In his attempts to escape our attention, Michael Jackson becomes, in a variation of Jonathan Swift's definition of satire, a mirror in which we catch glimpses of everything but him.

The real performance takes place in Neverland's main house, where Michael Jackson surrounds himself with mirrors and life-sized portraits of himself striking poses in the distinctive uniforms of European royalty. Everywhere he looks, he sees himself adorned with capes, swords, collars and crowns, in knight's armour donning angel wings or in a swirling firmament of seraphic children pointing toward Heaven. He develops an interest in acquiring work by the French academic painter William-Adolphe Bouguereau. 'It's funny,' Andy Warhol tells his diary, 'they're just the perfect paintings for Michael Jackson – like ten-year-old boys with fairy wings, around beautiful women.' No wonder witnesses report that Michael never leaves his bedroom without first putting on false eyelashes and makeup, applying it so thickly that it looks as though he is preparing himself to go onstage. His favoured brands include Fashion Fair, Honey Glow and Lancôme eye shadow, mascara and eyeliner. Ludwig II had his hair elaborately teased and styled each day before he could even bring himself to face breakfast. There are moments when both Ludwig and Michael share an equally performative pleasure in beauty. Michael Jackson perfects his Moonwalk, while Ludwig devised for himself a high stepping 'aesthetic' walk so extreme it nearly caused a diplomatic incident when he demonstrated it on the streets of Paris.

⁘ ✠ ⁘

Ludwig II's innocence made him subject to panderers and seductresses, courtesans and actresses. Sooner or later, everybody ends up pimping for the King – 'as if by magic,' runs one account, 'photos suddenly appeared, sent to Ludwig on request, of beautiful young men, not to be in private performances of Wagner operas but for his own personal enjoyment of classic Greek beauty.' Any display of sexual interest shown by women towards Michael Jackson is politely but firmly rebuffed. 'Neverland is a shrine to adolescence,' notes one of his main biographers. 'There are statues of youngsters and photographs of boys and girls all over the place. He's obsessed with kids.' It is also 'a monument to his confusion and conflict about childhood' in which the cracks are already starting to show. 'Mental love alone is permitted,' Ludwig sternly reminds himself in his private diary, 'sensual love by comparison is accursed.'

⁘ ✠ ⁘

Then came the accusations and allegations, the police raids and the TV reports, the investigations and the endless revelations.

XXIX

In the Shadow of Heaven

The Ninth Sphere Concluded

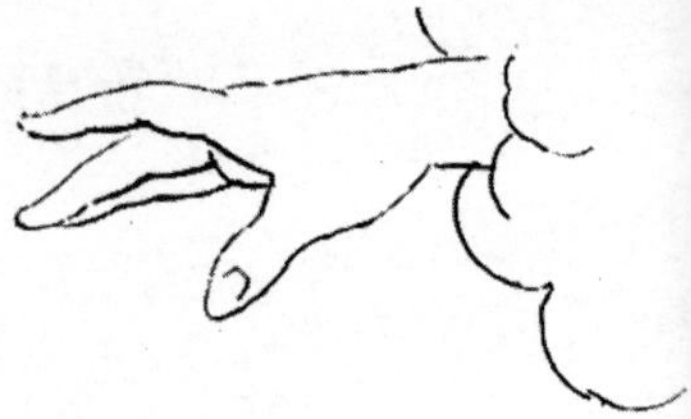

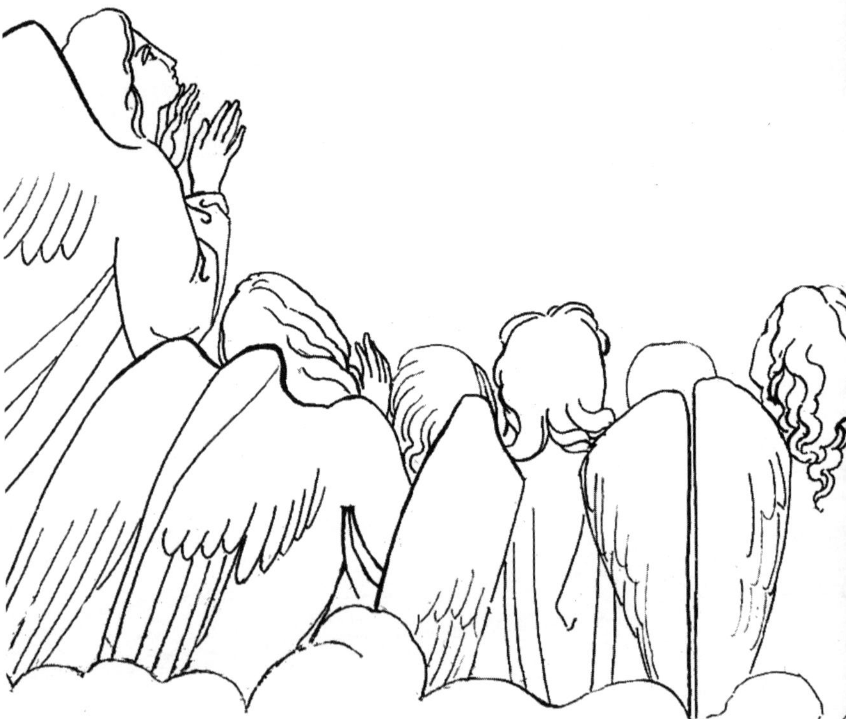

Preaching Trash to the World

Lisa Marie is staying at Flag Land Base, spiritual headquarters to the Church of Scientology in Clearwater Florida, when she gets the call. She has been invited to meet Michael Jackson at a mutual friend's house.

Flag is the largest Church of Scientology in the world. Flag represents the hub of the greater Scientology worldwide community as a dynamic, multilingual organisation. Flag not only ministers the most advanced levels of training available anywhere, but all advanced levels of auditing up to New OT VII, being the final pre-Operating Thetan level culminating in attainment of the state of CAUSE OVER LIFE. Planned to ensure the most important Scientology religious retreat continues to meet the increasing need for its services, Flag began with a single property in 1975 and now spans a complex of some fifty buildings over a nine-mile grid, totalling upwards of two million square feet.

Lisa Marie had been bingeing hard on pills, cocaine and alcohol as a teenager when she agreed with her mother Priscilla Presley to attend the Scientology Center in Hollywood to get herself off drugs. 'I felt that I had a responsibility to save him,' she later says of her early relationship with Michael Jackson. 'I don't know the psychology of it and what it had to do with my father. I only know what I felt.' Lisa Marie leaves her number at Flag Land Base with Michael and waits for him to call.

Michael Jackson has been travelling the world on the latest leg of his 'Dangerous' tour. 'For some imaginary Madame Tussaud's, he transformed himself into his own waxed, blanched figure,' *Time* magazine reports of his recent appearance. Past kings crowd in around him – stories circulate. Anxious and unable to sleep, Michael starts taking Percodan, Demerol and codeine as well as Valium, Xanax and Ativan in increasing quantities, quickly growing dependent upon painkillers and tranquilisers to function at all. Not so long ago he had been telling a *New York Daily News* reporter: 'I don't drink or take any drugs, and I don't want to experiment. If a person wants to get away from things, there are a million things to do outside of getting high.' Michael starts taking prescription drugs on tour to keep going, together with sleeping pills after his scalp is burned. He wears surgical tape on his fingers, and a black mask covers his nose and mouth as if the least physical contact with the world will injure him. His pain continues to be real. Michael severely burns his scrotum with bleaching cream and is treated by dermatological nurse Debbie Rowe, who will soon be revealed to the world as the mother of his children. Michael undergoes treatment for discoid lupus involving frequent injections directly into his scalp of hydroxychloroquine. He describes himself to a *Rolling Stone* reporter as withdrawing from the world 'just like a haemophiliac who can't afford to be scratched in any way'. It's the same scratch that Ludwig II felt indelibly inscribed upon the photographic plate of his inner world. 'Sometimes it hurts me so fuckin' much,' Elvis mutters into his microphone, live onstage one night on his last ever tour. 'But STILL I MUST Achieve I MUST seek Truth in all things,' Michael writes in a note to *People* magazine. 'I must endure for the power I was sent forth, for the World for the children BUT HAVE Mercy, for I've been Bleeding a LONG TIME NOW.'

Accompanying Michael Jackson on the 'Dangerous' tour is nine-year-old Prince Albert von Thurn und Taxis. Descended from the Wittelsbach line, Albert is the son of Eurotrash 'punk princess' Gloria von Thurn und Taxis. In a postmodern recreation of the times his ancestor Paul von Thurn und Taxis spent having fun on the Roseninsel with King Ludwig of Bavaria, Albert goes with Michael to Disneyland Paris. Protected from the crowds and the photographers by a dozen guards, they visit the Phantom Haunted House, then ride together on a space flight simulator and the Thunder Mountain rollercoaster and then do it all again. 'Michael's Plastic Face Is Melting,' the UK newspapers scream, claiming that his cosmetic preparations and constant surgery have caused it to collapse.

Publicly accused of sexually molesting an underage boy, Michael overdoses on Percodan in his five-room suite on the forty-second floor of the Hotel Presidente in Mexico City. Combined with Valium and all the other drugs he has been taking, it sends Michael spinning into a full psychotic episode: vomiting uncontrollably over the white carpets, scribbling *I love you I love you* on every available surface, crying violently and banging his head against the wall. At the Wailing Wall in Jerusalem, Michael is called an abomination and told to go home – except that he will not return to the United States while his case remains under investigation, unable even to attend the funeral of his grandfather Samuel, who dies at the age of 100 still believing that Michael is the Messiah. The War in Heaven will also be waged on Earth. Michael flies to London and checks into a detox clinic where his luggage is searched, and fifteen bottles of pills are confiscated.

••• ✝ •••

'I believed that he didn't do anything wrong, and that he was wrongly accused and yes I started falling for him,' Lisa Marie says of her growing feelings for Michael. 'I wanted to save him. I felt that I could do it.' Michael and Lisa Marie fly to the Dominican Republic and are married in a secret ceremony without their families' knowledge and with none of their friends present. 'There were no tears of happiness, no joy, no laughter,' the officiating judge recalls. Michael said he liked his Fred Flintstone tie. Donald Trump said he knew what was coming, having invited the celebrity couple to stay at his Mar-a-Lago estate in Palm Beach, Florida, where they had separate bedrooms. Trump said he saw them walking in the grounds, looking sharply dressed. Michael dropped to one knee and kissed Lisa Marie's hand. She pulled him to his feet, and they kissed staring into each other's eyes. Then Michael pulled a string of pearls out of his pocket.

For a while they were really getting it on, the former president insists, the whole scene must have been so perfect. It was where they first had sex.

⁂ ✝ ⁂

A former PR flack for Michael Jackson denounces the wedding as 'nothing more than a publicity stunt. Michael had no desire for a woman.' The President of the California Elvis Presley Fan Club is equally succinct: 'Oh God, no! Are you serious?' Lisa Marie's early life was spent at Graceland, where Elvis bought her fur coats and jewels before she was five years old. She understands Michael like no one else. 'He puts on an act for outsiders, this sort of victim thing,' Lisa Marie tells herself, believing that she can fix him.

⁂ ✝ ⁂

The newlyweds withdraw to separate villas five miles apart from each other at the holiday resort of fashion designer Oscar de la Renta.

XXX

In the Shadow of Heaven

The Empyrean

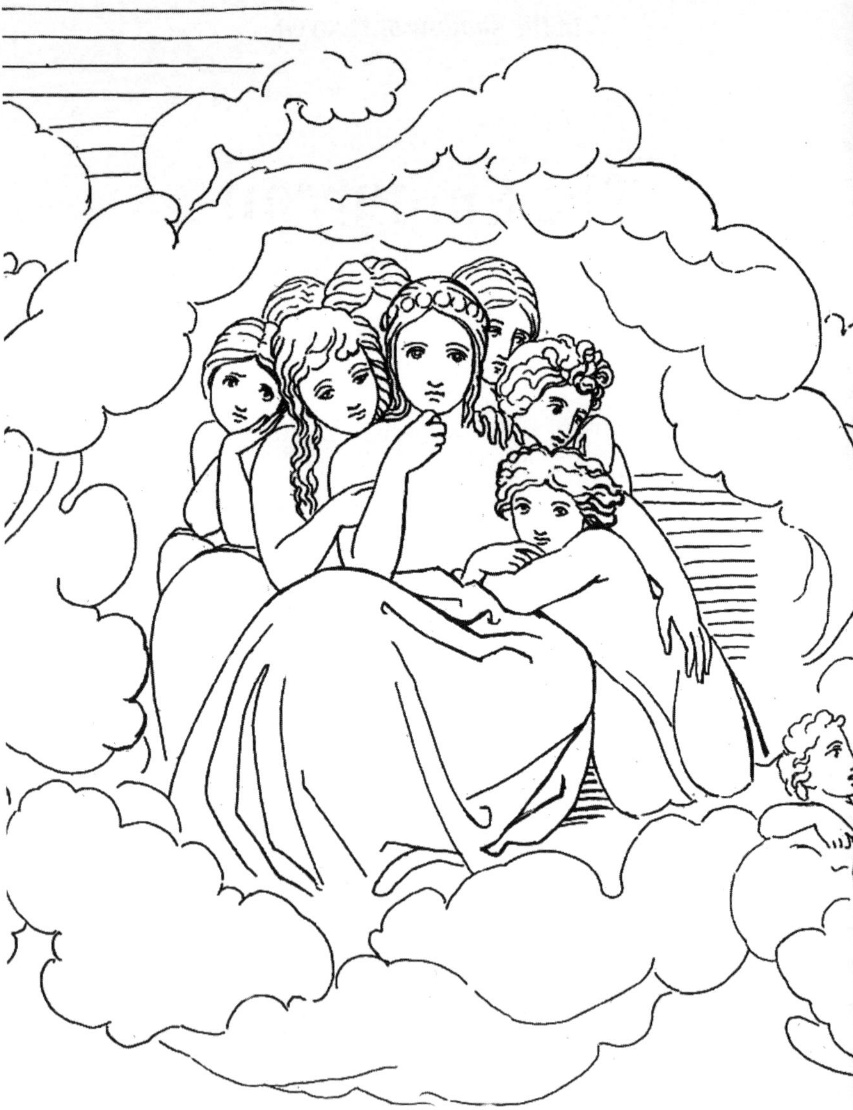

Infinite time and infinite space begin here

··· ✝ ···

And Michael now knows that he is bigger than Elvis – knows that he's already outsold him. Hasn't he suffered more – as much as any Messiah ever could? It's so unfair. Lisa Marie believes that you don't play the victim – that you run towards your problems, meeting them head-on. 'You're the biggest star ever, but the white man will never let you be bigger than Elvis,' promoter Don King tells Michael, getting inside his head during the 'Victory' tour. Stung by stories circulating in the media that Elvis would never have approved of Michael Jackson's marriage to Lisa Marie, the King of Pop suggests that they hold a séance to contact him. Lisa Marie shuts that idea down right away. Michael never mentions it again. 'I was a fucking little tyrant,' she says of her early childhood at Graceland.

··· ✝ ···

Michael's record company ask what more can they do for him. 'Build a statue of me,' he tells them, claiming it's needed to promote *HIStory – Past, Present and Future, Book One,* his 1995 album and tour package. When

Michael speaks of needing something, observes one of his handlers, the star is describing a 'psychological state that he required in order to function'. The executives at Sony order nine identical statues of Michael Jackson to be built from steel and fibreglass, each 32 feet tall. Michael is shown striking a straight-legged heroic pose: arms at his side, fists clenched, determined not to dance. The exact opposite of Elisabet Ney's statue of Ludwig II, the lightness and grace of the young king is replaced here by the heaviness and fixity of a despot. It takes a team of thirty people three months to build the nine statues. Michael is once again shown wearing a military tunic, embellished with braiding, crossed bandoliers and an armband, beloved of punks and agitators across the political spectrum.

In a single grand gesture, the nine statues of Michael are installed in various European locations to herald the coming of *HIStory*; life-size cardboard replicas are made available for instore displays. The next day movie theatres are running Michael's HIStory video 'teaser' – and never has the meaning of a word been so stretched out of shape. This is High Trash pop grandiosity so tasteless it parodies itself. The first thing you see is the statue of an Imperial eagle spreading its wings from the top of a column, followed by riot cops in futuristic visors marching against a red sky, jackboots stamping on cobbled streets – straight out of the Bronx and those late-night chase scenes in *Moonwalker*. The 'teaser' has no music: just the sound of troops marching in unison, chanting crowds, explosions, helicopters and rioting. Molten steel is poured out in a foundry; hot muscular men are shown hard at work on a giant five-pointed star. The video was shot in Hungary. Long columns of troops in dress uniform parade down a seemingly endless boulevard crowded with expectant fans who steadily lose their shit as the procession advances. Sony marketing executives are roused late at night: 'Michael wants more troops.' A couple of close-up shots identify a figure outfitted in black and silver marching in front. Two more reveal that it is Michael Jackson – for a few seconds you see him smiling, waving and blowing a kiss. Then the soldiers go into an elaborate drill, twirling their guns, getting jiggy with it. This is fascism as choreographic routine: totalitarian moves and empty expressions of power. At no point does Michael Jackson dance. Over the course of the entire video six individual females are shown either fainting or overcome by the sight of him. The crowd surges. Someone holds up a 'KING of POP' placard. A young boy shouts 'We love you,

Michael'. Glimpsed for only a few seconds, Michael Jackson hardly appears in his own teaser, even though he is rarely absent from it. All he needs is to see himself represented, especially in the reactions of the crowd that swarms around him. Cue apocalyptic shots of a helicopter silhouetted against a burning red sunset, blurred scenes of rebellion and rioting, a red flag being waved. The blurred masses gather together in the public square. A sacrificial flame is lit in the sudden darkness, banks of floodlights turned on. People are running, lost in wonder, pointing up at the night sky, while helicopters circle a towering object wrapped in huge white sheets. Explosive charges are ceremoniously detonated, and the covering falls away to reveal a statue of Michael so big that the helicopters can fly between his legs. He dominates the night sky. The masses can only look up at him, lost in collective feelings of wordless awe.

••• ✝ •••

Michael sees that he is really not the performer; he is the spectator. Michael sees that this is all for him. Michael sees that his very presence is only for him. If at this moment he does not sense death, Bataille observes, then he senses anguish: 'crowds sweat from the anguish provoked by shadows; death exists in it in a supressed state; but fills it up.' One eyewitness account has Michael Jackson praying to a wooden statue of Elvis. In a manner that Ludwig II would have understood, Michael tells Lisa Marie that 'I just met my father-in-law in the woods.' The more he embodies the kings who came before him, the more Michael loses himself in them. 'Indeed,' Bataille continues, 'he is the one who doesn't die, for he dies only to be reborn. He is not a man in the individual sense of the word, but rather a god; he is essentially the embodiment of the one he is but is not. He is the same as the one he replaces; the one who replaces him is the same as he is. He has no more regard for the limits of identity than he does for the limits of death, or rather these limits are the same; he is the transgression of all such limits.' The collars, tunics and cloaks that Ludwig, Elvis and Michael favour hide their majestic weakness. Each is wounded beneath their sovereign regalia. Uniforms serve simply to hide imperfections and frailties, disguise an individuality that is very different from the image in whose shadow everyone is forced to sweat with anguish. Michael announces that the 'HIStory' tour will be his last. One of Sony's nine promotional statues is sent floating down the Thames on a barge; another ends up outside a McDonald's in the Netherlands. Many of them have now disappeared entirely, their whereabouts unknown.

Rolling Stone reports Lisa Marie 'wanted to kill' Michael after he informs *TV Guide* that she had told him 'Elvis had a nose job'. They were asking Michael about his plastic surgery. 'I think it justified something in his mind,' she reveals. 'When you're the king of your own palace, there are no morals or ethics or integrity,' Lisa Marie later tells *Playboy* magazine.

'Everyone will kiss your ass,' she continues, 'and then give you the push that knocks you over.'

XXXI

In the Shadow of Heaven

The Empyrean Continued

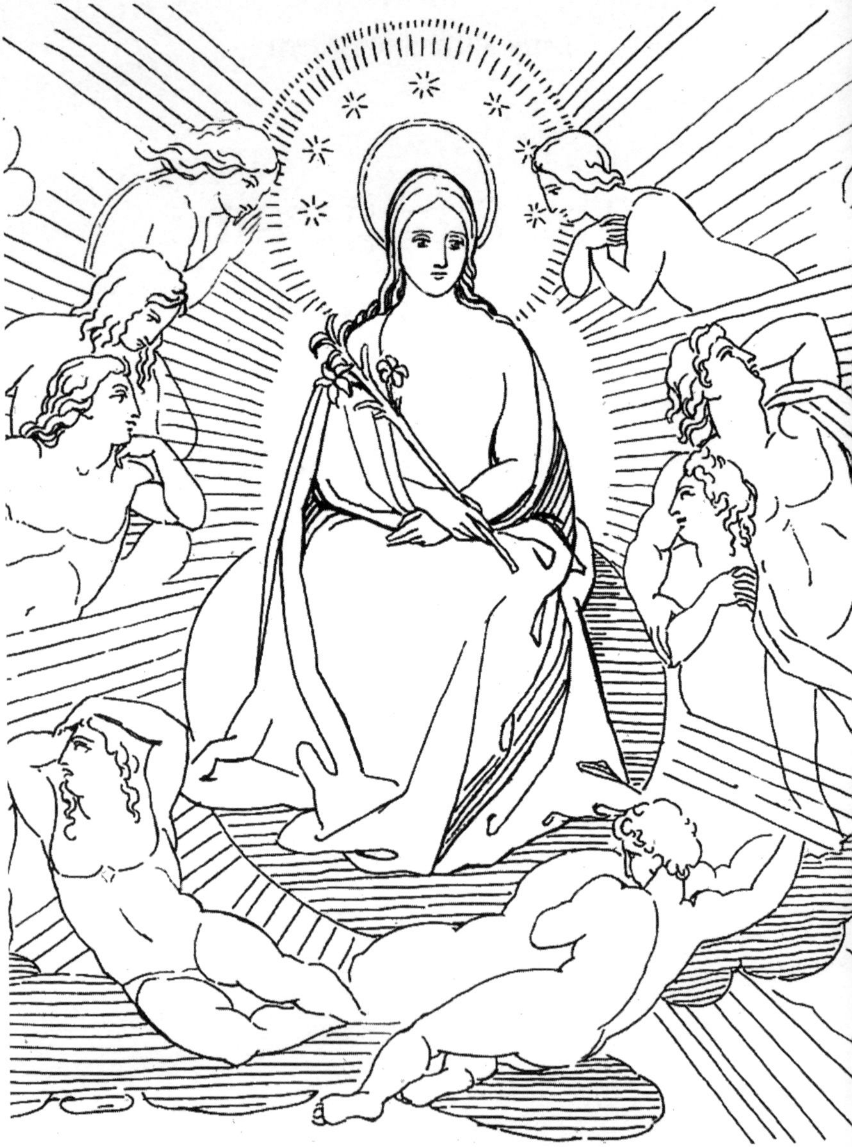

History begins and history continues

••• ✝ •••

But 'HIStory' never ends. According to the ancient Maya, a Grand Cycle in the human timeline will come to an end as another begins on 22 December 2012. The Winter Solstice and the Milky Way's Equator will align to mark this Great Occurrence. There will be plagues, fires and floods. A rogue planet, first discovered by the Sumerians, who named it Nibiru, is set to collide with the Earth, causing mass destruction. Michael stays up all night, unable to sleep, worrying about what is to come. 'We only have a little time left,' he keeps repeating to anyone who will listen. It was not so long ago that Michael couldn't sign his own name without adding the numbers '1998' to it, convinced that this marked the year when either he or the entire world would die. Ludwig's secret diaries are obsessed with the numerology of kings' reigns, especially that of Louis XIV. Elvis still consults his battered copy of *Cheiro's Book of Numbers*. Prognostication fractures and fragments time. Dante is certain that we are in the Final Age of the World.

Santa Maria, California, 13 June 2005: the woman on the aluminium stepladder at the front of the human cordon forming outside the courthouse releases one white dove after another into the blue sky as Michael Jackson is found not guilty on four charges of child molesting, one charge of attempted child molesting, one conspiracy charge and eight possible counts of providing alcohol to minors. One set free for each acquittal: the white doves are a real Neverland touch, sharing the same trashy aesthetic. 'All around her,' the *LA Times* reports, 'people wept, screamed, hugged each other, wailed into their cellphones.' The woman grows ecstatic. Her joy is unspeakable.

Michael has the best legal defence that money and fame can buy. Over the previous twelve years he has paid out almost 100 million dollars in settlements and legal fees; but while the criminal charges don't stick, the rumours and the stories do. Not guilty but not entirely innocent either, Michael flies to Bahrain, where he takes refuge in the magnificent palace of Sheik Abdullah bin Hamad bin Isa Al Khalifa, second son to the ruling monarch. The kingdom enthusiastically greets Allah's Great Angel *Mikaeel* and entertains him lavishly. However, as Bataille observes, such splendour is also dragged into the mire by the very services and divisions that raise it up. Soon the *National Enquirer* is reporting that Jackson has overdosed in Bahrain, injecting Demerol into his leg. A few months later it is reported that the King of Bahrain himself is obliged to intervene, dismissing charges and keeping the story out of the papers, when one of Michael's aides is arrested at Manama airport carrying a case packed with synthetic opiates.

••• ✠ •••

King Ludwig II increasingly seeks relief from pain and insomnia in larger doses of chloral hydrate, convinced that he is atoning for his grandfather's shameful abdication. His cousin, Crown Prince Rudolf of Austria, takes to morphine and alcohol, believing himself to be the reincarnation of the Roman emperor Caligula and that he must now pay for the latter's sins and excesses. Later Rudolf will kill his lover and then himself in a hunting lodge outside Vienna. According to Caligula, disasters are what make a reign unforgettable, so kings should always hope for the biggest and the worst. The ultimate cure for recurrence is not atonement but a wiped memory. That's why Ludwig's rooms reek of chloroform, while Michael seeks treatment for Demerol and morphine dependence brought on by anxiety and insomnia. Like Elvis before him, Michael uses dozens of different names to obtain opiates. 'If I stop using drugs, I'll die,' he tells a friend. 'I won't survive another day without them.'

••• ✝ •••

Michael can never return to his magic kingdom of Neverland, which contains too many painful memories for him now, so he remains constantly on the move. From palaces to penthouse suites and then on to the private mansions of friends, he never stays anywhere long. His main eating requirement when flying by private jet is a steady diet of original 'secret recipe' KFC with mashed potatoes, corn and biscuits with spray butter. Like Elvis, Michael likes to eat with his hands. Wine has to be served to him in Diet Coke cans. White wine is 'Jesus Juice', and red wine 'Jesus Blood' – it's a little sacramental joke of his. He's far from Neverland now.

••• ✝ •••

Ludwig's teeth are so rotten that he eats only soft foods but still insists upon being served cakes, sweets and dessert wines – even after seeing the royal dentist. Most of the king's good looks have vanished; 'when he spoke,' an eyewitness writes, 'several missing teeth disfigured his appearance and made it even more difficult to understand his words, which he sputtered out hastily.' Rubber dentures help to make his speech clearer; and the king holds a perfumed handkerchief over his mouth to mask the bad breath. 'I think growing old is the ugliest thing,' Michael Jackson remarks towards the end of his life. 'When the body breaks down and starts to wrinkle, I think that's so bad... I never want to look in the mirror and see that... I'd rather go out like Elvis.'

••• ✠ •••

By the time he turns 40, Elvis has earned 100 million dollars – approximately the same amount that Michael Jackson will pay in legal expenses – only to discover that he's almost broke. Too many fans have been beaten up or threatened by his bodyguards, leading to expensive lawsuits. Elvis fires Karate buddies Red West, Dave Hebler and Sonny West, who soon start work on a tell-all account of their time with him called *Elvis: What Happened?* To keep spending, Elvis borrows on future earnings, working himself to death on endless concert tours of the United States. A single routine endlessly repeated, part of sovereignty's mystique is the prospect of an eternal presence without end, stretching far into the future and back into the past. Elvis quickly squanders and consumes himself, leaving little for his audiences. 'The show was awful, a depressingly incoherent amateurish mess served up by a bloated and mumbling figure, who didn't act like "The King" of anything, least of all rock 'n' roll,' a reporter laments of a Houston appearance in the summer of 1976. Deeply in debt, Ludwig II is unable to pay the gas and water bills for his castles, but keeps on building anyway. Michael Jackson has his Black Amex card cancelled, while the power company threatens to turn off the fairy lights at Neverland. In preparation for a two-week tour that he will never commence, Elvis orders one hundred x three-gramme Amytal capsules; twelve half-gram ampules of amobarbital sodium; 150 x 300-milligram Quaaludes, 100 x five-milligram Dexedrine tablets; 100 twenty-milligram Biphetamine spansules; 100 Percodan tablets; fifty x four-milligram Dilaudid tablets plus twenty ccs of injectable Dilaudid in a two-milligram solution.

⁂

'You know, all he can do now is die,' his music director comments as the king's carefully maintained corpse is sent out onto the stage again.

XXXII

In the Shadow of Heaven

The Empyrean Continued

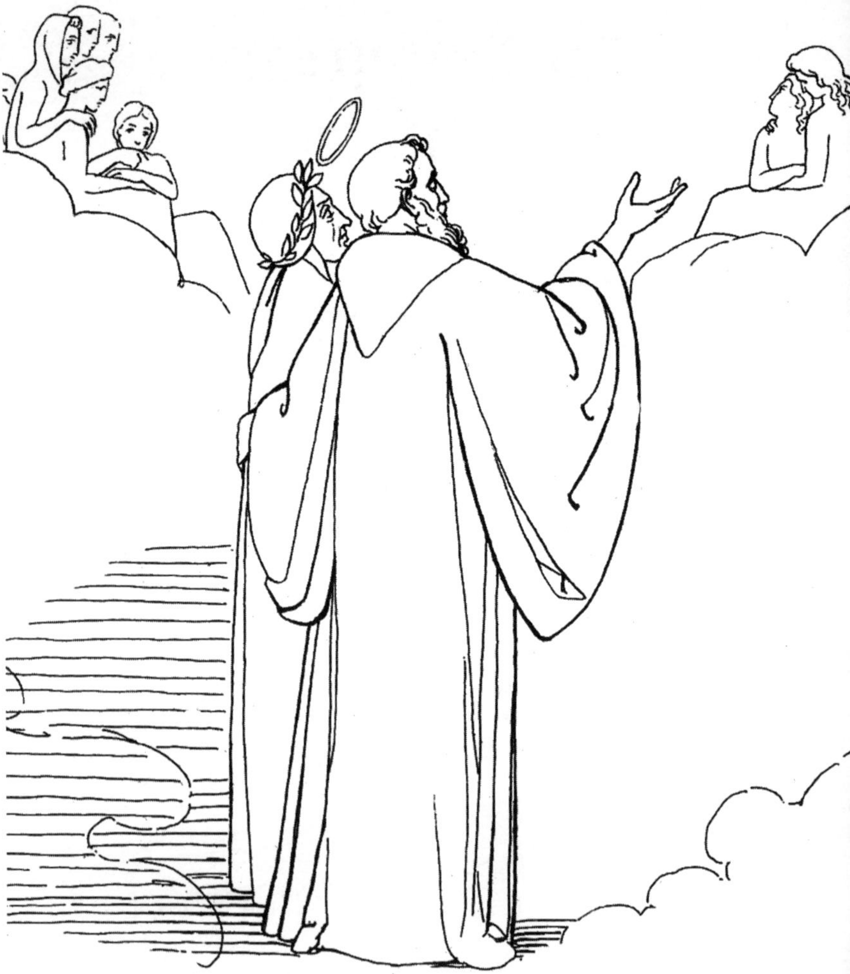

And now the end is near...

••• ✝ •••

Whether they know it or not, everyone comes to Las Vegas to destroy themselves, which can also be a step towards spectacular self-discovery. Michael Jackson is no different. After his long exile in Bahrain, Vegas becomes his glittering dark attractor. A private jet takes him there on 23 December 2006. He rents a home for himself and starts making plans for a 'Thriller' Casino with 'King of Pop' slot machines. A Michael Jackson-themed hotel will herald his return to live entertainment with one of the leftover HIStory statues out front. 'I want the hotel to encase it in the wall, and the nights I'm in performance the statue comes out on a conveyer belt,' Michael enthuses. A projected fifty-date residency will be promoted by a fifty-foot-tall Michael Jackson robot roaming around the Nevada desert, a gigantic walking billboard for the shows. The Michael Jackson Hotel and Casino will also feature an animated 'King of Pop' face that shoots laser beams. This has got to be the greatest comeback of all time. In the end, Michael Jackson makes his first public appearance on American soil since his trial at James Brown's funeral, where he approaches the Godfather of Soul in his gold-plated coffin and kisses him full on the lips. Michael had spent the previous night in the funeral home where the body was being prepared for burial, asking questions about the procedure – how the facial features are 'set' with eye caps and a needle injector. 'What type of fluids do you use?' he asks. 'And how do you put them in the body?'

◆◆◆ ✝ ◆◆◆

In Las Vegas Michael lives the life of a king in debt, which is another form of exile. He plans to buy a palatial $45 million residence from a member of Brunei's royal family; the place is large enough to house Michael's entire collection of paintings, sculpture, Baroque vases and gilded urns. Archive footage shows him on a buying spree in the Venetian Resort's luxury shopping mall, picking up *objets d'art.* 'Yoo-hoo,' he calls across the store. 'Did we get these?' Michael wants his new home to be a museum dedicated to his own life, according to one of his aides. 'We're going to do it like Graceland,' he adds. Michael makes it clear that he will never return to Neverland. The place holds too many painful memories for him. 'I don't ever want to set foot there again,' he tells his aide. 'Just get rid of everything.' An auction house is hired to remove 1,390 individual items of 'memorabilia' from his former home and place them in storage. 'Neverland is finished,' the same aide tells

··· ✝ ···

the *Wall Street Journal.* Deeply in debt, Ludwig II desperately requires funds to continue his building plans. He hears stories from Persia of an 'infinitely rich man' who can lend him the necessary millions and orders a trusted servant to go in search of him. Others are instructed to carry out bank raids in Stuttgart, Frankfurt and Paris or simply borrow money from the King of Sweden, the Duke of Westminster and the Sultan of Turkey. Most recognise the futility of such commands and discreetly ignore them. Rumours and stories circulate, questioning Ludwig's sanity. The auction of Michael Jackson's belongings, once they are removed from Neverland Ranch, is expected to bring in over ten million dollars. 'Michael was asked what he wanted to sell from Neverland,' recalls someone closely involved in the deal, 'and his answer was, "Everything." He said it twice: 'Everything".' Like any true king, he is betrayed by the people around him.

··· ✝ ···

A fifty-date Las Vegas residency means that Michael Jackson can embark upon another world tour without going anywhere. That had been Elvis Presley's big mistake. To create the illusion that he had never left home, the King ordered every hotel room to look and feel the same, aluminium foil across all the windows to keep out the day. Michael leaves Las Vegas after his money runs out, returning to LA to prepare for a residency at the O2 Arena in London. The series of shows will be called 'This is it'. At first Michael will play only ten concerts, but the number is extended to fifty, taking him from the summer of 2009 to the spring of 2010. 'When I say *this is it,*' Michael tells the world's press, 'it really means *this is it*. This will be the final curtain call.' It's the same comeback he'd been planning for himself in Vegas, only in a different city. The demand for tickets soars overnight.

Chemical analysis reveals fourteen separate drugs in Elvis Presley's system at the time of his death, including codeine, morphine, methaqualone, diazepam, ethinamate, Amytal, Nembutal, Demerol, amitriptyline and the decongestant Sinutab. Informed that members of his own cabinet were plotting to depose him, Ludwig II orders his aide-de-camp to bring him poison – from an apothecary, a chemist, from *anywhere*. 'I cannot go on living!' the king declares. It was during the 'HIStory' tour, when all his usual opiates failed, that Michael started to rely upon propofol to help him sleep. Propofol lays you out, then puts you under, leaving you alert and euphoric upon waking. Imagine what Elvis would have done with it. An intravenous anaesthetic, propofol is also extremely dangerous and must be administered carefully. Recreational use of the heavy white liquid can prove fatal.

⸭

The stresses and strains of preparing for his fifty-date London residency mean that Michael is soon asking for his 'milk' at bedtime again. His mental deterioration during rehearsals is striking. Depositions describe him as 'confused, easily frightened, unable to remember, obsessive, and disorientated.' In a recording made by his doctor, Michael's speech is so slurred that he sounds barely conscious. 'Elvis couldn't do it... Beatles couldn't do it... we have to be phenomenal,' he murmurs in a haze about the ambitious new show. He says he's doing it for the children of the world 'who don't have enough hope'. He speaks of songs he's written 'because I hurt, you know I hurt.' Beating his wings, Michael falls backwards into oblivion. 'I am asleep,' he says at the end of the tape.

⸭

Ludwig's drowned corpse is found floating in Lake Starnberg just days after he was declared mentally unfit to rule then confined to Berg Castle. Elvis dies alone on the carpeted floor of his private bathroom at Graceland. The last words anyone hears him say are 'I won't.' At the eleventh hour, Michael withdraws the contents of Neverland from auction but not before the world's media has had a chance to peer down their noses at it. 'Disneyland collides with the Louvre,' sniffs the show's chief curator about the items put on sale. Neverland stands empty and abandoned. 'What's weird is that within his house, there was no dust. It was immaculate. The carpet was vacuumed,' reports one late-night visitor to Michael's former home.

✝

'The house is foreclosed, it's basically derelict, defunct. You're in the valley, and you're on your own, and it's pretty desolate.'

XXXIII

In the Shadow of Heaven

The Empyrean Concluded

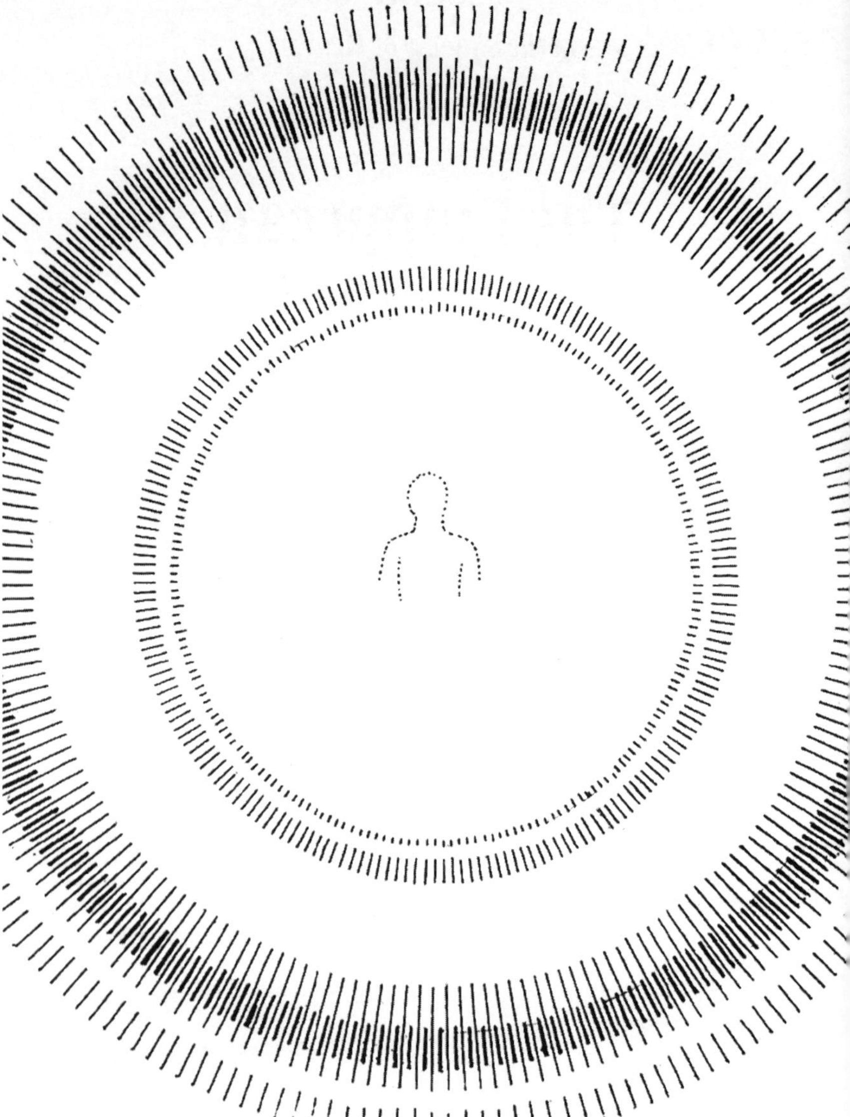

This is it

The dead are always out of fashion. Frozen in that final moment and then buried forevermore, their manners and their style become a quaint joke over time. Twelve bottles of propofol, along with innumerable tubes of skin whitening cream, are found in a medical bag stashed inside Michael's bedroom following his death. Further searches reveal stockpiles of lorazepam, diazepam, temazepam, trazodone, Flomax, clonazepam, tizanidine, hydrocodone and lidocaine, together with syringes, needles and IV catheters. 'When the autopsy comes, all hell's going to break loose,' Liza Minnelli remarks upon hearing that Michael had died.

And there is a War in Heaven. Michael will fight against the Dragon; and the Dragon shall not prevail, nor shall his place be found any more in Heaven. And the Great Dragon, who is called Satan and deceives the whole world, shall be cast out upon the Earth, and his angels with him. And a loud voice shall say in Heaven: 'Now is come Salvation, and Strength, and the Kingdom of our

God, and the Power of his Christ, for the Accuser of our Brethren is cast down.' In his death, Michael's fans see the beginning and the end of all things. In his death, Michael endlessly divides, multiplies and replicates. In his death, Michael becomes a sanctified American Jesus. In his death, Michael starts making more money than ever.

••• ✝ •••

'Elvis didn't die,' Colonel Parker tells the world. 'The body did. We're keeping up the good spirits. We're keeping Elvis alive. I talked to him this morning and he told me to carry on.' To prove his point, he stages 'Always Elvis', a merchandising extravaganza held at the Las Vegas Hilton to mark the first anniversary of the King's death. The main attraction is a life-size bronze statue of Elvis Presley. Weighing 450 pounds and costing $150,000, it shows him slim and young and dressed in a Bill Belew jumpsuit, a scarf around his neck, a guitar slung across his hips. He mutely turns his face away from a microphone held in his modestly bejewelled hand. The fans don't go for it, however. 'They prefer to go to Graceland,' observes one commentator. Plans are discussed to turn Neverland into a Michael Jackson museum 'in the style of Elvis Presley's Graceland', according to one source. This would involve burying Michael there, transforming 'Graceland West' into a public shrine. The number of trashy souvenir and gift shops across the street from Graceland grows in the weeks and months following Elvis' death. Joe and La Toya Jackson attend 'Long Live the King', a ticketed event taking place in New York before Michael's body is even in the ground.

··· ✝ ···

Let the world tremble as its kings depart. In a destructive gesture of Wagnerian proportions, Ludwig II had ordered that all his castles be dynamited after his death so that nobody but him could ever enjoy them. The Twilight of the Gods transforms the masses into mere spectators. Neuschwanstein is quickly overrun by tourists, anxious to see what had formerly been withheld from them: Ludwig's 'miracle fortress' as one the first tour guides calls it. The gates of Linderhof are flung open, his bedroom is hastily redecorated. Any great act of the will makes its subsequent desecration inevitable. The King's personal effects are sold off to clear his debts. Knickknacks, postcards and visitor centres mean the money continues to flow in. And still the crowds come, attracted by what is forbidden – they snap at its grandeur even as it consumes them.

On the 130th anniversary of Ludwig II's death, men in black robes and hoods visit the cross on Lake Starnberg marking the spot where the King's body was found. They place in the water a giant replica of his face with *'It was murder'* written across the forehead in Gothic script. Elvis either took his own life or faked his own death, depending on who you listen to, and the King is still known to speak from beyond the grave. Based on the autopsy and toxicology screenings, the doctor treating Michael Jackson for insomnia is found guilty of involuntary manslaughter and sentenced to four years in prison. His medical license is pulled. Elvis' personal physician serves as a pallbearer at the King's funeral. The doctor who had found Ludwig insane and was treating him at Berg Castle on Lake Starnberg drowns alongside his patient.

How did you expect them to die? Orpheus was torn to pieces. Narcissus faded away. One became little more than a head filled with song, the other a flower – both trashed themselves out of love for beauty. 'But,' observes Bataille, 'the object that fascinated in sacrifice is not only horrible, it is *divine*, it is the god who *agrees* to the sacrifice – who exerts an attraction and yet has only one meaning: losing oneself in death.' True sovereigns are sacred beasts cursed with the knowledge that they must inevitably waste and demean themselves. Try to picture such fabulous creatures passing away peacefully in contented old age. How little would we care for them, knowing they had settled for our dreams, not theirs – *our* mortality, not their own.

⋯ ✝ ⋯

What happens to ordinary desires given the freedoms enjoyed by a king? Imagine an ideal version of reality that revolves solely around watching Disney movies all day and all night. 'He lived in a fantasy world,' observes an artist once in Michael Jackson's employ, 'and if he didn't like something, you felt as if he could behead you. But the way he does it is by not calling you again. And somewhere along the line he stopped calling me and I thought I had been beheaded.' Michael Jackson lies in the Sanctuary of Golden Slumber in the Holly Terrace of the Great Mausoleum, where Paramahansa Yogananda's body remains at rest, in Glendale's Forest Lawn Memorial Park. Michael's gold coffin is the same model as the one in which James Brown was buried. The thousands of fans who attend Elvis Presley's funeral take away every single floral tribute afterwards as souvenirs, down to the last ribbon and leaf. Ludwig II is laid out in state in his rooms at Berg Castle, wearing the black robes of the Grand Master of the Order of St Hubertus. He holds in his hands a spray of white jasmine flowers picked by his cousin the Empress Elisabeth herself. They come from the garden of her private villa on Lake Starnberg and are preserved for later display in museum showcases. Having reached the end and limit to Paradise, we ask ourselves what brought us here. Ernst von Possart wrote of his first encounter with the young King Ludwig: 'But my gaze could not take in anything but the two powerful steel grey eyes, framed in dark eyelashes, which looked penetratingly into my own and then held them captive.' He could have been describing Elvis Presley or Michael Jackson.

••• ✝ •••

'Now the King was speaking to me in a quiet, kindly sounding tone, but I could not grasp the words – I just looked spellbound at those lofty shining stars.'

Glossary

Glossary

••• OF •••

NAMES, PLACES AND

REFERENCES

Respectfully dedicated to the memory of Ambrose Bierce – because in this world, as in the next, The Devil always has the last word.

A

Nick Adams

American actor. Befriended James Dean in Hollywood and subsequently did the same with Elvis Presley. Later starred opposite Godzilla in Toho Studios' *Monster Zero* AKA *Invasion of Astro-Monster*. Died of a drug overdose in his Beverly Hills home. What an amazing movie his life story would make. (XIII)

King Aeëtes

Father of Medea (qv). Descended from Helios the Titan and personification of the Sun. Played by the British actor Jack Gwillim in the 1963 movie *Jason and the Argonauts*. The name is derived from the ancient Greek word for 'eagle'. (XVIII)

Agamemnon

King of Mycenae. Commanded the Greeks and successfully laid siege to Troy. Returned home in triumph only to be immediately murdered by his wife and her lover. Now that's cold. (V)

The Aladdin

Las Vegas casino. A hallucination of a building originally built in 1962 and demolished in 1998, having hosted the hallucination of a marriage that lasted from 1967 until 1973. (XVI)

Joseph Albert

Appointed Court Photographer to the Bavarian royal family in 1857 when Ludwig II was still a boy, allowing him to document almost the entirety of the young king's reign. Developed the first photomechanical printing technique and later introduced Albertype, making the mass production of photographic copies possible. These biographical details are by no means unrelated. Albert died in 1886, about six weeks before Ludwig II. (III, IV, VI)

Amfortas

King of the Grail Knights in the opera *Parsifal* by Richard Wagner (qv). A fictional character, his presence onstage is burdened by a wound that never heals and way too much backstory. (VI, VII)

Alfred Apaka

Hawaiian baritone related to the politician Luther Aholo and the educator Lydia Ka'onohiponiponiokalani Aholo. Made numerous appearances on *Hawaii Calls*, produced by Webley Edwards (qv) and later performed at Don the Beachcomber in Waikiki (qv) before becoming a permanent fixture at Henry Kaiser's Hawaiian Village Hotel (qv). Died in 1960 and was buried in Hawaii holding a microphone in his hand. (XIV)

Apollo

'*Apollo's* deception: the eternity of the beautiful form; the aristocratic law that says *"Thus shall it be forever!"*' – Friedrich Nietzsche (qv). (*Purg.* I, XV, XVII, XXXIII) (*Para.* I, II, X, XVII)

Ariadne

Greek princess and daughter of King Minos. Helped Theseus kill the Minotaur, who was her half-brother; later she married Dionysus. Life gets complicated. Sometimes you have to make choices. (XXII)

Frankie Avalon

Hollywood actor and singer. *Beach Party* (1963), *Muscle Beach Party, Bikini Beach* (both 1964), *Beach Blanket Bingo* (1965). He was nothing without Annette Funicello. (XIII)

B

Alice Bailey

Former Theosophist who took telepathic dictation from the Tibetan Masters of the Ancient Wisdom. This resulted in a series of esoteric texts including *Letters on Occult Meditation* (1922), *A Treatise on Cosmic Fire* (1925) and *The Reappearance of the Christ* (1947). These were works read and appreciated not only by Elvis Presley but also by The Mole People closely associated with the original Warhol Factory. (XII)

Joe Don Baker

American screen presence. Followed up *Golden Needles* with such Trash classics as *Mitchell* (1975), *The Shadow of Chikara* and *Checkered Flag or Crash* (both 1977). Not to be confused with Josephine Baker. (*Inf.* II) (*Para.* XX)

Josephine Baker

American-born French diva, dancer and civil rights activist – also the first black woman to star in a major motion picture. Encouraged Bill Belew (qv) to become a stage costume designer. Not to be confused with Joe Don Baker. (XVI)

George Barati

Hungarian-born cellist, composer and conductor. Any further information at this point would only strain the bounds of relevance. (XIV)

Pat Barringer

Actress and exotic dancer and the golden thread connecting Hell with Purgatory and Heaven. (*Inf.* XVIII) (*Purg.* XVII) (*Para.* XVII)

George Barris

Automotive engineer, car designer and 'Kustom King' whose restless energies connect the Sun with Mars. The wise will seek him in Hell only to find him again in Heaven. (*Inf.* XIV, XV, XXI, XXXI) (*Para.* XII, XV)

Georges Bataille

French writer and philosopher who understood the vital necessity of antagonising the heavens, making him the closest equivalent to Dante's Beatrice in this particular version of Paradise. (*Purg.* XXIX, XXX, XXXII) (*Para.* IV, VI, XV, XVII, XXI, XXII, XXVII, XXVIII, XXX, XXXI, XXXIII)

Charles Baudelaire

Nineteenth-century French poet. 'Baudelaire patterned his image of the artist after the image of the hero. From the beginning, each is an advocate of the other' – Walter Benjamin. (*Purg.* XXX) (*Para.* VIII, XXIV)

Bayreuth Festspielhaus

Bavarian opera house and an early experiment in the technological domination of an audience conducted by Richard Wagner (qv) in 1876. The following year Thomas Edison publicly demonstrated the phonograph for the first time, which hardly seems that surprising in retrospect. (VII)

Bill Belew

Designer of glitzy stage costumes to the stars and best known for his work for Elvis Presley. Covered the King's ass on more than one occasion. (XVI, XVII, XVIII, XIX, XX, XXXIII)

Joseph Sieber Benner

Spiritual writer and medium much admired by Elvis Presley. Born in Akron, Ohio. Took dictation directly from God. Books include *The Impersonal Life* (1914), *Christ in You* (1918), *The Way to the Kingdom* (1932). (XII)

Helmut Berger

Austrian movie actor and sex symbol. Perfect as Ludwig II. Perfect as Dorian Gray. Just all-round perfect really. (*Purg.* XXXII) (*Para.* XVIII)

Annie Besant

Theosophist and freemason. 'The pilgrimage of humanity during its present cycle of evolution consists in passing seven times round a chain of seven globes; on each globe a stay is made of many millions of years, and of these stays there are forty-nine – seven globes each dwelt on seven times.' (XII)

Madame Blavatsky

Occultist and one of the prime movers and shakers of the Theosophical Society. Born in Ukraine. 'Discovered' Tibet and the hidden Masters of the Ancient Wisdom. Key works include *Isis Unveiled: A Master-Key to the Mysteries of Ancient and Modern Science and Theology* (1877), *The Secret Doctrine: The Synthesis of Science, Religion and Philosophy* (1888) and *The Voice of the Silence* (1889). (XII)

William-Adolphe Bouguereau

Highly collectible French painter and the last word in realism. *Nymphs and Satyr* (1873), *The Birth of Venus* (1879), *The Return of Spring* (1886), *The Youth of Bacchus* (1884), *The Abduction of Psyche* (1895). Died 1905. (*Purg.* IX) (*Para.* XXVIII)

James Brown AKA 'The Hardest Working Man in Show Business' AKA 'Mr Please Please Please', AKA 'Mr Dynamite' AKA 'The Godfather of Soul' AKA 'The Godfather of Funk'

AKA 'The Minister of the New New Super Heavy Funk' AKA 'Soul Brother Number One'

He was all of the above and more. Lived in America. (XXXII, XXXIII)

Ludwig von Bürkel

German lawyer and son of the landscape painter Heinrich Bürkel. Responsible to Ludwig II for the financing of the building work at Neuschwanstein (qv) and Herrenchiemsee (qv). Acted as the King's envoy to Richard Wagner (qv) in February 1883 and accompanied the composer's body on its funeral procession back from Venice to Bayreuth (qv). (II)

C

Caesars Palace

Luxury hotel and casino located on Las Vegas Strip in Paradise, Nevada. Boasts a wide selection of fountains, fake Greek and Roman statuary, fake Roman architecture and Hollywood-era antiquities. A twenty-foot-high statue of Caesar hailing a taxi stands on a marble plinth in its driveway. (XVI)

Roger Caillois

French intellectual freebooter and cofounder with Georges Bataille (qv) of the Collège de Sociologie. Works published in English include *The Mask of Medusa* (1964) and *The Writing of Stones* (1985). (XIII)

Caligula AKA Gaius Julius Caesar Augustus Germanicus

Rome's third emperor. 'In reckless extravagance he outdid the prodigals of all times in ingenuity, inventing new sorts of baths and unnatural varieties of food and feasts; for he would bathe in hot or cold perfumed oils, drink pearls of great price dissolved in vinegar, and set before his guests loaves and meats of gold, declaring that a man ought either be frugal or Caesar' – Suetonius. (XXXI)

Captain Marvel

American superhero and early rival to Superman. Commonly known as Shazam for reasons too complicated to address here. Played by Tom Tyler in the 1941 movie serial *The Adventures of Captain Marvel*, featuring Dr Maldor's 'Scarab' costume from *Captain America* and Kenne Duncan from Ed Wood's *The Sinister Urge*. See *Inferno* IV and IX for more details. (XVI, XVII, XIX)

John Carpenter

American filmmaker and auteur. Relevant movies of note include *Dark Star* (1974), *Assault on Precinct 13* (1976), *Halloween* (1978), *Elvis* with Kurt Russell (qv) (1979), *The Fog* (1980), *The Thing* (1982) and *Big Trouble in Little China* (1986). There have been others to be sure. There are always others, are there not? (XXIV, XXVI)

Casimir of Poland AKA Casimir III AKA Casimir the Great

King of Poland from 1333 to 1370 and King of Ruthenia from 1340. Makes a brief appearance in *The Warriors* running with the Van Cortlandt Rangers. This entry may not be altogether historically accurate. (IV)

Enzo G Castellari

Italian filmmaker and auteur. *Renegade Riders* (1966), *Kill Them All and Come Back Alone* (1968), *Cold Eyes of Fear* (1970), *Heroin Busters* (1977), *Day of the Cobra* (1980), *The Last Shark* (1981) and *Light Blast* (1985). (XXIV, XXV, XXVI)

Renee Shin-Yi Chen

Born in Taiwan 1 April 1976. Died on a movie set 23 July 1982, aged six. Buried in Forest Lawn Memorial Park, Glendale, Los Angeles County. (XXV)

Cher

Goddess of Pop. Made her screen debut in the 1965 beach party movie *Wild on the Beach* and has blessed us with her presence ever since. (XVII)

Circe

Semi-divine enchantress related by blood or myth to Helios the Titan and the sea nymph Perse, as well as Hecate, Aeëtes (qv) and Pasiphaë, mother to the Minotaur. Her shapeshifting impact upon poetry, art and dance remains mutable and diverse. Remember her. (*Purg.* IV, XX) (*Para.* XVIII)

Queen Clothilde of France

Burgundian Catholic princess who married King Clovis I of Gaul in 493. Convinced her husband to renounce his Frankish ways and embrace Christianity in 496. Venerated as the patron saint of queens, brides, widows and exiles. Could find her way in and out of Heaven blindfolded. (IV)

Nat King Cole

African-American singer and pianist. Appeared as himself in countless movies and TV shows throughout the 1950s and early 1960s. Collapsed onstage at the Sands in Las Vegas in 1964 and was later diagnosed with terminal lung cancer from which he died the following year. 'Smile', one of Cole's biggest hits, was later covered by Michael Jackson, who included the track on *HIStory: Past, Present and Future,* claiming it was his favourite song. (XV)

Augie Colón

Percussionist and exotica vocalist supreme. Born August Borero Colón on Honolulu in 1922. Officially joined Martin Denny (qv) and his quartet when they first played Henry Kaiser's Hawaiian Village Hotel (qv) in 1956. Recorded several classic albums with Denny in the late 1950s, as well as the solo releases *Sophisticated Savage* (1959) and *Chant of the Jungle* (1960). 'This marks the passing of a giant, as far as I'm concerned,' Denny remarked on Colon's death in 2004. (XIII)

Cythera

Located in the Mediterranean with a secure place in Greek mythology. The original *Love Island*. (II)

D

Bette Davis

Hollywood actress. *What Ever Happened to Baby Jane?* (1962), *Who is Buried in My Grave?* (1964), *The Nanny* (1965), *The Anniversary* (1968), *Burnt Offerings* (1976). (*Purg*. XXIII, XXIV) (*Para*. XII)

Doris Day

Hollywood actress, singer and animal activist. Star of *The Doris Day Show* from 1968 to 1973. (XII)

Martin Denny

American arranger, composer and pianist. *Exotica* (1957), *Exotica Volume II* (1958), *Forbidden Island* (1958), *Primitiva* (1958), *Hypnotique* (1959), *Exotica Volume III* (1959), *Quiet Village* (1959), *The Enchanted Sea* (1960), *Exotic Percussion* (1961). 'Marty was one of the classiest guys in the business' – Don Ho. (XIII, XIV)

Frank Dileo

American entrepreneur. Michael Jackson called him 'Uncle Tookie'. Appeared as rock music manager Frankie 'Mr Big' Sharp in *Wayne's World* (1992) and *Wayne's World 2* (1993). Not to be confused with Frank Lideo (qv). (XXVII, XXVIII)

Walt Disney

One of the Fixed Stars Under Heaven, but only because there is no longer any room for him in Hell. (*Inf*. XVI) (*Para*. XXVI, XXVII, XXXII, XXXIII)

Fats Domino

African-American singer and composer. The *real* King of Rock and Roll, according to Elvis Presley. 'Rock 'n' roll was here a long time before I came along,' Elvis later added. 'Let's face it: I can't sing like Fats Domino can. I know that.' (XV)

The Dominoes AKA Billy Ward and his Dominoes

African-American close harmony group specialising in R&B and Doo-Wop. Launched the singing career of Jackie Wilson (qv). Hits included 'Stardust' and 'Deep Purple' (both 1957). (XV)

Don the Beachcomber

Legendary Tiki bar franchise founded by former rumrunner Donn Beach, who opened and ran a branch on Waikiki Beach – you can see where this is going already. Rum-based cocktails on offer included the PiYi, which came to your table in a miniature pineapple, the Missionary's Downfall, the Vicious Virgin, the Never Say Die, the Cobra's Fang, the Tahitian Rum Punch and the Zombie. Justly deserves its place in Paradise. (XIII)

Dorian Gray

Sooner or later, every sovereign sees Dorian staring back at them from the mirror. (*Inf.* VIII) (*Purg.* IV, V, VI, VII, IX, XII, XXIV, XXV, XXXI, XXXII) (*Para.* VII)

Bobby Driscoll

Hollywood child star and American tragedy. Dead at 31. 'His own family didn't know he was the one in the pauper's grave with a heroin overdose. He was a Disney giant, the voice of Peter Pan' – Michael Jackson. (XXVII)

E

Max Thomas Edelmann

German engineer, physics professor, inventor and industrialist. Founded the Physical-Mechanical Institute in Munich. Appointed head of all stage lighting and mechanical engineering for the Court Theatre by Ludwig II before going on to create elaborate special effects for His Majesty's pleasure. (VIII)

Edward the Confessor

Anglo-Saxon king. Not to be confused with Edward the Martyr for obvious reasons. Canonised by Pope Alexander III in 1161. The rest is history. (IV)

Webley Edwards

American broadcaster and former WWII correspondent. As well as his regular live Hawaiian music shows, he released several easy-listening albums over the 1950s and 1960s in association with his music director Al Kealoha Perry. Releases include *Hawaii Calls: Fire Goddess* (1958), *Island Paradise* (1959), *Hula Island Favorites* (1959) and *Waikiki After Dark* (1965). (XIV)

Empress Elisabeth of Austria AKA Sisi

Sister to Sophie in Bayern (qv), cousin to Ludwig II and mother to Crown Prince Rudolf of Austria (qv). Considered one of the great beauties of nineteenth-century Europe; but, unlike her cousin Ludwig, avoided being photographed whenever possible. Died in 1898 after being stabbed by an Italian anarchist on the shore of Lake Geneva. (VI, VII, VIII, XXXIII)

Landgravine Elisabeth von Thuringen AKA Elizabeth of Hungary, AKA Saint Elizabeth of Hungary

Married Ludwig IV of Thuringia (qv) at age 14 and was widowed at age 20 when her husband died on his way to join the Sixth Crusade. Devoted the remainder of her life to helping the poor. Associated with numerous miracles, most notably after her own death. Canonised in 1235. (IV)

Joanie Esposito

Matron of Honour to Priscilla Presley (qv) at her wedding to Elvis. Following her divorce from Joe Esposito (qv), Joanie married Robert Kardashian's brother Tom. She's a Kardashian now, which is a lot like being canonised these days. (XV)

Joe Esposito

One of the King's fixers and source of the story about Elvis dancing with an erection on the set of *Girls! Girls! Girls!* (XIII, XIV, XV, XVII, XXI, XXII)

Ettal Abbey

Benedictine Abbey founded by Ludwig the Bavarian (qv) to placate the Pope. Dedicated to the Assumption of the Blessed Virgin, so maybe the Grail connection is a little fanciful. Was expanded and renovated in the Grand Baroque manner in the mid-nineteenth century when many of the original buildings were consumed by fire. Geographically close to Linderhof (qv) if not quite in spirit (qv). (IV)

F

Ferdinand III of Spain

Founded hospitals, monasteries, churches and cathedrals as well as the University of Salamanca. Canonised in 1671, which was a lot like becoming a Kardashian back then. (IV)

The Finks

Acid rock band whose whole existence is confined to the Lana Turner (qv) movie *The Big Cube*. They are a reminder of the deep cultural influence of Big Daddy Roth's Rat Fink. See *Inferno* XVI for more details. (XII)

Ella Fitzgerald

African-American singer and jazz virtuoso. 'If you'd like to hear Ella Fitzgerald's voice crystal clear, you'll record on new Memorex MRX3 cassette tape. It reproduces live sound with such crystal clear fidelity, you'll have to ask: is it Ella or MRX3? Is it live or is it Memorex?' (XVI)

The Flamingo

Las Vegas casino and hotel located firmly in the House of Mars. Opened by American mobster Bugsy Siegel on 26 December 1946, it closed again two weeks later. A slow return on gangland investment following its reopening resulted in Siegel's death six months later, shot multiple times in the head and lungs, a stray bullet shattering a white marble statue of Dionysus on a nearby piano. Viva Las Vegas. (XVI)

Flegetanis

Muslim astronomer and a descendant of Solomon whose divinations are recalled by the medieval knight and poet Wolfram von Eschenbach. *'He declared there was a thing called the Grail, whose name he had read clearly in the constellations. A host of Angels left it on Earth.'* (IV)

Flora

Roman goddess of flowers, youth and the spring. Her festival is celebrated between 28 April and 3 May, the rites of Flora still being observed to this day at Daytona Beach. (II)

Larry Fortensky

Probably the most blessed construction worker since Jesus and consequently the most cursed as well. Seventh and final husband to Elizabeth Taylor (qv). They met each other while drying out at the Betty Ford Clinic in 1988. (XXVII)

Bob Fosse

American choreographer and all that jazz. Had a thing for fishnet tights, bowler hats and amphetamines. (XXIV, XXVI)

Frank Lideo – AKA 'Mr Big'

Principal villain in *Moonwalker* (1988). Heavily into spiders and world domination. *'You wanna know why I'm doing this, do you? I just wanna get everybody high, man. You know, some good drugs. That's all.'* Not to be confused with Frank Dileo (qv). (XXVII, XXVIII)

Fred Flintstone

Prehistoric working stiff originating in the early Hanna-Barbera era. From the town of Bedrock. He's a page right out of hist-o-ree. (XXIX)

Buckminster Fuller

Architect, writer and theorist. One of the few inhabitants of this planet who actually thought it could be a paradise. (XIV)

G

Ghidra AKA King Ghidorah AKA Kingu Gidora

Gilded space dragon noted for having three heads. His one ass has been handed to him by Godzilla and his friends on numerous occasions, most notably in *Ghidra: The Three-Headed Monster* (1964), *Monster Zero* (1965), *Destroy All Monsters* (1968), and *Godzilla vs. Gigan* (1972). Has returned to the screen several times since, despite the unpromising start. (XVIII)

Ennio Girolami AKA Thomas Moore

Italian movie actor. Brother to Enzo G Castellari (qv). *The Fury of Achilles* (1962), *The Hellbenders* (1967), *Between God, the Devil and a Winchester* (1968), *Tenebrae* (1982), *Operation Nam* (1986). (XXVI)

Goethe

German poet. One of the first to realise the romantic appeal of damnation without going to Hell first himself. (*Purg.* XX) (*Para.* V)

Graceland

All roads lead here. Built in 1939, added to the National Register of Historic Places in 1991 and declared a National Historic Landmark in 2006. (X, XI, XII, XIII, XIV, XV, XVI, XVIII, XIX, XXII, XXVI, XXVIII, XXIX, XXX, XXXII, XXXIII)

The Grail

A fable and a dream. Either a stone that fell from Heaven or the cup that once held the blood of Jesus Christ, everything it touches becomes the object of myth and veneration, thereby maintaining and extending its reality, which is a miracle in itself. (III, IV, V, VI, VII, X)

Abbé Grégoire AKA Henri Jean-Baptist Grégoire

French priest and revolutionary. As deputy of the Third Revolutionary Assembly in Paris, he proposed the abolition of the monarchy and demanded that Louis XVI (qv) be brought to trial. So much for ruling by divine right. (II)

Mark Gregory AKA Marco de Gregorio

Italian action movie star. Also appeared in *Thunder Warrior* (1987), *Thunder Warrior II* (1985) and *Thunder Warrior III* (1988). An impoverished recluse, he died from a drug overdose in 2013. (XXIV, XXVI)

Grotta Azzurra, AKA The Blue Grotto

A natural sea cave located on the Island of Capri renowned for its crystalline blue water. Several scenes in Mario Bava's *Danger: Diabolik* (1968) were filmed here. See *Purgatory* XXVI and XXVII for more details. (I, II)

Gurnemanz

Grail Knight and hermit who appears in *Parsifal*, the last opera by Richard Wagner (qv). Knows more about what's going on than anyone else, and that includes the main character. Tends to elaborate upon this at some length. (VII)

H

Hagia Sophia

Formerly the spiritual centre of the Eastern Orthodox Church in Constantinople, now the Grand Mosque in Istanbul. Dedicated to Holy Wisdom. The true underside of Heaven can be found in the early history of the Holy Roman Empire. (IV, VII)

Hammer

Violent corporate stooge played by Vic Morrow (qv) in *The Bronx Warriors*. Laughs a lot. Good with a flamethrower. Not to be confused with Fred 'The Hammer' Williamson (qv). (XXIV)

Olivia de Havilland AKA Dame Olivia Mary de Havilland

British-American screen actress. *A Midsummer Night's Dream* (1935), *The Dark Mirror* (1946), *The Snake Pit* (1948), *Lady in a Cage* (1964), *Pope Joan* (1972), *The Screaming Woman* (1972). (XII)

Hawaiian Village Hotel

Beachfront resort developed by Henry J Kaiser (qv) in 1954. Now the Hilton Hawaiian Village. 'Best pools and slides in Waikiki.' (XIII, XIV, XIX)

Hayvenhurst

The Jackson family home in California and an early draft of Neverland (qv). (XXVI)

Dave Hebler

Bodyguard and martial arts instructor to Elvis Presley from 1972 to 1976. Holds a tenth-degree black belt in Kenpo Karate. Co-author with Red West (qv) and Sonny West (qv) of *Elvis: What Happened?* (1977). (XX, XXI, XXXI)

Hecate

Greek goddess of magic, witchcraft, ghosts and necromancy. The 'threefold goddess' is closely associated with crossroads and torches. Works from afar. (XVII, XVIII)

Heinrich der Vogler AKA Henry the Fowler

Duke of Saxony, King of East Francia and founder of the mediaeval German State. Also found time to appear in *Lohengrin*, one of Ludwig II's favourite operas by Richard Wagner (qv). (VI)

Emperor Heinrich II AKA Saint Henry the Exuberant

Holy Roman Emperor from 1014 to 1024. Member of the Bavarian branch of the Ottonian Dynasty and grandson to Heinrich der Vogler (qv). Still working on the 'Exuberant' bit, though. (IV)

Piero Heliczer

Filmmaker, poet and haunting presence on the New York underground movie scene of the 1960s. Founded Dead Language Press. Worked with Jack Smith (qv) and the Velvet Underground. Has his own place in Hell. (XXVII)

Lord Henry Wotton

Key character in *The Picture of Dorian Gray*, an invaluable work of fiction by Oscar Wilde (qv). 'Et in Arcadia ego'. (*Inf.* VIII) (*Purg.* V, VII, XVI, XXIII, XXV, XXXI, XXXII) (*Para.* VII)

Herrenchiemsee

Ludwig II's palace located on the Herreninsel, the largest island on Chiemsee lake in Southern Bavaria. Building work commenced on 21 May 1878. First opened to the public a few weeks after the King's death in 1886. (IX, X, XXVIII)

Walter Hill

American cineaste. That he should have directed *The Warriors* (1979) is a miracle; and miracles are the way things ought to be. (XXIV)

Hoerselloch

Mountain situated between Gotha and Eisenach, near the Wartburg (qv). 'It is said that strange noises issue from it, and that is why the mountain itself bears in the old chronicles the name of *mons Horrisonus*; the Hoerselloch is a gate to Hell or at least to Purgatory; the noises heard there are nothing else, it is said, than the complaints and groans of the damned' – *Mémoires de l'Académie des sciences, inscriptions et belles-lettres de Toulouse* (1893). (I)

Prince of Hohenlohe Schillingsfürst AKA Chlodwig Carl Viktor, Prince of Ratibor and Corvey

Minister-President of Bavaria under Ludwig II. Enjoyed the favour and support of Richard Wagner (qv) and Otto von Bismarck. You can already see where this is heading. (VIII)

Hohenschwangau

Palace in southwest Bavaria built by Maximilian II (qv) and the childhood home of Ludwig II. (IV, VI, XXVI)

The Holy Sepulchre AKA The Church of the Holy Sepulchre AKA Church of the Resurrection

Sacred site in Jerusalem built around the Tomb of Jesus together with a fragment of the Angel's stone that was used to seal it. (III)

Lena Horne

African-American singer, dancer and actress. Screen appearances include *Meet Me in Las Vegas* (1956) as herself and as Glinda, the Good Witch of the South in *The Wiz* (1978), which also starred Michael Jackson as The Scarecrow. (XVI)

I

The International

Las Vegas resort and Elvis Presley's Calvary. Has been lost to itself ever since. Started as the International Hotel in 1969, became the Las Vegas Hilton in 1971, then the LVH – Las Vegas Hotel and Casino in 2012, then the Westgate Las Vegas in 2014. You get the picture. (XVI, XVII, XX, XXXIII)

Iphigenia

Daughter of King Agamemnon (qv) and a tragic reminder of what can happen when your dad is a loser – fatherhood in this case being little more than a Trash version of sovereignty. (V)

The Iron Men

Vicious and disciplined street gang who, along with the Zombies, the Jackals, the Scavengers and the Sharks, defend their own little piece of turf in *The Bronx Warriors*. They would have killed on Broadway. (XXIV, XXVI)

Isolde

Nineteenth-century pinup girl. (*Purg*. XV, XXII) (*Para*. III, V, VII, VIII)

J

Joe Jackson

No king can ever permit their father to be alive, happy or at peace. (XXV, XXVI, XXVII, XXXIII)

Marlon Jackson

The 'dancingest Jackson'. His words. (XXIII)

Michael Jackson

King of Pop. Died 25 June 2009 at the age of fifty. (XXII, XXIII, XXIV, XXV, XXVI, XXVII, XXVIII, XXIX, XXX, XXXI, XXII, XXXIII)

The Jacksons

What remained of the Jackson 5 after they left Tamla Motown. (XVII, XXII)

James Bond

Elegant British thug. Constantly changing and therefore incapable of change. (*Inf.* XVII, XVIII) (*Purg.* XVII, XXV) (*Para.* XVII)

Christian Jank

Scenery designer whose work for Ludwig II was heavily inspired by the operas of Richard Wagner (qv). Painted the Parsifal (qv) murals and the woodland backdrop for the Singers' Hall in Neuschwanstein (qv) for which he also supplied architectural drawings, as well as for Ludwig's unrealised Schloss Falkenstein. Much better at depicting places than people. (V, VIII)

Jason

Greek hero and mythic love rat. Betrayed his wife Medea (qv), abandoning her for a younger woman, thereby bringing about the deaths of his two sons and breaking his vow to the goddess Hera. Died a sad and lonely death. The tabloids would have loved him. (XVII, XVIII)

The Jungle Room

Former converted patio at Graceland (qv) where Elvis recorded his final studio sessions. Lisa Marie recorded there – as did Kid Rock. History is a practical joke we keep playing on ourselves. (XIV)

Jupiter

Ruler of all the ancient Gods of Imperial Rome and father to Venus. Last seen as Zeus spraying his sperm all over the civilised world in Purgatory. Currently occupying the Sixth Sphere of Paradise. Names become our destiny only if we let them. (*Purg*. VIII, XVII, XIX, XXII, XXIII, XXIV) (*Para.* II, XVIII)

The Emperor Justinian AKA Justinian I AKA Justinian the Great

Byzantine ruler of the Eastern Roman Empire from 527 to 565. Occupies the Sphere of Mercury in cantos V, VI and VII of Dante's *Paradise*, while also receiving a brief mention in canto VI of *Purgatory* – he gets his first mention here. (IV)

K

Josef Kainz

Born into the Austro-Hungarian Empire and considered one of the greatest actors of his generation. Worked with Ernst von Possart (qv) at the National Theatre in Munich, where he came to the attention of Ludwig II, quickly becoming one of the king's favourites. Their relationship ended during a boat trip across Lake Lucerne after Ludwig invited fourteen alp-horn players aboard to perform all night, driving the actor into a sleepless frenzy. (VI)

Henry J Kaiser

American industrialist involved in the mass production of ships, steel, aluminium, suburban housing and the mass consumption of holidays, television and healthcare packages. (XIII, XIV, XIX)

The Kaiser Aluminum Dome

A miracle of rare device located in the crystal Sphere of the Sun, otherwise known as the Hawaiian Village Hotel (qv) in Waikiki. Erected in 1957, it was one of the first functioning geodesic domes in the West, only to be demolished in 1999. (XIV, XIX)

Anna Kanakis

Italian beauty queen and film actress. Her movie credits include *2019: After the Fall of New York* (1983) and *The Final Inquiry* (2006) where she played Claudia Procula, the otherwise unnamed wife of Pontius Pilate. (XXV)

Kato

Sidekick and chauffeur to the Green Hornet. Played by Bruce Lee (qv), he became the *real* hero of the franchise. (XX)

Jim Kelly

African-American Karate champion and movie star. As well as appearing in *Enter the Dragon* (1973), *Black Belt Jones* (1974) and *Golden Needles* (1974), he made *Three the Hard Way* (also 1974) with Fred 'The Hammer' Williamson (qv). (XX)

Abdullah bin Hamad bin Isa Al Khalifa

Personal Representative of His Majesty King of Bahrain. President of the Supreme Council for the Environment. Senior Member of the Civil Judiciary. Chairman of the Primary International Sanctioning Body for Kart Racing. (XXXI)

Don King

Legendary African-American sports promoter. 'This is the Don King show and The Jacksons are an opening act. Can't you see how bad this looks?' – Michael Jackson. (XXIII, XXX)

Klingsor

Magician first mentioned in Wolfram von Eschenbach's epic thirteenth-century poem *Parzival*. Carried out a reign of terror with a silk handkerchief, a dove and a fake pack of cards before going on to play the villain in the Wagner (qv) opera *Parsifal*. (IV, VII)

Gladys Knight

Empress of Soul. Considered to be one of the greatest singers of all time. Performed 'America the Beautiful' at WWF WrestleMania IV in Atlantic City in 1988, which is pretty epic when you think about it. (XVI)

Nancy Kovack

Hollywood actress. Appeared with Dean Martin (qv) in the Matt Helm (qv) movie *The Silencers* (1966) and with Elvis Presley in *Frankie and Johnny* (also 1966) then rounded out the same year with *Tarzan and the Valley of Gold*. (XVII)

John Kramer

Bass player and flautist who started out with Martin Denny (qv) and ended up playing with Arthur Lyman (qv). Knows better than most musicians what the inside of a geodesic dome sounds like. (XIV)

The Kreeton People

An ancient race who ruled the entire Earth. Looked a lot like angry Muppets. Very angry Muppets indeed. (XXIII)

Kundry AKA Condrie

'High Messenger of the Grail', according to poet and knight Wolfram von Eschenbach. 'The First Sorceress', 'Hell's Rose', Herodias and Gundryggia, according to Richard Wagner (qv). (V, VI)

L

Lake Shrine

The Self-Realization Fellowship's Retreat at Pacific Palisades. An exotic easy-listening album cover brought to life. The memorial service for The Cramps' lead singer Lux Interior was held there at the Windmill Chapel on 21 February 2009. (XIII)

John Landis

American cineaste. Wrote, directed and starred in *Schlock* (1973), which he later described as 'terrible'. It's been downhill ever since. (XXV, XXVII)

Morris Lapidus

Russian-born but very American architect. Claimed that most of the people who stayed in his hotels 'weren't essentially cultured people. Some of them may have been, but they'd forgotten their culture.' His son Alan Lapidus designed the Trump Plaza Hotel and Casino in Atlantic City, which was blown up in 2021, delighting crowds of cheering onlookers. Always give the public what it wants. (XVII)

Myca Dinh Le

Born in Vietnam 7 January 1975. Died on a movie set 23 July 1982, aged seven. Buried in Forest Lawn Memorial Park, Cypress, Orange County. (XXV)

Bruce Lee

An enigma wrapped in muscles, wrapped in discipline. (XX, XXI, XXVI)

Liberace AKA 'Mr Showmanship'

One of the great pianists of the twentieth century – and certainly the greatest ever to play Las Vegas. (*Inf.* XVI) (*Para.* XVII)

Linderhof

Ludwig II's Graceland and his Neverland rolled into one and therefore the quintessential Trash Palace. (I, II, VII, IX, X, XII, XIV, XXVI, XXVIII, XXXIII)

Lohengrin

The son of Parzival (qv), according to Wolfram von Eschenbach. Arrives in a boat drawn by swans to defend Elsa of Brabant against accusations of murder in the Wagner (qv) opera of the same name. This is also the name that Elsa isn't supposed to know – even though it's right there in the title. (III, IV, V, VI, VIII)

Longinus

Roman centurion present at the Crucifixion who pierced the side of Christ with the 'Holy Lance'. Was later venerated as a Christian Saint. It figures. (VII)

Jack Lord

American actor and handsome star of TV and movies. Appears to have been made entirely out of Naugahyde. (XIX)

St Louis IX

Devout Catholic. Led the Seventh and Eighth Crusades and died of dysentery in Carthage. Devoted considerable time and effort to the spiritual instruction of his son Philip III, who also died of dysentery while on a crusade – this time in Catalonia. Was clearly doing something wrong. (II, IV, V, VI, IX)

Louis XIV

The human incarnation of Apollo (qv) on Earth. *L'État, c'est Louis.* (I, III, VIII, IX, X, XVII, XXVI, XXXI)

Louis XV

A recurring figure in the fictional works of the Marquis de Sade. (IX, VIII, XIX)

Louis XVI

The human incarnation of the *Acéphale* on Earth. His beheading was a sacrificial act that redefined sovereignty while at the same time ushering in the age of the masses. The king's death took place in what was then called the Place de la Révolution and is now the Place de la Concorde. (II, IX)

Louis XVIII
How many more of these *are* there? (V)

Lucifer
The star that fell from Heaven and is now at the centre of Hell. The real hero of this book, if not this entire glossary. (V)

Ludwig I
King of Bavaria, father to Maximilian II (qv) and grandfather to Ludwig II. His affair with Lola Montez pretty much started it all. (*Purg.* VI, VII, VIII, IX) (*Para.* II, VI, VII)

Ludwig II
King of Bavaria. Died 13 June 1886 at the age of forty. (II, III, IV, V, VI, VII, VIII, IX, X, XI, XII, XIV, XV, XVI, XVII, XVIII, XIX, XXI, XXII, XXIII, XXIV, XXV, XXVI, XXVIII, XXIX, XXX, XXXI, XXXII, XXXIII)

Ludwig the Bavarian AKA Louis IV
Holy Roman Emperor from 1328 until his death in 1347 – a role Arnold Schwarzenegger might well have played in the early stages of his Hollywood career. (II, IV)

Ludwig of Kelheim AKA Louis I, The Duke of Bavaria
Crusader and fixer for the Holy Roman Empire. In other words: a Wittelsbach. Assassinated in 1231 on a bridge in Kelheim, Southern Bavaria. (II)

St Ludwig Landgrave of Thuringia AKA Louis IV AKA Blessed Louis of Thuringia
Married to Elizabeth of Hungary (qv). Embarked on the Sixth Crusade in 1227. Died of the plague having reached Southern Italy. Serves him right. (II)

Duke Ludwig the Rich AKA Ludwig IX of Bavaria
Fifteenth-century Duke of Bavaria-Landshut. To date historians have been unable to establish quite what it was people found so attractive about 'Ludwig the Rich'. (II)

Bela Lugosi
Enduring myth without whom cinema would be considerably the poorer. Movies include *Dracula* (1931), *White Zombie* (1932), *The Phantom Creeps* (1939) and *Plan 9 from Outer Space* – sort of (1959). (*Inf.* IV, V, X, XVIII, XXXII) (*Para.* XVIII)

Arthur Lyman
Hawaiian musician, arranger and recording artist whose ghost used to haunt the Kaiser Aluminum Dome (qv) at night, making exotic music until the first garbage trucks came crashing through the dawn. *Taboo* (1958), *Taboo 2* (1960), *Hawaiian Sunset* (1961), *Paradise* (1964), *Latitude 20* (1967). (XIV)

M

Bob Mackie

American costume designer. Used to do everybody's Vegas act, but remains best known for helping Cher (qv) to the top of the 1991 All Time Worst-Dressed List, ahead of Elizabeth Taylor (qv), Queen Elizabeth II of England, Dolly Parton and Jayne Mansfield (qv). (XVII)

The Maenads

Beloved and intoxicated followers of Dionysus, they have been known to draw fresh milk and honey from the land with their bare hands. They are impervious to injury and therefore cannot be kept out of Paradise. (*Purg.* VIII, IX) (*Para.* VI, VII, XI, XXVI, XXVII)

Stéphane Mallarmé

French Symbolist poet of breath-taking complexity and delicacy who more than deserves his place in the Sphere of Venus but is probably too refined to say so. (VIII)

Jayne Mansfield

Hollywood actress, singer and Playboy Playmate for February 1955. Movies include *Female Jungle* (1955), *The Girl Can't Help It* (1956), *The Loves of Hercules* (1960) and *The Wild, Wild World of Jayne Mansfield* (1968), the last one only being released after her death, at age 34, in a high-speed auto collision. (XVII)

Charles Manson

An American institution. 'You invented the words, and you made a dictionary and you gave me the dictionary and you said "These are what the words mean" I could never say what someone else said. I can only say what I said' – from his trial testimony, 19 November 1970. (*Inf.* XXV, XXX, XXXI, XXXII, XXXIII, XXXIV) (*Para.* XX, XXIV)

Margaret of Provence

Queen of France and the only woman ever to lead a crusade. She even managed to come back from it alive – unlike her husband Louis IX (qv) and their son Philip III. Just try finding her grave, however. (VI)

Marie Antoinette

Born a Habsburg, the eleventh daughter of the Holy Roman Emperor Francis I and Empress Maria Theresa. The last queen of France, she has become a far more popular media personality today than she was back then. Accepted the same fate as her husband Louis XVI (qv) and was beheaded in the Place de la Révolution in 1793. (I, IX)

Marie of Prussia AKA Marie Friederike Franziska Hedwig von Preußen

Queen of Bavaria and mother to Ludwig II, who did his best to avoid her as much as possible. (*Purg.* VI) (*Para.* III, VI)

Dean Martin

American entertainer and host of NBC's *The Dean Martin Show*. Elvis Presley worshipped him, according to the official Dean Martin website. (XX)

Maximilian II of Bavaria

No king can ever permit their father to be alive, happy or at peace. (II, III, XXVI)

Matt Helm

Fictional assassin created by American author Donald Hamilton and portrayed by Dean Martin (qv) in a fun but forgettable series of movies: *The Silencers* and *Murderers' Row* (both 1966), *The Ambushers* (1967) and *The Wrecking Crew* (1968). (XX)

Medea

Deathless sorceress and daughter of King Aeëtes (qv). Her golden presence holds sway over the spheres of Mars and Jupiter. Managed to cause the deaths of both her sons but not that of their father Jason (qv). It's complicated. (XVII, XVIII)

Medusa

The greatest side-eye in the business. Our understanding of art and beauty is meaningless without her eternal gaze. (*Purg*. VIII, IX, XIX, XXV) (*Para*. IV)

Burgess Meredith

'I loved Burgess Meredith, what he did with the Penguin... so funny, comedic and elegant... he really filled that costume – beautifully' – Adam West. See *Inferno* XXI for more details. (XX)

Archangel Michael

One of the Seven who enter before the Glory of the Lord and stand at His Right Hand. The other six being Raphael, Gabriel, Uriel, Sariel, Raguel and Remiel, in case anyone is interested. (XXIII)

Liza Minnelli

One of the Four who posed for an official group photograph on the day she married David Gest. The other two being Michael Jackson and Elizabeth Taylor (qv), in case anyone is interested. (XXXIII)

Monsalvat

The name of the 'savage mountain', hidden deep within a forest somewhere on the wildest hem of Northern Spain, where the castle of the Grail Knights is to be found – 'here time becomes space,' according to Gurnemanz (qv), and he should know. (IV, VII)

Robert de Montesquiou

French poet descended from the Montesquiou-Fézensac family of Gascony. His presence can be strongly detected in the work of JK Huysmans, Oscar Wilde (qv) and Marcel Proust (qv). Montesquiou's teeth were quite as black as Ludwig II's in later life and had to be just as carefully hidden. His poetry has often been called 'untranslatable', so you can guess what that means. (IX)

Lola Montez

Irish dancer and adventuress whose affair with Ludwig I (qv) deprived Ludwig II of his right to absolute rule. (*Purg*. VI, VII, VIII, IX) (*Para*. VI, VII)

Vic Morrow

American actor and everybody's favourite knife-wielding teenage maniac. Stabbed Elvis Presley during a street fight in *King Creole*. (XXIV, XXV)

N

Napoleon Bonaparte

A set of lies that have been agreed upon. Not entirely his fault. (*Purg*. I, VI) (*Para*. III, V, XVII)

Narcissus

Greek mythological figure embodying the indolence behind all real beauty. Needs to take a long hard look at himself. (*Purg*. IV, V) (*Para*. XXXIII)

Neuschwanstein

An historicist hallucination set in stone. Supposedly the location for Adolf Hitler's sex orgy at the start of Russ Meyer's *Up!* (1976), it was an aesthetic obsession for Walt Disney (qv) and the subject of a 1987 painting by Andy Warhol (qv). Requires a lot more believing than seeing. (V, XII, XXI, XXVI, XXVIII, XXXIII)

Neverland

The most commonly known name for the fantasy island first introduced in the fictional works of JM Barrie. Also, the most commonly known name for Sycamore Valley Ranch, Santa Barbara County, California. (XXVI, XXVII, XXVIII, XXXI, XXXII, XXXIII)

David Newman

Hollywood scriptwriter. Cowrote with Robert Benton 'The New Sentimentality', which first appeared in the July 1964 issue of *Esquire*. See *Inferno* XVII, XIX and XXIV for more details. (XXVII)

Elisabet Ney

German-born sculptor who worked predominantly in plaster and marble. Her subjects included Wagner (qv), Otto von Bismark, Lady Macbeth and a large number of other worthies you've probably never heard of. (V, XXX)

Marshal Ney

First Duke of Elchingen, First Prince of the Moskva and Marshal of the Empire. A victim of circumstance. (V)

Friedrich Nietzsche

German philosopher and poet. Died 1900. One day the world will be ready for him. (*Inf*. XIX) (*Purg*. I, III, VI, VIII, XVI) (*Para*. III, X, XXII, XXIV)

Nipper

A phantom presence rendered visible by the British painter Francis Barraud. The very picture of mortality. (X, XI)

Chuck Norris

It's all true. American martial artist and movie actor. Appeared in the kind of movies Elvis secretly wanted to make but then never did. *Silent Rage, Forced Vengeance* (both 1982), *Missing in Action* (1984), *Missing in Action 2: The Beginning, Invasion USA* (both 1985), *The Delta Force* (1986), *Braddock: Missing in Action III* (1988), *Delta Force 2: The Colombian Connection* (1990), *Hellbound* (1994). (XX)

Nymphenburg

A favoured summer residence of the Bavarian royal family, the land for which was purchased in 1663. The gift shop on the ground floor of the central building was opened in 2008. (II, VI, XV)

O

Orkowski Twins

Sometimes all that remains is a photograph or two and a name. May all such lives be happy ones. (X)

Orpheus

Poet, musician and singer capable of charming both the natural world and the underworld. There would be no Paradise without him. (*Purg.* IV, VIII) (*Para.* X, XI, XXXIII)

The Osmonds

American family music group. Danced like the Jacksons. Dressed like Elvis. Mormons, obviously. (XVII)

Ovid

Roman poet who, like Dante, died in exile. (*Purg.* I, IX, XIV, XXIII, XXX) (*Para.* XVIII)

P

George Pal

Hollywood producer and sometime director. Credits include *Destination Moon* (1950), *When Worlds Collide* (1951), *The War of the Worlds* (1953) and *Conquest of Space* (1955). (XII)

Ed Parker

Senior Grand Master of American Kenpo Karate. Author of *Inside Elvis.* (XIX, XX)

Colonel Tom Parker

He had his reasons. (XV, XVI, XVIII, XXI, XXXIII)

Parsifal AKA Parzival

The redeemed Redeemer of the Grail Legend and the missing link between innocence and idiocy. In other words, God's Pure Fool. Once killed a swan just to brag about it. Prick. (IV, V, VI, VII, IX, XI)

Walter Pater

Victorian art critic and aesthete. Set out to rediscover the art and poetry of the Renaissance and awakened the sensibilities of the early modernists instead. (I)

Maria de la Paz

Spanish Infanta and daughter of Queen Isabella II. Married Prince Ludwig Ferdinand of Bavaria, thereby joining the House of Wittelsbach. Died in Schloss Nymphenburg (qv) in 1946. It was, for the record, Beatrice and not Virgil who led Dante into Paradise. The Roman poet was not even allowed into the Earthly Paradise at the top of Mount Purgatory, so he can just forget about Heaven. (VIII)

Minnie Pearl, AKA Sarah Ophelia Colley Cannon

American comedian. Ruled over the Grand Ole Opry and Kornfield Kounty without ever once removing the price tag from her bonnet. (XI)

Peter Pan

Long-term fictional resident of Neverland (qv) and an enduring modern myth thanks to JM Barrie, Michael Jackson and an animated feature film by Walt Disney (qv) that would keep most people awake at night if they ever really thought about it. (XXVII)

The Petit Trianon

Neoclassical *petite maison* built by Louis XV (qv) for successive mistresses within the park of the Grand Trianon, which in turn is located within the grounds of the Palace of Versailles (qv), which in turn can be found within the Sphere of Venus. (IX)

Friedrich Wilhelm Pfeiffer

German landscape and genre painter. His twenty-six portraits of Ludwig II's favourite horses are on permanent display in the former stables at Nymphenburg (qv), while Ludwig I's *Gallery of Beauties* can be found in the main part of the palace. For more details on the latter, see *Purgatory* VI, VII and VIII. (VI)

The Playboy Mansion

The Petit Trianon (qv) of every lonely man's dreams. (I)

Ernst von Possart

German actor, theatre director and a mean Mephisto, by all accounts. (XXXIII)

Milton Prell

Vegas casino-owner. Started with a bingo palace then made it big by introducing camels to the Sahara (qv) and the Arabian Nights to the Aladdin (qv). (XV, XVI)

Elvis Presley

King of Rock and Roll. Died 16 August 1977 at the age of forty-two. (*Inf.* VII) (*Para.* X, XI, XII, XIII, XIV, XV, XVI, XVII, XVIII, XIX, XX, XXI, XXII, XXIII, XXIV, XXVI, XXVII, XXVIII, XXIX, XXX, XXXI, XXXII, XXXIII)

Gladys Presley

Elvis Presley's mother and therefore both the beginning and the end of him. (XIII)

Jesse Garon Presley

Yes, but what if he'd *lived?* (XXII)

Lisa Marie Presley

American entertainer and media personality. Daughter of Elvis Presley, former wife of Michael Jackson. Former serial substance abuser and Scientologist. That's a heavy enough burden for anyone to carry. (XXII, XXVIII, XXIX, XXX)

Priscilla Presley

Former wife of Elvis Presley and mother to Lisa Marie Presley (qv). Her on-again, off-again relationship with Detective Sergeant Frank Drebin has been exhaustively chronicled in *The Naked Gun: From the Files of Police Squad!* (1988); *The Naked Gun 2½: The Smell of Fear* (1991) and *The Naked Gun 33+⅓: The Final Insult* (1994). An American icon. (XIII, XV, XVI, XVII, XX, XXIX)

Vernon Presley

No king can ever permit their father to be alive, happy or at peace. (XIV, XVIII)

Marcel Proust

French novelist and early modernist sensibility. Seldom read. Often cited. (*Inf.* XIX) (*Purg.* I, II, X) (*Para.* I)

Patrick Purdy

Mass murderer who used a Chinese-made variant on the AK-47 semi-automatic assault rifle to deprive five young Southeast Asian children of their lives. Most of them were born in refugee camps after their families had fled the killing fields of Kampuchea. Welcome to America. (XXIV)

R

Della Reese

African-American gospel singer, movie actress and TV personality. The only ordained minister to make it into Paradise. (XV)

Oscar de la Renta

Dominican-born American couturier. Dressed a succession of First Ladies, including Jackie Kennedy, Nancy Reagan, Hillary Clinton, Laura Bush and (eventually) Michelle Obama. Belongs in the outermost moving sphere of this universe. (XXIX)

The Residenz

Sprawling royal palace belonging to the Wittelsbach monarchs and occupying a great deal of central Munich real estate. Cordially loathed by Ludwig II. (III, IV, VII, VIII, X)

The Riders

Prominent biker gang featured in *The Bronx Warriors.* Not as vicious or as disciplined as the Iron Men (qv), but they certainly knew how to carry a movie. (XXIV)

Roseninsel

The Rose Island, located on Lake Starnberg, featuring a villa and a rose garden commissioned by Ludwig II's father Maximilian II (qv). Visitors included Richard Wagner (qv) and Empress Elisabeth of Austria (qv). (VIII, XXIX)

Crown Prince Rudolf of Austria

Born a Habsburg, son of Emperor Franz Josef and Empress Elisabeth (qv). Heir presumptive to the Austro-Hungarian Empire. Liked sex and skulls, drugs and guns. Loved his mistress Mary Vetsera so much that he shot her and then put a bullet through his own head. Their scandalous deaths were kept a desperately guarded secret in order to preserve the empire. Sovereigns' houses are never as solid as they might appear. (XXXI)

Kurt Russell

Hollywood actor and former child star. A top earner for Walt Disney (qv), just like Bobby Driscoll (qv). One of his earliest onscreen appearances is as a young kid kicking Elvis Presley in *It Happened at the World's Fair* (1963). Goes on to play Elvis in the 1979 biopic of the singer directed by John Carpenter (qv). (XXVI)

S

Hassan-i Sabbah

Legendarily devout and ascetic Ishmaelite beloved of Betty Bouthoul, Vladimir Bartol, William S Burroughs and Brion Gysin. Understood Paradise in his own austere way better than just about anyone else – Dante included. (II)

The Sahara

Las Vegas casino. A desert within a desert, right on the corner of Sahara Avenue. Began as Club Bingo, but then Milton Prell (qv) brought in his fake camels. (XV, XVI, XXII)

Sardanapalus

Legendarily decadent and depraved monarch beloved of Lord Byron, Eugène Delacroix, Hector Berlioz and Franz Liszt. Dante placed him in the Fifth Sphere of Paradise as a lesson to others, but it clearly didn't take. (XV)

Satan

Servant of Lucifer carrying out his wishes on Earth, according to the mystics of the Early Church. There would simply be no show without him. (XXIII, XXV, XXXIII)

Josefine Scheffsky

Took the role of Sieglinde, mother of Siegfried (qv), for the first ever performance of the complete *Ring* cycle at Bayreuth (qv) in 1876 in the presence of Ludwig II, who never attended again. (VII)

Lalo Schifrin

Film and television composer. Wrote the soundtrack to the violence inside your head. Credits include *Murderer's Row, Hell in the Pacific, The Hellstrom Chronicle, Magnum Force, The Amityville Horror, Class of 1984*. (XX)

Max Schreck

German actor. Worked with Max Reinhardt, Bertolt Brecht and Karl Valentin but is best known for his portrayal of Count Orlok in FW Murnau's *Nosferatu: A Symphony of Horror* (1922). (XI)

Alex Shoofey

Las Vegas casino manager, former Club Bingo employee and one-time vice-present of the Nevada Resort Association. Inducted into the Hotel Industry Hall of Fame in 1969. (XVI)

Siegfried

The opera world's answer to Hulk Hogan. Not to be confused with Siegfried Wagner (qv). (*Inf.* XXII, XXVI, XXIX) (*Para.* V)

Henry Silva

American character actor. *Crowded Paradise* (1956), *Johnny Cool* (1963), *Almost Human* (1974), *Megaforce* (1982), *Above the Law* (1988). (XXVI)

Frank Sinatra

American entertainer. Used to play regular residencies at The Sands in Las Vegas before things got ugly. 'I built this hotel from a sandpile, and I can tear the fucking place down,' he's supposed to have said before driving a golf cart through a plate glass window and signing a three-million-dollar contract with Caesars Palace (qv). (*Inf.* XXIX) (*Para.* XVII, XVIII, XX)

Jack Smith

American artist. 'I want to be uncommercial film personified. That's the...oh wait...' – extract from *What's Underground about Marshmallows?* (*Inf.* VIII, IX, XII, XIII, XVII, XVIII, XXIX, XXXIV) (*Para.* XXVII)

Duchess Sophie Charlotte in Bayern

Sister of Empress Elisabeth of Austria (qv). After her engagement to Ludwig II fell apart, she went on to marry Prince Ferdinand of Orléans and Duc of Alençon. She died in the tragic Bazar de la Charité fire in Paris on 4 May 1897. Insisting everyone be rescued before her, she was last seen kneeling in the flames to pray. Her body was so badly burned that she could only be identified by the gold fillings in her teeth. (VI, VIII)

Stephen I of Hungary AKA King Saint Stephen

Canonised in 1083. Makes a brief appearance in *The Warriors* alongside the Jones Street Boys, although historical accounts diverge sharply on this matter. (IV)

Mike Stone

Hawaiian-born martial artist. Tenth degree black belt. Won the 1968 World Professional Karate Championship and was the author of the *Globe* tabloid story 'How I Stole Elvis Presley's Wife From Him'. Moved to an isolated island paradise in the Philippines, so that's how *that* goes. (XX)

Richard Strauss

German composer. Wrote the entrance music for Elvis Presley's later stage shows but very little of note after that. What a waste. (XVII)

Suetonius

Roman historian and author of *The Lives of the Twelve Caesars*. He wrote a lot more books, but nobody alive today has ever read them. (II)

Gloria Swanson

Hollywood actress. Appeared as a washed-up screen diva in *Sunset Boulevard* (1950) and as herself in *Airport 1975* (1974). (XVII)

Jonathan Swift

'Satire is a sort of glass wherein beholders do generally discover everybody's face but their own; which is the chief reason for that kind reception it meets with in the world, and that so very few are offended with it.' (*Purg.* XIX) (*Para.* XXVIII)

Hans-Jürgen Syberberg

Prussian filmmaker. Frequently misunderstood – especially by himself. (XVIII)

T

Russ Tamblyn

Film and television actor. Movie credits include *Peyton Place* with Lana Turner (qv) (1957), *High School Confidential!* with Mamie Van Doren (qv) (1958), *The War of the Gargantuas* (1966) and *Black Heat* (1976). (*Inf.* XXXII) (*Para.* XIII)

Tannhäuser

Franconian poet and Teutonic knight. The start of his story may have been lost in time, but it always ends the same way in the Wagner (qv) opera of the same name. (I, III, V, VII)

Sharon Tate

Hollywood actress and murder victim. Starred opposite Dean Martin (qv) in *The Wrecking Crew* (1968), her last movie appearance before her death. (*Inf.* XXXII) (*Para.* XIII)

Elizabeth Taylor

Hollywood icon and former child star. Movies include *Cleopatra* (1963), *Doctor Faustus* (1967), *Ash Wednesday* (1973, *The Driver's Seat* with Andy Warhol (qv) (1974) and *The Flintstones* (1994). (*Inf.* XII) (*Para.* XXVII, XXVIII)

The Templars

Fanatical postapocalyptic order of warriors featured in *The New Barbarians*, dedicated to purifying the Earth through sodomy and mass murder. Not to be confused with the Knights Templar, who would never do any of that sort of thing. (XXV)

Albert von Thurn und Taxis

German aristocrat and philosopher. Onetime regular visitor to Neverland. Owns six castles and his own bank. (XXIX)

Gloria von Thurn und Taxis

'Went to dinner and then had to go to Heaven and met Gloria von Thurn and Taxis and her husband Johannes. She was sort of cruising for him' – Andy Warhol (qv), diary entry for 10 July 1986. (XXIX)

Paul Thurn und Taxis

Confidant and playdate of Ludwig II. Later disowned by his family and rejected by his king when he married a soubrette from the Munich People's Theatre. (VI, VIII, XXIX)

Tiberius

Roman Emperor. Could have been a god like the others, but flesh was his weakness. (II)

Trash

Pretty-boy leader of the Riders (qv) bike gang in *The Bronx Warriors*. Seventeen years old and walks like he's wearing a scoliosis brace. (XXIV, XXVI)

Trauttmansdorff Castle

Located in Merano in the Southern Tyrol and noted for the splendour of its botanical gardens. Safely contained within the Sphere of Venus, visits by the Empress Elisabeth of Austria (qv) helped keep it on the map. (VIII)

Tristan

Nineteenth-century poster boy. (*Purg.* XV) (*Para.* III, V, VII, VIII)

Donald Trump

So done with him now. (*Inf.* XXXIV) (*Para.* XXIX)

Lana Turner

Hollywood actress who never fully appreciated the subtle difference between gravitas and looking mildly offended. *The Prodigal* (1955), *Peyton Place* (1957), *Imitation of Life* (1959), *Portrait in Black* (1960), *Madame X* (1966). (XII)

U

Pope Urban IV

Papal fixer who earned eternal damnation for refusing to absolve Tannhäuser (qv) of his sins and receive him back into the Church. (I)

V

Mamie Van Doren

Hollywood sex symbol and American legend. Movies include *Running Wild* (1955), *Star in the Dust* (1956), *Untamed Youth* (1957), *High School Confidential!* with Russ Tamblyn (qv) (1958), *Sex Kittens Go to College* (1960), *The Navy vs. the Night Monsters* (1966) and *Voyage to the Planet of Prehistoric Women* (1968). (XVII)

Venus

Roman incarnation of Aphrodite, the Greek goddess of beauty, love and youth – inevitably trashed since birth. (*Purg.* II, XV, XVI, XXV) (*Para.* I, II, VI, VII)

The Venus Grotto

An early form of Virtual Reality located in the grounds of Ludwig II's Schloss Linderhof (qv). (I, II, XIII, XIV)

Venusberg

A mediaeval retirement home for poets grown too tired of this world. (I, IV)

Versailles

Seventeenth-century trailer park located outside of Paris and reserved exclusively for aristocrats. (I, II, III, IX, XVI)

Victory

Allegorical figure and therefore not intended to be taken seriously – also the title of the 1984 North American tour undertaken by the Jacksons (qv) to promote their album of the same name. (I)

Luchino Visconti

Italian count, filmmaker and opera director. A cultural elitist born in the wrong century and consequently a profound pessimist. (XVIII)

W

Cosima Wagner

Daughter of Franz Liszt, second wife of Richard Wagner (qv). Helped found Bayreuth (qv) and then preserved its repertoire to within an inch of its life. (III, XXII)

Richard Wagner

German composer and cultural nightmare. *The Trash Project* would be unthinkable without him. Had many sublime moments, but most of them happened offstage. (*Inf.* XXIX) (*Purg.* I, III, VIII, XIII, XV, XXII) (*Para.* III, IV, V, VI, VII, VIII, XXVIII, XXXIII)

Siegfried Wagner

Son of Cosima Wagner (qv). Not to be confused with Siegfried (qv), son of Sieglinde. (III)

Bill 'Superfoot' Wallace

American kickboxer and actor. Most people think his foot isn't all that big, but then they rarely see it coming. Movie credits include *A Force of One* with Chuck Norris (qv) (1979), *Sword of Heaven* and *LA Streetfighters*, AKA *Ninja Turf* (both 1985). (XX)

Andy Warhol

'I always thought I'd like my own tombstone to be blank. No epitaph and no name. Well, actually, I'd like it to say "*figment*."' (*Inf.* VII, X, XII, XIII, XIV, XVI, XVII, XIX, XX, XXI, XXIII, XXIV, XXV, XXVII, XXVIII, XXIX, XXXIV) (*Purg.* I) (*Para.* XII, XXVII, XXVIII)

Wartburg

Home of Landgravine Elisabeth von Thuringen (qv) and the inspiration for Ludwig II's castle at Neuschwanstein (qv). You'll also find Martin Luther and Richard Wagner (qv) lurking about its ancient corners. (V)

Dionne Warwick

Why do you have to be a heartbreaker? (XVI)

Dinah Washington AKA 'Queen of the Blues'

African-American singer and pianist. Died at age 39 of a secobarbital and amobarbital overdose prescribed for insomnia. (XV)

Antoine Watteau

French Rococo painter too gentle for this world. (II)

Joseph Werner

Swiss Baroque painter too subservient for this world. (XVII)

Pat West

Imagine Elvis telling you what his favourite drug is. She doesn't have to. (XIX)

Red West

Friend and former bodyguard to Elvis Presley. His performance in *Road House*, alongside the monster trucks, the strippers, the endless barfights and a glistening half-nude Patrick Swayze doing Tai Chi, is what makes this movie so great. (XVIII, XIX, XX, XXI, XXXI)

Sonny West

Cousin of Red West (qv), friend and bodyguard to Elvis Presley (qv). Sometime actor. Had a bit part in *The Navy vs. the Night Monsters* with Mamie Van Doren (qv) (1966). Later appeared in a ton of Elvis documentaries – really quite a lot when you look at them. (XIII, XIV, XX, XXXI)

Oscar Wilde

Irish poet and philosopher. Died 1900. One day the world will be ready for him. (*Inf.* IX, XVII) (*Purg.* II, III, IV, V, VI, IX, X, XII, XXIII, XXIV, XXXI, XXXII) (*Para.* I)

Fred 'The Hammer' Williamson

African-American athlete, legendary movie star, director and cineaste. Has many film credits to his name, including *That Man Bolt* (1973), *Three the Hard Way* with Jim Kelly (qv) (1974), *Warriors of the Year 2072* (1984), *Delta Force Commando* with Mark Gregory (qv) (1987) and *Vegas Vampires* (2007). Not to be confused with Hammer (qv), the psycho from *The Bronx Warriors*. (XXV)

Jackie Wilson AKA 'Mr Excitement'

African-American singer and one of the greatest ever. (XV)

Y

Paramahansa Yogananda

Hindu guru who came to America in 1920, thereby introducing yoga and meditation to the West. Met Calvin Coolidge at the White House in 1927: an example Elvis Presley would follow in 1970 – only with Richard M Nixon in his case. (XIII, XXXIII)

Z

Pia Zadora

Singer and actress. Made a strong debut as 'Girl Martian' Girmar in *Santa Claus Conquers the Martians* (1964). Her career has spun gloriously out of control ever since. The last name you'd expect to see on a list like this. (XVII)

Index

m

A guide to the illustrations used in Paradise

The front cover is a composite of *Le Purgatoire [et le Paradis] de Dante Alighieri*, Gustave Doré, public domain, and *Schloss Neuschwanstein*, Percival Gaskell, listed by The Cleveland Museum of Art as public domain. The back cover is adapted from *Opere di Dante Alighieri. v. 1–3. La Commedia di Dante Alighieri con varie annotazioni*. Gio. Scaggiari inv., Zul. Zuliani scv, public domain.

The front and back flaps are edited graphics featuring *The Creation of Trees and Herbs* by Paul Nash, listed by Wiki Art as public domain.

The image on page 27 is adapted from *Le Purgatoire [et le Paradis] de Dante Alighieri*, Gustave Doré, public domain.

The chapter heads throughout the main body of the text are from John Flaxman's *Paradiso*, accessed online from JSTOR.

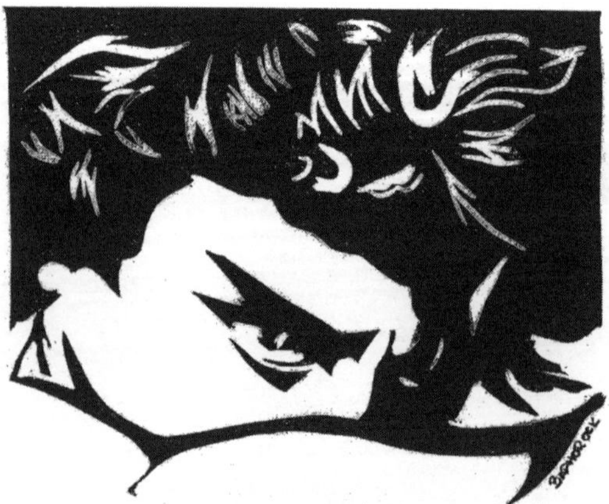

2024